HARRY S.
TRUMAN
HIS LIFE AND TIMES

HARRY S.
TRUMAN

HIS LIFE AND TIMES

BRIAN BURNES

EDITED BY DONNA MARTIN

KANSAS CITY STAR BOOKS
Kansas City, Missouri

HARRY S. TRUMAN

HIS LIFE AND TIMES

AUTHOR:
BRIAN BURNES

EDITOR:
DONNA MARTIN

DESIGNER:
BRIAN GRUBB

COPY EDITOR:
CLAIRE CATERER

KANSAS CITY STAR BOOKS
Kansas City, Missouri

PUBLISHED BY
KANSAS CITY STAR BOOKS
1729 Grand Blvd.
Kansas City, MO 64108
All rights reserved.
Copyright © 2003 by The Kansas City Star Co.

To order copies, call StarInfo, (816- 234-4636)
www.TheKansasCityStore.com

First edition, first printing
Printed in the United States of America by
Walsworth Publishing Co.

ISBN: 0-9740009-3-0
Library of Congress Control Number 2003114076

CONTENTS

FOREWORD

By Clifton Truman Daniel

I think one of the things that made my grandfather such a great president is that until history caught up with him, he was a normal human being, a middle-class guy trying to make a decent life for himself and his family. It helped that he wanted the same for everyone else. He was proud to have served his country, but prouder still just to be an American. He never forgot who he was or where he came from.

Back in the early 1950s, after Grandpa had retired to Independence, a driver blew a tire in front of the house on Delaware Street. The man didn't know where he was, that it was any place special, so he walked up and rang the doorbell. Grandpa answered the door in his shirtsleeves and the man said, "I've got a flat. Can I use your phone?" Grandpa said, "Sure. Come on in and help yourself." He did, called the local mechanic, who told him it would be twenty minutes or so before he could get out there. Well, the man didn't want to be a bother, so he said he'd wait by the car. Grandpa wouldn't have it, told him to sit in the living room and make himself at home, and they sat and talked until the wrecker showed up. When it did, the man shook Grandpa's hand, thanked him for his hospitality, and walked out the front door. He was halfway down the front steps when he turned, looked back up, and said, "You know something? You look like that son of a bitch Harry Truman." Grandpa just smiled at him and said, "I *am* that son of a bitch."

I can't think of any other United States president who has been as straightforward. In writing his memoirs and building his presidential library, he laid it all out for anyone who was interested. And he strongly believed that Americans should be interested, that it behooved them to understand the presidency, especially the men who had held the office and how they came to their decisions. You couldn't do that, he thought, unless someone put it all, public and private, under your nose. (He was alone in his family in this belief. He came home one afternoon and found my grandmother tossing handfuls of his letters to her into a roaring fire. "Bess, what are you doing?" he said. "Think of history!" She said, "*I have*," and kept right on tossing.)

In the following pages, you'll meet Harry S. Truman, the average guy who became president of the United States. That's the man I knew, the towering figure, the world leader who, when asked to bestow the wisdom of the nation's highest office on his young grandson said, "Keep your feet off the table and don't run in the house." You have a fine guide for the trip. Brian Burnes has written about Grandpa and my family for years, and he's always taken the time to get it right and make it interesting. I hope what you take away from his work is not only an understanding of Harry S. Truman the man, but a feeling of possibility, of hope. The promise of democracy is that anyone, usually anyone with enough money, can be president of the United States. But it takes a common man with common sense and uncommon values to do it better than just about anybody else.

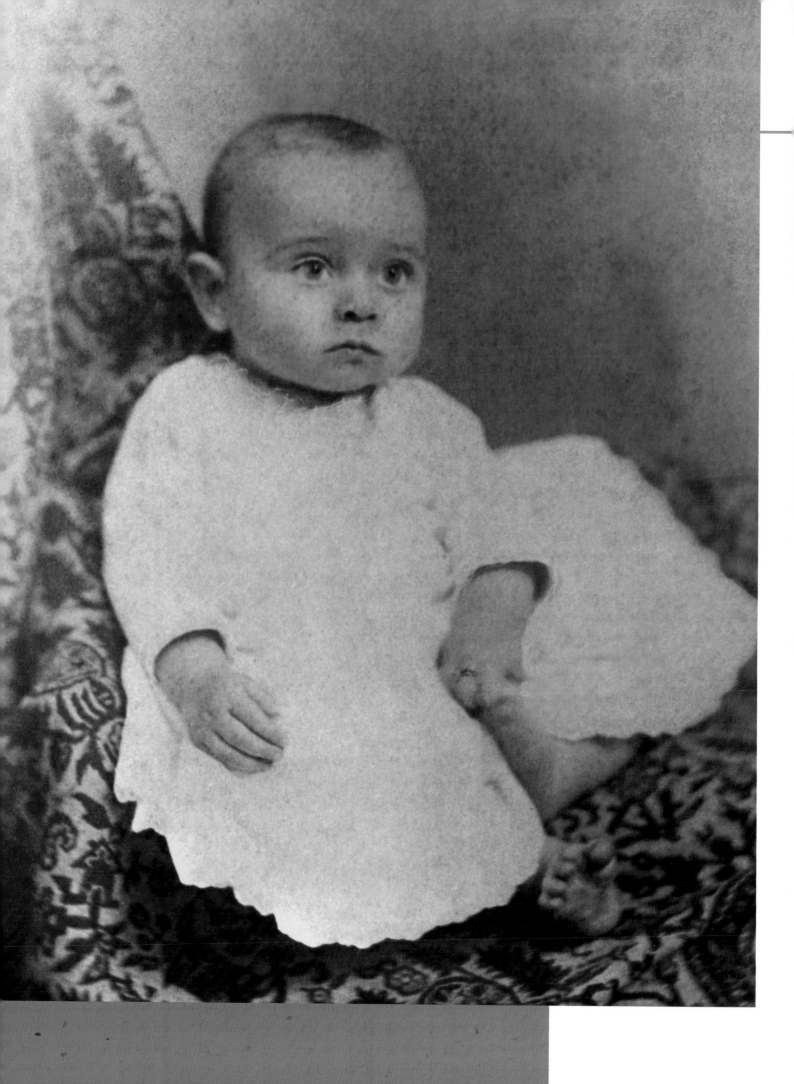

YOUTH

At first glance he seemed a delicate boy.

He had worn glasses since age six, his eyes large behind the thick lenses. Instructed well in the cost of the spectacles, he had stayed away from ballgames and roughhousing.

Instead, he read. Decades later, in his memoirs, he would exaggerate, insisting that he had read every book in the Independence library. While that was perhaps impossible, he had given every appearance of at least intending to do so, as his teachers later often recalled seeing the young Harry bent over a volume there.

He was considered a bright boy; he skipped the third grade. He played piano and studied with instructors in Kansas City. Friends would later recall seeing him hurrying by on the Independence sidewalks, hustling to catch a streetcar to ride downtown.

He helped edit the high school annual. During high school he also worked at an Independence Square drugstore, cleaning hundreds of medicine vials with a feather duster. His class of forty-one students contained thirty girls, yet he was often shy around young women. "I was always afraid of girls my age and older," he once recalled years later. And yet, there was a resiliency about him that many of his classmates were never asked to exhibit.

As a teenager he worked retail, reporting to the drugstore before class and then returning to it after. Following graduation from high school, he took jobs not all his classmates might have considered. For several months he monitored the work hours of laborers laying railroad track, paying them off in saloons. For several summer weeks he wrapped newspapers in a daily newspaper's stifling mailroom.

The house in Lamar, Missouri, where Harry Truman was born. His father traded livestock here.

WELCOME to LAMAR

'HARRY' APRIL 19, 1959

Harry Truman returns to his birthplace in Lamar, Missouri, on April 19, 1959. The United Automobile Workers had bought the house in which he was born and was turning it over to the state of Missouri for preservation..

Considered today, Truman's youth was rich in the range of experience. In twenty-two years, from 1884 through 1906, the young Truman encountered every lifestyle Jackson County then could offer: farm, small town, big city.

As a toddler and boy, the life Truman knew was rural. In 1884 he was born in Lamar, Missouri, where his father traded livestock. From 1885 through 1887, his family lived on a seventy-one-acre farm about four miles southeast of Belton, in Cass County, just south of Jackson County. From 1887 through 1890, the Truman family lived on the farm of Solomon and Harriet Louisa Young, Truman's maternal grandparents, in

what is now Grandview.

His earliest memory, as recalled in his memoirs, was a pastoral one: following a jumping frog through the brush and slapping his knees with laughter. Lest anyone think the future president a solemn boy, the older Truman offered evidence to the contrary. He once recalled the small red wagon his family owned and how on one occasion he pulled his brother, Vivian, and a neighbor boy into a mud hole, and then upset the wagon. "It seemed a good thing to do and it was repeated several times," Truman wrote.

From 1890 through 1903, from age six through his late teens, Truman's world was that of small-town Independence, population

HARRY S. TRUMAN: HIS LIFE AND TIMES

six thousand in 1890. It was his mother's wish that Truman and his younger siblings benefit from the schools maintained by the Jackson County community just east of Kansas City. Harry's first Independence home was at 619 South Crysler Avenue. His father, John Truman, bought several acres to keep livestock. In 1896 John Truman upgraded, buying a home at 909 West Waldo Avenue, a "nice house," Truman later remembered, located near the heart of genteel Independence.

The Democratic National Convention was held in Kansas City's Convention Hall in 1900. It's easy to imagine the impression that may have had on the sixteen-year-old Truman, who watched from a balcony as William Jennings Bryan accepted the party's nomination for president.

From 1903 through 1906 Truman – unable to afford college – made downtown Kansas City his campus. Truman worked at two banks, drilled with the Missouri National Guard, and discovered the theater, seeing shows after work and, in one case, taking a job as an usher to see still more.

Finally, in 1906, Truman left Kansas City and returned to the Young farm in Grandview. It was there that the young man evolved into the recognizable Harry Truman. He filled out, joined the Masons, grew interested in politics, and shouldered great responsibility in operating a large farm after the 1914 death of his father. If the young Truman ever felt unduly burdened by fate or circumstance, the older Truman left perhaps only one ambiguous hint in his memoirs.

"It was a very happy time," Truman once wrote of his youth, "not fully appreciated until a long time afterward."

In fact, to know Truman's youth and then read his later recollection of it is to discover not only an almost total lack of sour grapes or score settling, but even any acknowledgment that he ever knew disappointment or doubt.

Yet there was plenty of occasion for both.

In January 1894 Truman and his younger brother, Vivian, contracted diphtheria, an acute bacterial disease sometimes characterized by fever, respiratory difficulty, swelling of the palate, and malaise. While Vivian Truman recovered quickly, older brother Harry did not. Such was his listlessness that his mother moved him around the house by baby carriage. The illness lingered with

John Anderson Truman and Martha Ellen Truman, Harry's mother and father, in 1881, the year they were married. John Truman taught his children that honor was everything. As much as he admired his father, the future president enjoyed an abiding relationship with his mother, who lived for almost thirty-three years after his father died.

Truman for some six months, through his tenth birthday.

The thoughts of the elder Trumans can be imagined; they shipped younger sister Mary Jane Truman off to relatives. What young Harry himself thought can only be imagined as well, because in his memoirs, written decades later, Truman shrugged off the experience.

for Bess through the years was not especially noticed by her, even though the alphabetical seating arrangement used by Independence teachers often placed her in the desk just behind Truman.

"She sat behind me," Truman wrote in one of the essays he later would write when taking refuge in Kansas City's Pickwick Hotel while serving as Jackson County presiding

Mary Ethel Noland, first cousin to Harry Truman.
On the diphtheria suffered by Harry Truman:

"At one time he was so low that they thought he might not live. Dr. Twyman, Dr. G. T. Twyman, was their physician and he was concerned about that boy. He had a boy of the same age named Elmer who was afterwards a lifelong friend of Harry. He told Harry's mother to give him some ice. We didn't have ice the way you have ice now. It was wintertime and it had snowed and she raised the window and reached out and got a handful of snow and gave it to him, and it brought up the mucus out of his throat and he began to get better."

"My arms, legs and throat were of no use, but I recovered and went back to school and skipped the third grade," Truman wrote.

Another challenge may have been the social status the Truman family knew. Truman himself never suggested that he was anything less than the equal of his classmates. "The grand times we had!" he wrote of his family's experience on West Waldo Avenue. "Halloween parties and all sorts of meetings after school, making bridges by Caesar's plans and discussing what we'd like to be when grown up."

Yet the Truman family's Baptist affiliation appeared to leave young Harry somewhere below the community to which the family of Bess Wallace belonged. This was no small matter to Truman, who had been smitten by Bess Wallace since he, at age six, first glimpsed her at Sunday school at the nearby First Presbyterian Church. The torch he carried

judge. "I could not keep my mind on lessons or anything else."

Bess, however, did notice the heavy work schedule of her classmate at Clinton's drugstore on Independence Square. Mary Paxton Keeley, Bess's best friend, described in a memoir published several years after her 1986 death a day when she, Bess Wallace, and a companion named Nellie were riding a surrey around the square. Upon spying young Harry Truman sweeping out the drugstore, the three waved as they turned a corner.

"Poor Harry," Keeley recalled Bess saying. "It's not fair. He has to work all the time and never has any fun like we do."

"Oh well, we can't help it if he is poor and a Baptist," Nellie replied.

There were dreams deferred. As a high school student Truman had imagined attending West Point and found time to prepare for

Harry, age four, and Vivian, two.

the examinations with tutors. But his poor eyesight scuttled that notion.

While that would have been disappointment enough, the loss of an appointment to a service academy meant that the entire college experience was no longer an option for Harry Truman. In the early 1900s, just as Truman was nearing his high school graduation, his father John squandered his family's finances speculating in grain futures. One estimate of the elder Truman's loss was $40,000 in cash, stocks, and personal property. So complete was the disaster that the Truman family had to sell their West Waldo Avenue home and eventually move to Kansas City, where John Truman found work as a night watchman at a grain elevator.

"Difficulties overtook us," Truman wrote.

The family needed cash flow and young Harry Truman, after his 1901 graduation, contributed. His first long-term job could not have been further from the Independence library: He served as a timekeeper with a railroad that was doubling its tracks east of Kansas City.

For thirty-five dollars a month, Truman spent ten hours a day, six days a week tabulating the work hours of railroad laborers at several tent construction camps, transporting himself from site to site by hand-powered railcar. Truman paid the workers every second Saturday night, often distributing the money in saloons and then watching as the men drank up enough of their wages to force them back to work the following Monday.

That job ended several months later, when the railroad track was completed.

Permanent work was hard to find. At *The Kansas City Star*, for a few weeks in August of 1902, Truman had "wrapped singles" in the newspaper's mailroom. That job, which likely left Truman's hands black from the inky newsprint, paid either seven or nine dollars a week. But ultimately a friend approached Truman about a job at Kansas City's National Bank of Commerce, which was looking for a clerk in its basement bank vault.

Truman started at the bank in 1903, at a salary that he remembered as thirty-five dollars a month. He applied himself, and eventually earned forty dollars a month – perhaps more than what his father was making. More important, however, was that the job demanded downtown residency. At first he lived with his parents. But in 1905, when John Truman decided to raise farm crops in Clinton, Missouri, young Truman was on his own. He took a room with an aunt, but later found space in a Kansas City boarding house at five dollars a week.

His interests changed. Back in 1901 he had enrolled at Spalding's Commercial College, which instructed students in skills such as shorthand and accounting. But now he abandoned that curriculum. He also quit his piano lessons – so faithfully followed before – to save more money. At the bank, Truman asked for a raise. Refused it, he took a similar position at the nearby Union National Bank, making seventy-five dollars a month and then later a hundred dollars a month – a "magnificent salary," Truman later remembered.

Accounting courses and piano lessons should have been within reach now, but again, he had found new enthusiasms. In June 1905 he joined the Missouri National Guard, paying twenty-five cents a week for the privilege of drilling in a local armory. The pride he took upon joining was keen. "I was twenty-one years old in May of that year and could do as I pleased," he wrote.

Solomon Young, Harry Truman's maternal grandfather, died in 1892, but his influence on his grandson was profound. Decades later Harry Truman came to appreciate the grit that Grandfather Young had displayed leading wagon trails west to California and Utah.

Harriet Louisa Young, Truman's maternal grandmother, had emigrated with her husband, Solomon, from Shelby County, Kentucky, in 1841.

In 1844 they acquired eighty acres in southern Jackson County, which along with several parcels added over the years, came to be known as the Young farm. Grandmother Young was the grandparent Harry Truman knew best.

Mary Jane Holmes Truman, Harry's paternal grandmother, died in 1879, five years before his birth.

There were limits to Truman's bravado, as he never considered rejecting his family or the responsibilities that came with it.

Of his four grandparents, he knew three. His paternal grandmother, Mary Jane Truman, had died in 1879, five years before his birth. Mary Jane's husband – and Harry Truman's paternal grandfather – was Anderson Shipp Truman, who had come to western Missouri from Kentucky in 1846. With his bride he accepted a slave as a wedding present from his mother-in-law, Nancy Tyler Holmes, and the young couple settled on a farm on land that later became part of Kansas City. Decades later, Anderson Truman would live on the Grandview farm of Solomon and Harriet Louisa Young, Truman's maternal grandparents. Anderson Truman died when the future president was a toddler.

The Youngs made such a lasting impression on their young grandson that he would write of them often decades later. Both Solomon and Harriet Young emigrated from Shelby County, Kentucky, in 1841. Settling first near the Missouri River in what later became Kansas City, in 1844 the Youngs acquired eighty acres in southern Jackson County, in a district called Blue Ridge.

This land, as well as several parcels added to it over the years, became known as the Young farm, which would eventually serve as home for the three-year-old Harry Truman, whose parents brought him there in 1887.

Both Young grandparents captured

Truman's imagination. As a boy Harry Truman knew Solomon Young as the grandfather who took him along to horse races in Belton. But it was decades later that Truman really came to appreciate the grit that Grandfather Young had displayed as a freighter on the overland trails leading out of Independence and Kansas City. From the 1840s through the 1860s, Solomon Young helped lead wagon trains west to California and Utah.

About a century later the freighter's grandson thought often of Young, especially while traveling west in the presidential aircraft. In 1950, after flying from Kansas City to Salt Lake City in three hours, Truman couldn't resist comparing his route with his grandfather's. "It took Grandpa Young three months to make that trip one way," he wrote cousin Nellie Noland.

Young died in 1892, when Truman was still a boy. But his influence on Truman remained profound even in his absence. When the future president invested family capital in an oil-drilling business in 1916, his mother, Martha, told him to keep close the memory of Solomon Young – her father – as he had known economic ruin several times, only to eventually prevail as an overland freighter.

In 1948, as a president campaigning during an election few thought he could win, Truman stopped to speak in Salt Lake City. "Oh, I wish my grandfather could see me now," he told the crowd. In 1953, when he was back in Independence from the White House and considering plans for his presidential library, Truman made rough sketches of how he remembered the first Young farm

Anderson Shipp Truman, Harry Truman's paternal grandfather, had come to western Missouri from Kentucky in 1846 with his bride, Mary Jane. Anderson Truman died when Harry was a toddler.

home, before it had burned in 1894.

He wanted his library to look like it.

Also in the 1950s, when he was writing his presidential memoirs, Truman couldn't resist seeing parallels in his early life and his professional one. "I used to watch my father and mother close to learn what I could do to please them, just as I did with my school-teachers and playmates," he once wrote. "Because of my efforts to get along with my associates, I usually was able to get what I wanted. It was successful on the farm, in school, in the Army and particularly in the Senate."

His experience clearing checks in the basement vault of the National Bank of Commerce may have given him confidence, some forty years later, to lead a Senate committee investigating waste in the defense industry.

He apparently resented the sight of personal power being abused. In one memoir the older Truman reached back several decades to identify Charles H. Moore, an executive at National Bank of Commerce.

"His job was to do the official bawling out," Truman wrote. "He was an artist at it. . . . He was never so happy as when he could call some poor inoffensive little clerk up before him in the grand lobby of the biggest bank west of the Mississippi and tell him how dumb and inefficient he was because he'd sent a check belonging in the remittance of the State Bank of Oakland, Kansas, to Ogden, Utah."

It's unclear whether the "little clerk" referred to is Truman or a colleague. But it's not hard to imagine the young man bristling at the sight of such an upbraiding, given the tenacious nature of his parents and the frontier achievements of his grandparents.

The grandparent he knew best, Harriet Louisa Young, would live seventeen more years than her husband, dying in 1909. Of the three grandparents he knew, it was Grandmother Young that Truman mentioned first in his memoirs, describing how she laughed while he was chasing that frog as a two-year-old.

It was to her farm that Truman would return in 1906, and not as a child but as a young man with other options. She apparently never forgot that. Upon her death Grandmother Young willed the Grandview farm to Martha Ellen Young – Truman's mother – and her brother Harrison, for whom the future president was named.

She cut off her five other children.

Uncle Harrison, meanwhile, figured in the young Truman's life in crucial ways. Harrison lived much of his life in Kansas City. When he brought the Truman children presents and candy on his frequent visits, the young Harry may have associated him with the possibilities that that lay beyond his parents' home. "When he came," Truman once wrote of Uncle Harrison, "it was just like Christmas."

But that was not all. For several years Uncle Harrison lived with Grandmother Young on the Grandview farm, but he eventually decided that he was not suited for the work. He resolved to return to Kansas City. That meant John Truman, who then was trying to grow corn in Clinton, Missouri, had an opportunity in Grandview. John Truman's bad luck forced the matter, as a flood had ruined his corn crop in Clinton.

It was here, perhaps, that Harry Truman's youth ended. The future president, twenty-one years old, acted as the designated grown-up, persuading his parents to move back to the family farm. "I took the word to them at Clinton and urged them to move," Truman wrote.

"So in 1906 we all moved to the old home place at Grandview."

CLINTON'S DRUGSTORE

Harry Truman's first real job was at Clinton's drugstore, on the northeast corner of Independence Square.

Truman was about fourteen, and he worked there for several months, reporting to the drugstore before school at 6:30 A.M. and sometimes working several hours on Saturdays and Sundays.

His responsibilities included opening the store in the morning, sweeping the sidewalk, mopping the floor, and dusting the hundreds of small vials in which owner J.H. Clinton offered his various tonics and remedies.

"There must have been a thousand bottles to dust and yards and yards of patent-medicine cases and shelves to clean," Truman wrote in his memoirs. "At least it seemed that way, because I never finished the bottles and shelves by schooltime and had to start the next morning where I'd left off the day before. By the time I got around them all, it was time to start over."

His first week's wages were three silver dollars. That money, he later wrote, was "the biggest thing that ever happened to me." He tried to give the money to his father, who refused it. Ultimately his father suggested that he quit the drugstore and use the time to better pursue his studies.

But Truman's principal memory from his time at Clinton's was the hypocrisy he saw exhibited by some of the town's champions of temperance. Behind the drugstore's prescription case, which faced the front and shut off the view of the back end of the drugstore, there was a secluded spot. That is where, for these clients,

Clinton kept several bottles of whiskey. The customers would walk back, throw back their shots, look through an observation hole in front the prescription case, and leave. The price: ten cents an ounce.

Truman resented the practice. "There were saloons aplenty around the square in Independence," Truman later wrote, "and many leading men in town made no bones about going into them and buying a drink. I learned to think more highly of them than I did of the prescription-counter drinkers."

Truman, the son of a Baptist mother, never attempted to hide his occasional drink of bourbon.

The original Clinton's drugstore burned down in 1906. The building later was rebuilt and the drugstore re-established in it. Today Clinton's Soda Fountain, a restaurant and coffee shop, operates on the same site at 100 West Maple Avenue.

As a youth, working at Clinton's drugstore, Harry Truman observed the hypocrisy of some of the town's champions of temperance, who would put down ten cents and take a shot of whiskey in a secluded part of the store. Items recovered from the drugstore in recent years include these medicine bottles and a shot glass.

One day about forty years ago, a researcher handed Harry Truman a letter he'd once written to his mother, Martha Ellen Young Truman.

The researcher told Truman he wanted to get the former president's voice on tape. Maybe, he suggested, Truman could read aloud one of his letters to his mother, who had died in 1947. But this request proved an awkward one. On the audiotape that survives of this moment, there is a pause.

"I can't do it," Truman finally said. "I can't do it."

Since the mid-1990s Truman Museum researchers have been processing the eighteen thousand film and audio clips that were generated during the early 1960s production of a twenty-six-part documentary called *Decision: The Conflicts of Harry S. Truman.* In the spring of 2003, the museum released approximately seventy-five minutes of film and eleven hours of sound recording from the collection – including the moment when the former president choked up. It was new audio evidence of just how emotional Truman could get about his mother and father.

John and Martha Truman married in 1881. John was thirty years old, Martha twenty-nine. They moved to Lamar, Missouri, some ninety miles south of Jackson County, where John Truman bought and sold live-

stock. Their first child, a boy, was stillborn. The second child, also a boy, was born on May 8, 1884. They named him Harry. Two other children, John Vivian and Mary Jane, followed.

John Truman instructed his children that honor was everything. Decades later, Truman told a story describing how, as a young man, he had bought a soda at the Kansas City candy store operated by Jesse James Jr., son of the Missouri outlaw. When Truman discovered he didn't have enough change to pay for the soda, James merely told him to settle the account the next time he came in.

"I paid the nickel the next day!" Truman wrote years later. "My father stood for honesty."

John Truman was a perfectionist, often criticizing his son Harry if he didn't plow a straight line on the family's Grandview farm. He rode him hard, routinely finding other chores that needed doing when Harry's mind was elsewhere. "I have to write this on the installment plan," Harry wrote Bess Wallace on November 26, 1912. "As usual, Papa keeps wanting something."

John was a risk taker, gambling his family's resources in the early 1900s on grain futures. He

stood five feet four inches tall, two inches shorter than his wife, and often was described as bantamlike. He was combative. One story details how the elder Truman chased a lawyer out of the Jackson County Courthouse after the lawyer charged him with embroidering the truth.

It's easy to see this John Truman in his son, the future president, who during his 1948 whistlestop presidential election campaign seemed to be the only one who thought he had a chance.

Ultimately, John Truman's tenacity was literally the end of him, in that while working as a Jackson County road overseer in 1914, he had refused to quit trying to move a boulder on a road. In continuing his efforts, the elder Truman injured himself. An X-ray revealed a hernia that caused an intestinal blockage. An operation in Kansas City's Swedish Hospital followed that October, but John Truman began to fade. He died November 2, 1914.

As much as he admired his father, the future president enjoyed an abiding relationship with his mother, who lived for almost thirty-three more years.

Martha Ellen Young Truman was educated, attending

Lexington Baptist Female College as a young woman. She was fun, sometimes referring to herself as a "lightfoot" Baptist, meaning that she would dance on occasion.

And, on several important matters, she would intervene on behalf of her eldest son and his two siblings.

It was she, according to one story, who noticed how young Harry was not responding to the glare of the Fourth of July fireworks one year, but to their sounds. She took him to a Kansas City optometrist, who fitted the young boy with glasses.

Martha Ellen apparently handled the physical discipline of the Truman children. "She kept a good switch and a slipper handy for application to the spot where the most good could be accomplished on young anatomy," Truman later wrote. But it was also his mother who, after seeing her son receive eyeglasses, encouraged him to read and play the piano.

In 1914 Martha Ellen underwent emergency surgery for a hernia. The procedure took place in the family's Grandview farmhouse, with Harry holding a lantern for the doctors. It wasn't long after this episode that Harry purchased his used Stafford automobile, transforming his life and allowing him to court Bess Wallace of Independence in far better style. Some scholars believe Martha Ellen encouraged her son to buy the car.

After the 1919 wedding of Truman and Bess Wallace, Truman's friend Ted Marks spoke with Martha Ellen Truman.

"Well now, Mrs. Truman, you've lost Harry," Marks said.

"Indeed I haven't," Mrs. Truman replied.

She wasn't kidding. Martha Ellen enjoyed a special relationship with her eldest son until her death in 1947. She was a partner in his political career.

She was present during an August 1944 appearance by Truman at his Lamar, Missouri, birthplace after being nominated as Franklin Roosevelt's vice presidential running mate.

"Am I proud of him?" she said, responding to a reporter's question. "Say, I knew that boy would amount to something from the time he was nine years old. He could plow the straightest row of corn in the county."

In the eyes of Harry Truman, those who sought to injure him through his mother represented the lowest form of political life. In 1940 the judges who controlled the Jackson County Court decided to foreclose on a court-held mortgage on the Truman farm in Grandview. On Tuesday, July 16, officials sold at auction 195 acres of the farm on the Kansas City courthouse steps. Truman suspected it had been done for political reasons, to humiliate him during his U.S. Senate re-election campaign. He did not have the money to save his mother from eviction.

"Old man Montgomery as presiding judge foreclosed to embarrass me," Truman told Truman biographer Jonathan Daniels, referring to George S. Montgomery, elected Jackson County presiding judge in 1940. "They sold it under the hammer without giving us any chance to refinance and moved Mamma off

the farm. She broke her hip in the house I got for her."

Martha Ellen visited Washington for the first time for Mother's Day in 1945, staying in the White House.

She grew ill two years later, suffering a stroke in the spring of 1947. Truman checked into Kansas City's Hotel Muehlebach and, for thirteen days, traveled between the hotel and his mother's Grandview home. She rallied sufficiently for Truman to return to Washington. But on July 26, 1947, Mary Jane notified her brother that their mother was suffering from pneumonia and might not last through the day. Truman ordered his presidential plane, the *Sacred Cow*, to be made ready.

She died not long before noon. She was ninety-four.

"In 1947 my mother lay for weeks on a rocking bed suffering no end," Truman wrote in a 1952 diary entry. "When she finally passed on I was over Cincinnati and instinctively I knew she'd gone. I'd been dozing and dreamed she'd said, 'Goodbye, Harry. Be a good boy.' When Dr. [Wallace] Graham came into my room on the *Sacred Cow* I knew what he would say."

To his daughter, Margaret, Truman wrote, "Someday you'll be an orphan just as your dad is now."

Theodore Roosevelt took several pairs of glasses to Cuba for the Spanish-American War.

So did Harry Truman to France during World War I.
But it had little to do with his regard for Roosevelt.

The relationship Harry Truman had with his eyeglasses was lifelong.

It is the rare photograph that captures Truman not wearing them. He took them off for his high school graduation class picture, while attending a 1920 reunion of his World War I artillery battery in Kansas City, and while getting a haircut as president.

David Lilienthal, chairman of the Atomic Energy Commission, was sufficiently startled when the president took off his glasses during a 1949 conversation that he later made a note of it. "He took off his glasses, first time I saw him without them, large, fine eyes," Lilienthal wrote.

He received his glasses at age six. His mother, Martha Ellen Truman, concerned about her son's vision, took him to a Kansas City optometrist. He diagnosed a malformation that he called "flat eyeballs," or hypermetropia, and Mrs. Truman paid ten dollars for a pair of wire-rimmed glasses.

Decades later, Truman still remembered the moment.

"When I first put the glasses on I saw things and saw print I'd never seen before," he wrote. "I learned to read when I was five but could never see the fine print."

The downside of wearing glasses Truman also learned right away. Spectacles, common on adults in 1890, were a curiosity on such a young child. Told to protect the glasses, he did not play sports such as baseball, and instead concentrated on reading and playing the piano.

In later years, after Truman became president, some former boyhood friends remembered things differently. Henry Bundschu, longtime Independence resident, circulated a pamphlet that included a description of how young Harry had joined one baseball game when the neighborhood boys had found themselves a player short.

"He took his place at first base and it wasn't but a few minutes before we found out that he could holler louder, throw the ball harder, and play just as rough as any kid on the lot," Bundschu wrote. "If there was anybody there that harbored the idea that because Harry Truman played the piano he couldn't play baseball, it vanished that day."

Truman, reading this account, told Bundschu that he remembered joining the game as an umpire, and then later taking the field.

As he courted Bess Wallace, Truman conceded that his eyeglasses might not render him a dashing romantic. "I could die happy doing something for you. (Just imagine a guy with spectacles and a girl mouth doing the

Mize Peters, friend of Truman's since childhood. On Truman wearing glasses as a boy:

"It was very unusual for children to wear glasses then. Kids had a tendency to make fun of people who wore glasses. They'd call him four-eyes. But it didn't seem to bother him to be called that."

Sir Lancelot)," he once wrote Bess.

As an adult, Truman took off his glasses for another photograph, this one for his American Expeditionary Forces identity card. He had done the same thing for a portrait in his Missouri National Guard uniform. Maybe it was just a coincidence. Or maybe he was taking care to rid himself of the

Harry Truman first started wearing glasses when he was six years old. This pair was worn circa 1930.

assumptions of others – especially military officers – regarding men who wear glasses.

As a teenager, his thoughts of landing an appointment to the U.S. Military Academy at West Point, New York, ended with his poor eyesight.

Asked how, when he first joined the Missouri National Guard a few years later in 1905, he passed the eye exam, Truman simply said, "They needed recruits."

It grew more complicated as he grew older. When the Missouri Guard was brought into federal service in 1917, Truman finessed

the vision examination by memorizing the eye chart, said his brother, Vivian Truman. And yet Harry Truman still wasn't free of curious Army physicians. In February 1918, while training at Camp Doniphan in Oklahoma, he did some quick talking after an Army doctor quizzed him on his vision.

"They almost sent me home on a physical, too, yesterday, but I talked to the M.D.," Truman wrote Bess Wallace that month. "He turned my eyes down twice and threatened to send me to division headquarters for a special examination and then didn't. I guess I can put [on] a real good conversation when circumstances demand it."

To be sent home on the eve of leaving for Europe would have been a crushing blow to Truman. Perhaps that's why, upon arrival in New York, he sought out an oculist recommended by a New York optician who was a fellow Mason.

"Bought two pairs of glasses, which make me six pairs so I don't suppose I'll run out," Truman wrote Bess on March 27, 1918.

All six pairs of glasses were pince-nez models, and it was not because he was so enamored of Teddy Roosevelt. He had been advised that ordinary glasses with side stems would interfere with wearing a gas mask.

Truman's glasses did not go unremarked upon in France. Many members of Battery D, remembering the day Truman first took command of them in France, later recalled how the glasses contributed to the professorial look he presented. Those battery members who assumed Truman was a pushover would soon learn otherwise.

In action, there was at least one close call. Harry Vaughan, Truman's military aide during his presidency, once repeated the story that Truman had told him. Battery D was mounted and ready to move out on a night march when a low branch swept Truman's glasses off his face.

This was big trouble, since night troop movements in France were synchronized with the movement of other outfits. Still, Truman told Vaughan, he felt he had no choice but to halt the battery and find his baggage to dig out another pair of glasses.

Then luck intervened.

"As he turned to the rear," Vaughan said, "he put his hand on his horse's rump to turn around and he put his hand right on his glasses."

The battery moved out.

In 1895, an upright piano arrived at the Truman home in Independence. Good thing. A piano came in handy fifty years later when the young piano student in the Truman home, Harry, helped reorganize the free world during the post-World War II Potsdam conference in Germany.

With Winston Churchill and Joseph Stalin, Truman divided up the German Navy and accepted the Soviet Union's pledge to enter the war against Japan. Truman also ordered Staff Sergeant Eugene List, a concert pianist, flown from Paris to Potsdam to play Chopin at a banquet Truman arranged for his two fellow world leaders. The young pianist played, accompanied by a violinist. Then Truman himself took a turn at the keyboard.

Stalin was pleased and to accompany his own dinner, a few days later, ordered two pianists and two violinists.

If the presence of a piano at Potsdam did not deter the Soviet strongman in his designs for dominating eastern Europe, neither did it derail the ultimate agreements among the big three world leaders. A few months later, visiting a county fair in Caruthersville, Missouri, Truman sat down at a piano keyboard. "When I played this," he said, "Stalin signed the Potsdam agreement."

Truman's love for music and his fondness for the piano figured in several ways in the man's life and politics. Gathered around

Truman's various pianos at one time or another, beyond his friends and family, were Stalin and Churchill, actress Lauren Bacall, and even Richard Nixon, one of Truman's least favorite Republicans. Throughout his political life Truman was the target of mild jabs for his piano playing. But no one ever suggested that Truman's regard for music wasn't authentic.

"Did you ever sit and listen to an orchestra play a fine overture and imagine things were as they ought to be and not as they are?" Truman asked Bess Wallace in a November 1, 1911, letter. "Music that I can understand always makes me feel that way."

In 1890 the six-year-old Truman had received his eyeglasses, which changed his life in several ways. With the traditional sports of boys now denied him, Truman took to reading and the piano.

In 1895 the piano was delivered, an upright Kimball model that cost perhaps two hundred dollars. The Truman family then enlisted a next-door neighbor, Florence Burrus, to instruct young Harry. At about age fourteen Truman began walking to catch

Kansas City streetcars, due for appointments with piano instructor Grace White.

The boys of Independence noticed as he walked by, and the young Truman, at least now and then, felt their stares.

"You could see him watching the boys play," said Ardelia Palmer, an Independence teacher of Truman. "He would put his books and music roll down on the ground – he'd usually hide that music by putting his books on top of it."

Charlie Ross, Truman's friend and future press secretary, was among the boys who watched Truman go by.

"I distinctly recall, when we were together in high school, seeing the president on the street with his music roll," Ross said decades later. "He would be on his way to his music lessons. Mothers held him up as a model, so he took a lot of kidding. It required a lot of courage for a kid to take music lessons in a town like Independence."

Grace White was a demanding instructor, and Truman often awoke at five A.M. to practice before leaving for school. She was Truman's entrée to music royalty, having studied under pianist Theodore Leschetizky. When in 1900 the Polish pianist Paderewski – who had instructed Leschetizky – appeared in Kansas City, White and Truman attended his concert. Then they waited backstage, where Paderewski instructed the future president in playing *Minuet in G.*

Yet Truman ultimately let his lessons slide.

"When I got to be eighteen or nineteen and started to work, I decided it was sissy stuff," Truman recalled years later. "I joined the National Guard and then I worked on the farm. You know the rest. The country might have got a first-class pianist in a music hall. Instead it got a president."

Still, he played now and then, and his piano background came in handy in unexpected ways. When, while courting Bess Wallace, Truman was occasionally invited to the Wallace home for dinner, he sometimes would play afterward. The hard-to-impress Madge Gates Wallace was pleased, as she had attended a Cincinnati conservatory in her youth.

Truman never gave up the piano entirely. When, in 1935, he arrived in Washington as a new senator, he found an apartment first and then found a piano to rent for five dollars a month. Late on election night in 1944, Kansas City radio listeners heard, instead of election returns, a brief moment of Mozart's *Ninth Sonata.*

It was Truman, waiting out the election in a piano-equipped suite in Kansas City's Muehlebach Hotel.

Once his piano playing landed Truman into mild trouble. In 1945, two months before becoming president, Truman agreed to play an event for servicemen at the Washington Press Club. Also attending was actress Lauren Bacall. Soon, for the benefit of photographers, she was boosted onto the top of the vice president's piano. Truman kept playing to the enjoyment of all except, apparently Bess Truman, who told him to limit his public piano playing.

As president, Truman was asked who his favorite composers were. He often listed Chopin, Mozart, Bach, and Beethoven, adding on other occasions Cole Porter and George Gershwin.

He was proud when his daughter, Margaret, pursued a career as a concert singer. When one critic, Paul Hume of the *Washington Post*, derided Margaret in print, Truman wrote a letter defending her. "Someday I hope to meet you," Truman wrote Hume. "When that happens you'll need a new nose, a lot of beef-steak for black eyes, and perhaps a supporter below!" Yet Truman and Hume's mutual love of music ultimately overcame their animosity. Once, before attending a performance by Maria Callas in Kansas City, Hume went out to Independence to see Truman Museum and received a tour from the former president.

As president, Truman accepted the original manuscript for "I'm Just Wild About Harry" from composers Eubie Blake and Noble Sissle. The American Federation of Musicians sponsored a float in Truman's 1949 inaugural parade, with musicians playing that song again and again. In 1952, Truman played part of Mozart's *Ninth*

Sonata for a national television documentary of the just-restored White House.

After his presidency, Truman had more time to indulge in music. When visiting Salzburg, Austria, in 1956, Truman played a portion of Mozart's *Sonata in A Major* on the composer's own clavichord. In 1961, President John Kennedy invited Harry and Bess Truman to the White House. For the occasion, Eugene List again played for Truman, who

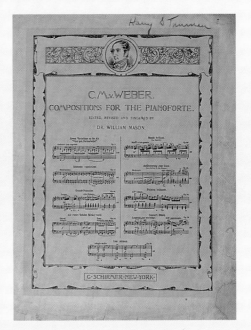

Truman's sheet music collection included "Rondo Brilliant," one of Carl Maria von Weber's compositions for the pianoforte.

again took a turn at the piano. The next year, when pianist Van Cliburn played Kansas City's Music Hall, Truman was there.

For all this, Truman should have sufficiently signaled his regard for quality composition. Yet he was saddled for much of his life with a song he didn't like: "The Missouri Waltz."

Delegates to the 1944 Democratic National Convention heard the song. So did voters in almost every town lining up to see Truman during his 1948 whistle-stop campaign trip. In 1949, the Missouri legislature adopted "The Missouri Waltz" as the state song. Yet when asked about the song during one national television interview, Truman shrugged off diplomacy.

"It's a ragtime song and if you let me say what I think – I don't give a damn about it, but I can't say it out loud because it's the song of Missouri," he said, adding, "It's as bad as 'The Star Spangled Banner' as far as music is concerned." On another occasion, Truman said it was merely a case of hearing one song too many times.

"I just got tired of it," he said.

In 1969, only two months after moving into the White House, President Richard Nixon, with wife, Pat, visited the Trumans in Independence. The Nixons arrived first at 219 North Delaware Street, and then left for the Truman Museum with Harry and Bess Truman.

There Nixon sat down at a piano and played "The Missouri Waltz."

In 1969, President Richard Nixon, with wife, Pat, visited the Truman home and, with Harry and Bess, the Truman Museum. There Nixon sat down at a piano and played "The Missouri Waltz."

READING AND WRITING

Harry Truman graduated from Independence High School on May 30, 1901. Of the forty-one members in his class, several either performed, spoke, or received awards during the graduation ceremony. The future president was not one of them.

The star of the class, in fact, may have been Truman's friend Charlie Ross, who during the ceremony delivered a short speech on William Shakespeare. At the event's conclusion Matilda Brown, who had taught both Ross and Truman, climbed onto the school's stage and bestowed a kiss on Ross.

Truman, standing nearby, asked if he would receive one as well.

"Not until you have done something worthwhile," Brown said.

The Independence school district had high standards. But if Truman apparently was just one of the rank-and-file members of the Class of 1901, that was no small thing. The Independence schools were a source of pride to the town's residents, and Truman's nine years of instruction from the community's teachers had been, for the Truman family, worth leaving the Young farm in Grandview back in 1890.

By the time of his graduation Truman had completed high school courses in geography, history, English, algebra, geometry, science, mathematics, and Latin.

He had been a member of the debate team. He and several other students had published the high school's first annual, which

they called *The Gleam*, after "Merlin and the Gleam," an Alfred Tennyson poem. "And, ere it vanishes / Over the margin / After it, follow it / Follow the Gleam," the poem read. (Today the annual yearbook produced by William Chrisman High School of Independence is still entitled *The Gleam*.)

Truman's achievement in math convinced one teacher, Ardelia Palmer, that his success in figuring artillery firing problems during World War I was thanks in part to the instruction he received in the Independence, Missouri, schools.

When Truman attended high school, such higher education was still a novelty for many young people. The district's first high school class in 1889 included seven students; the 1890 class, two. Instead of going to high school, many boys simply went on to work. Truman's class of forty-one included thirty young women.

It was a school district of its time and place. Among the responsibilities of the schools' janitors was to keep the inkwells filled. The district's library, according to a 1909 district handbook, was open to "all white residents . . . on furnishing satisfactory

guarantee of proper handling of books." One of Truman's favorite teachers, Ardelia Palmer, could not teach during Truman's last year of high school, as she had married the district's superintendent, W. L. C. Palmer. Married women did not then teach in Independence schools.

Truman aimed high. With another student he studied with tutors, hoping to do well enough on examinations to qualify for a service academy appointment. Truman's studying colleague received an appointment to the U.S. Naval Academy in Annapolis, Maryland. Truman's eyesight, however, did not meet military academy standards.

Likely the greatest legacy left by the Independence school district on young Harry Truman was his regard for reading and writing.

He had arrived an eager student. An 1893-94 report card included these

Harry Truman and several other students published Independence High School's first annual, which they called *The Gleam*, after an Alfred Tennyson poem titled "Merlin and the Gleam."

grades: Spelling, 95; Reading, 96; Writing, 92; Language, 99; Numbers, 99; Deportment, 95. Such marks are perhaps one reason why, after Truman missed much schooling due to a bout with diphtheria, he was allowed to attend summer school and then skip the third grade.

"The teachers loved him," Palmer said.

But in some subjects, Truman went well beyond his teachers. For her son's tenth birthday in 1894, Martha Ellen Truman presented him with a four-volume set of books entitled *Great Men and Famous Women*. The books included biographies of historical figures

far more than romantic adventure," he later recalled. "It was solid instruction and wise teaching which I somehow felt that I wanted and needed."

He descended upon the Independence library, apparently resolving to read every book there. Some Truman biographers have tried to estimate whether the young Truman could actually have done this. The Independence library began in 1894 with the donation of about four hundred volumes from a local library society. By 1909, the library offered some four thousand volumes.

The point is, young Harry Truman read in the library and he

in the end he'd win the Battle of Waterloo," Truman once recalled.

While he read, he also wrote. Truman's sturdy penmanship remains a revelation to historians, who are routinely amazed at the sheer number of his letters. In the more than twelve hundred letters Truman mailed just to Bess Wallace in his lifetime, the first was written on December 31, 1910, almost ten years after their graduation from high school. (That letter's first line: "I am very glad you liked the book.")

Truman's correspondence, through the years of his courtship of Bess Wallace, often featured updates regarding the content of

such as Napoleon, Sir Francis Drake, Benjamin Franklin, and Robert E. Lee. From all accounts this particular set of volumes changed Truman's life, and altered what he thought might be possible for his own life.

"Reading history, to me, was

read at home. He read while on duty at Clinton's drugstore, the job he reported to for several months as a teenager. "I spent many of my odd moments and many that belonged to my employer reading the life of Napoleon – always hoping that

Harry Truman's high school books included Shakespeare's *Macbeth* and *The Merchant of Venice*, George Eliot's *Silas Marner*, Alfred Lord Tennyson's *Idylls of the King*, and poems of Robert Burns. Truman wrote his name in most of his books. In this edition of *Macbeth*, he also added the initials of Independence High School.

particular magazines. In the same letters he expresses solemn concerns about stationery: its varieties, or the constant need for more.

"That's an awful smear," he says, beginning one letter in February 1912, "but my Santa Fe deluxe stationery is on the wane and every sheet counts."

Commercial College in downtown Kansas City, and later, the Kansas City School of Law. He left both institutions when other responsibilities or enthusiasms commanded his attention. Even as a senator, upon arrival in Washington, Truman announced that he would be attending Georgetown University.

officer who served as a companion and bodyguard for the former president during his later years, often drove the Trumans to and from a nearby library. In the late 1960s and early 1970s some Independence residents said it was sometimes possible, when passing by a window on the Truman home's north façade, to glimpse

Henry Chiles, longtime friend of Harry Truman since boyhood:

"I saw Harry go home many a time with two or three books on weekends, and I guess by Monday he had them all read. The rest of us just read Jesse James, these little paperback books, Jesse James stories. We were reading those in the barn loft."

His spelling grew sloppy as an adult. "The English language so far as spelling goes was created by Satan I am sure," Truman wrote Bess in 1912. This attitude followed him throughout his life. When, in 2003, the National Archives released a 1947 presidential diary just recently discovered, one historian remarked that it was further proof that the thirty-third president was an indifferent speller.

In all, Truman attended six grades of grammar school and three years of high school. Some biographers have wondered whether Truman felt sheepish about his lack of higher education. After high school he enrolled at other schools: first, Spalding's

And yet, if he never earned a traditional college degree, neither was Truman unschooled. In one instance, Truman corrected the Latin of Fred Vinson, who served as chief justice of the United States Supreme Court. On another occasion, his grasp of central Asian history startled Secretary of State Dean Acheson, a graduate of Yale University and Harvard Law School.

And, in 1956, Truman received an honorary doctor of civil law degree at Oxford University.

Truman spent his last days as he did many of his earliest, reading.

Mike Westwood, an Independence, Missouri, police

the silhouette of the former president seated, presumably with a book.

For the record, the Truman colleague who received the appointment to the Naval Academy left Annapolis not long after his arrival.

Truman, of course, became president. In 1945, after Truman named Charlie Ross as his press secretary, the two of them placed a call to Matilda Brown, who more than forty years before had challenged Truman to do something worthwhile.

"Do I get that kiss?" the president asked.

An early photo of the Grandview
house with Harry Truman's mother,
Martha Ellen Truman, his grandmother,
Harriet Louisa Young, and Harry.

CHAPTER 2

ON THE FARM

arry Truman spent about ten years on the family farm in Grandview, in southern Jackson County, between 1906 and 1917.

The experience changed the young man in ways he may not have anticipated. Truman came to the farm as a twenty-two-year-old banker used to spending his work-day examining checks and ledgers. Then, one morning, he woke up on his grand-mother's six-hundred-acre farm. Most likely he awoke to his father's voice before dawn, hailing him and his younger brother, Vivian.

"He taught us not to fear work," Vivian said of his father some forty-five years later.

Truman's mother described the farm's effect on her son in another way. "It was on the farm that Harry got his common sense," she once said. "He didn't get it in town."

But there was still another consequence of the future president's farm interlude. It was on the farm that Harry Truman had to be a grown-up.

Truman came to the property in 1906 because his Uncle Harrison, who had helped operate the farm since the 1892 death of his father, Solomon, finally decided that the farm life wasn't for him. He wanted to move to Kansas City.

The responsibility of running the Young farm then fell to John and Martha Truman, the future president's parents. But at the time they were in Clinton, Missouri, trying to raise corn. So young Harry Truman traveled

to Clinton and sold his parents on returning to the Grandview farm.

They came back in 1905, with Truman following the next year.

Soon, there were six in residence: his grandmother, Harriet Louisa Young; his parents, John and Martha; Vivian; his younger sister, Mary Jane; and himself.

Grandmother Young died in 1909.

Then, in December 1910, when a horse pulled over a beam on his father, breaking his leg, young Harry considered himself in charge. "I don't think I'll ever make much of a mark as a farmer or anywhere else, but sometimes I have to come across," he wrote to Bess Wallace the next month.

Vivian married in 1911 and left the Young property for another farm. Perhaps in view of his added responsibilities, Truman left the Missouri National Guard the same year.

John Truman died in 1914. At least one Truman family acquaintance, hired farmhand Brownie Huber, noticed a similarity between that occasion and another traumatic moment more than thirty years later.

"Harry and I often got up really early and very quietly so as not to awaken his mother and sister," Huber once recalled. "He would make biscuits, cook oatmeal, and fry eggs. That is the way it was the

Truman lived in this Grandview farmhouse from 1906 to 1917. During this period, Truman was a farmer, working the six-hundred-acre farm. In his mother's opinion, it was on the farm that Truman got "common sense." *Photo by Ray Geselbracht*

morning his father died. I was eating breakfast while Harry went in to stay with the old gentleman, when he appeared the door and said, 'Dad just passed away.'

"I thought of that moment and of the way Harry carried on the other day when I heard that President Roosevelt was dead."

Upon his father's death, it was Harry Truman's lot to run the farm with his mother and sister. But by then he was thirty years old, with eight years of experience, and he went on to operate the farm with the help of hired men.

Truman prided himself on being a progressive farmer. Coming to the farm from the bank, he kept careful books charting the Truman farm's livestock. He practiced crop rotation, not universal practice at the time, and this led to increased yields. Wheat on

the Young-Truman farm grew from thirteen to nineteen bushels per acre.

Like his father, Truman did everything. "I plowed, sowed, reaped, milked cows, fed hogs, doctored horses, baled hay, and did everything there was to do on a six-hundred-acre farm," Truman once remembered. Power for the Truman family's various farm implements, such as a gangplow or corn planter, was supplied by animals like mules or horses. Sometimes Truman would yell at the animals in his sleep.

His talent at plowing a straight row was part of the Truman legend when he began running for senator. He was good at it, Truman later recalled, because his father would not permit the occasional empty space in a field of corn or wheat. "I'd hear of it for a year," Truman once explained.

There were many farm tasks young Harry disliked, such as milking the dairy cows. He didn't enjoy placing rings in the noses of the farm's hogs. Hogs provided reliable cash flow so the animals, he wrote Bess, were a "necessary evil." When, in 1914, Harry brought a load of hogs to a stockyards operation, he couldn't get away fast enough.

"I suppose I'll carry some of the malodorous dust from those hog yards in my clothes for sixty days," he wrote Bess. "I wouldn't work down there for fifteen dollars a day."

Life on the farm, wrote Truman scholar Robert Ferrell, "properly increased the solitude that must be a part of everyone's makeup if that person is to do large things." And yet in

Winter photograph of the Truman farm in Grandview, Missouri. Circa 1915

the midst of this isolation – or perhaps because of it – Truman grew more social.

He joined the Masons. He joined the farm bureau in his township in 1913 and became an officer the next year. When, in 1914, he bought a used Stafford automobile, he spent much of his free time driving to Independence to court Bess Wallace. Also in 1914, he was appointed Grandview postmaster, but gave the post and its fifty-dollar-a-month salary to a local widow.

He attended meetings of the Washington Township Improvement Association, which agitated for better roads.

He surprised his neighbors in small ways. He never wore overalls on the farm. He played the piano, sometimes in the presence of other men. "He seemed to be more interested in National Guard work and in reading and in music," Gaylon Babcock, one neighbor, recalled. Babcock remembered a day when he and several others were helping out on the Truman farm. Prior to a meal, Babcock said, Truman, "instead of coming out and associating with us men, who were waiting for a short time before we ate, he played the piano. It was very noticeable." Truman, Babcock added, "liked his music, he liked his lodge work. Frankly, I would say he was a little less rugged in his likes and dislikes."

Yet few things were more rugged than Jackson County politics, in which Truman soon took an interest. When his father was named an area election judge, he named Harry an election clerk. John Truman later was named a Jackson County road overseer and upon his death, his son took over the position. In 1916 Truman ran for committeeman in the Washington Township of Jackson County, and lost.

Ultimately, the farm could not hold Truman's attention. He tried his luck with a lead and zinc mine in Oklahoma, and then entered the oil business. When war beckoned in 1917, Truman rejoined the Missouri National Guard and ultimately served in France. When he returned from World War I in 1919, Truman remained on the family farm for only a few weeks.

He stayed long enough to perform one more neighborly act. Stephen Slaughter, a member of the family whose property adjoined the Young-Truman farm, remembered a 1919 hog cholera outbreak when Slaughter and his father decided to vaccinate their hogs. Wrestling with the animals was work and, as Slaughter's father could not handle the task, they asked Mrs. Truman if Harry could help.

Harry, just a few weeks away from being married, showed up at 4:30 A.M. the following morning.

"We finished the job, brushed the dirt off our clothes, and Harry rode away," Slaughter recalled. "All part of being a neighbor."

But ultimately Truman decided to open a downtown Kansas City haberdashery. That September he organized a farm sale,

Mary Jane Truman, Harry Truman, Martha Young Truman, Myra Colgan (Truman's cousin), Vivian Truman, and Nellie Noland on a wagon at the Truman farm, circa 1908.

Mary Ethel Noland, Nellie Tilford Noland, Harry Truman, and Mary Jane Truman ice skating on the Grandview farm circa 1911.

Belton Masonic Lodge. Truman petitioned for membership in the Belton Masonic Lodge in December 1908. He was accepted soon after and quickly passed through the different degrees of membership.
Photo by Ray Geselbracht

offering at auction more than two hundred hogs, eighteen horses and mules, plus many farm implements.

That November he was back in downtown Kansas City, standing behind the counters of his haberdashery. Bess Wallace, whom he had married several months before, had never shown much interest in being a farmer's wife.

Throughout Truman's political career, voters heard a lot about Truman's farm background. "You folks won't get a chance very often to vote for a farmer for United States senator," one Dade County, Missouri, resident said when introducing Truman during his first Senate campaign in 1934. "Why, his hands fit cultivator handles just like owl's claws fit a limb."

Voters associated Truman with the farm as much as they did the piano. Roy Roberts, *The Kansas City Star* editor to whom Truman granted an interview at the White House just after becoming president in 1945, wrote what an amazing story Truman's rise was. After all, less than thirty years before, Truman had been forced to watch the rears of the draft animals pulling his plows.

During a stop at Dexter, Iowa, during his 1948 whistlestop presidential campaign, Truman detailed how 223,000 farmers had lost their farms under a Republican administration in 1932. Further, the Republican Congress of 1948 had "stuck a pitchfork in the farmer's back," Truman said, referring to a bill that had inhibited the acquisition of

additional grain-storage bins during a heavy harvest season.

Few questioned Truman's farm credentials. His grandfather Solomon Young had begun acquiring land in southern Jackson County in the 1840s, and began adding to his holdings just after the Civil War. Harry Truman, then three years old, first arrived on the Young farm with his parents in 1887, when the now elderly Solomon requested that John Truman help out on the farm.

Then the John Truman family had left for Independence and its schools in 1890.

When Harriet Louisa Young died in 1909, she willed her acreage to Harrison Young and Martha Ellen Young Truman, Harry Truman's mother. Her five other children received five dollars each, and the litigation that followed dragged on until 1919.

The farm bailed the Truman family out of occasional financial difficulty. Martha Ellen sold about two hundred acres to a developer in 1922. Martha and Mary Jane continued living there through 1940, with Vivian farming the land.

In 1938, in need of money, the Truman family took out a $35,000 mortgage on the farm from the Jackson County School Fund. State law permitted county judges to lend school money not currently needed. The loan was extended for two years, and in 1940 the county court, then predominately Republican, foreclosed on the loan during Harry Truman's Senate re-election campaign.

The candidate's mother and sister were forced from the home, something Truman never forgot.

In 1945, Truman friends organized a syndicate to repurchase the farm property with the understanding that it would be sold back to the Truman family. In 1945 Harry and Vivian Truman purchased eighty-seven acres, which included the old farm house. Harry Truman purchased another parcel in 1946.

In 1958 much of the Truman farm land in Grandview was sold to a Kansas City developer. The sale made life comfortable for the Trumans.

"It wasn't Truman's rise to political power or his world renown, his books or lectures, or the legacy of his wife's family that saw him through in the end, but the old farm at Grandview," Truman scholar David McCullough wrote.

Today the Truman farm at 12301 Blue Ridge Boulevard in Grandview rests uneasily amid strip malls and fast-food restaurants.

Although a federal grant in 1979 helped acquire the property, the farm home had been vacant and in disrepair as recently as 1983. After local Truman admirers led efforts to restore the property, the Jackson County Parks and Recreation Department took it over in 1987. In 1993, President Bill Clinton signed legislation making the home and the approximately five acres on which it stands part of the Harry S Truman National Historic Site, which also operates the Truman home in Independence.

Now, during summer weekends, the Grandview home is accessible to visitors. It is inside the house, standing on the second floor and while looking to the west through a front window, where it is easiest to imagine how things once were.

In the distance two stone pillars stand in the parking lot of a steakhouse. A century ago these posts marked the entrance to the Truman farm. In July 1914, Mary Jane Truman, who had persuaded her older brother to teach her how to drive the Stafford, ran the car into the farm's front gate.

"The gate looks rather sickly," Harry wrote Bess. "I am very thankful that she hit the gate instead of a stone post."

One of the two stone pillars that then marked the entrance to the Young-Truman farm has been knocked over twice in recent years by errant steakhouse customers. Both times it has been repaired.

Truman on plow circa 1910.

Bess Wallace in pigtails at age thirteen, February 1898.

CHAPTER 3

BESS TRUMAN

In 1952 Washington correspondent Inez Robb wrote this about Bess Wallace Truman:

"Most of her life has been spent in two large white houses, both of which dominate their respective communities."

Robb first was referring to the White House in Washington. She also was speaking of the large house at 219 North Delaware Street in Independence, which Bess would consider her real home for seventy-eight of her ninety-seven years.

The comparison was apt. Journalists faced with covering Bess Truman often tried to reconcile the distance between the Bess Truman presented to official Washington, and the Bess Truman whom her Independence friends insisted they knew. One problem was that, upon her husband's arrival in the Washington White House in 1945, Bess Truman felt no need to honor Eleanor Roosevelt's press conference policy. She announced that there would be no press conferences. Nor would there be any interviews or speeches. For a Washington press corps that craved access, there was no access.

Thus kept at arm's length, some reporters wrote about receiving a courteous note from the First Lady or winning a smile from her at a reception. These scraps of personality then were pondered in attempts to divine the "riddle" of Bess Truman, as one headline in *Collier's* magazine declared in 1952.

"She gives the impression of being anxious to be elsewhere," wrote *Collier's*

contributor Helen Worden Erskine. "The lines in her forehead have been described by a Washington society reporter as 'in-a-hurry-lines.' Mrs. Truman can look bored – and often does."

Those words identified another issue: the seemingly bottomless reserve of decorum that her formal photographs suggested. "Mrs. Truman's mien suggests to many that she is digging her heels in and saying to people, 'I dare you to like me. I won't admit I want you to,' " added Erskine.

The divide between perception and reality was such that more than one person reported incidents of Mrs. Truman shopping unrecognized in both Washington and Independence. The manager of one Washington grocery told Erskine that Mrs. Truman appeared several times a year.

"She wanders through the store, picks out items – like preserves – stands in line, pays her check, and walks out," he said. "She is rarely recognized."

Others had similar experiences, even in Independence. Hazel Graham, a neighbor of the Trumans, told of running into Mrs. Truman at an Independence grocery after her husband had returned for good from Washington.

Harry Truman circa 1903.

"When she went on, I said to the clerk, 'Do you know who you were taking care of?' " Graham said. "She said, 'No.' I said, 'Mrs. Truman.' 'Oh my goodness, I didn't know that.' But this was not uncommon."

Writers working the Bess Truman beat began with the fundamentals.

Mrs. Truman was born February 13, 1885, in Independence. She was the eldest child of David Willock Wallace and Madge Gates Wallace. She and Harry Truman were married in June 1919, and their daughter, Mary Margaret, was born in 1924.

As the various profiles of the First Lady were published, a body of Bess Truman intelligence built up.

As a girl, she could whistle between her teeth.

Very early, she had a presence noticed by others. "I remember her walking in . . ." Ardelia Palmer, a former teacher at Independence High School once said, "and she would put them [her books] down and take her seat and look at you as if to say, 'Well, there they are.' "

Mary Paxton Keeley, one of Bess Truman's best friends, later recalled that she envied Bess's ability to appear more stylish than others but not spend more to do so. Keeley also recalled that young Bess Wallace was formidable, and sometimes restored order during occasional rows between neighborhood boys. During his 1948 whistlestop campaign tour, Bess Truman's husband, merely the president of the United States, introduced his wife to crowds as "The Boss."

Their daughter Margaret testified to her mother's role in the family. "She runs the show wherever she is," she told *Look* magazine in 1949.

Young Bess Wallace indulged in some of the proprieties of her time. She hosted teas that received notice in the *Examiner* of Independence. She had personal cards printed that read "Miss Bessie Wallace."

Then again, *Life* magazine in 1949 published a photograph depicting a post-high school party in the backyard of 219 North Delaware. In the picture, for the benefit of the photographer, a younger version of the current First Lady buried her face in a slice of watermelon.

She wasn't the delicate type. Her prowess as an athlete was beyond dispute. She wasn't considered one of the town's best woman tennis players – just one of the best tennis players.

After graduating from high school in 1901, she played on a basketball team organized by her friends. Bess's position: forward. Her coach was Forrest "Phog" Allen, a fellow student at Independence High who, some fifty years later, would coach the University of Kansas men's basketball team to the national title.

Bess Wallace's team was thoroughly modern. "We considered ourselves quite daring because we refused to wear over our bloomers the skirts that were considered by gym teachers as essential to modesty," teammate Keeley wrote in a 1952 article for *The Kansas City Star*.

"If you tossed Bess the ball," Keeley added, "you could be fairly sure she would score, even at a phenomenal distance."

Keeley also described their games as

Bess Wallace and friends at a picnic, sitting on an embankment in the early 1900s. Bess is fifth from left.

Bess's parents, Madge Gates Wallace and David Willock Wallace.

"rough," so much so that the girls' parents finally prevailed on them to dissolve the squad. Unhindered, Bess Wallace went off to Barstow, a Kansas City finishing school, where, at one school field day, she prevailed in the shotput competition.

The young men who began visiting her home found themselves tested in a unique way. Bess Wallace led them on long walks – really long walks. Margaret Truman, in her biography of her mother, insisted that one beau was led on a hike from Independence to Lee's Summit – not quite the length of Jackson County, but close.

Harry Truman also was treated to some of these walks, and apparently gave as good as he got. "Be ready to walk Sunday," he wrote in one letter to Bess in 1913.

The future president first encountered Bess Wallace at Sunday school at the First Presbyterian Church in Independence in 1890.

"I met a very beautiful little lady with lovely blue eyes and the prettiest golden curls I've ever seen," he wrote. "We went through Sunday school, grade school, high school and we're still going along hand in hand. She was my sweetheart and ideal when I was a little boy – and she still is." In another account, Harry Truman said, "She sat behind

Henry Chiles, longtime friend of Harry Truman since boyhood. On young Bess Wallace:

"They [the Wallace boys] lived right next to the Paxtons. The Paxtons were all boys. They were about equal in number and they would get in a big row, the Paxton boys and the Wallace boys, then they'd send Bess in there to settle it. They were all afraid of her; she didn't fool around with them."

me in the sixth, seventh and high school grades and I thought she was the most beautiful and the sweetest person on earth."

Truman's pursuit of Bess Wallace made life complicated for the future first lady. Though some of the biographers of Bess Truman during her White House years mentioned her father's death in 1903, none mentioned that he had committed suicide. The thought of this becoming public knowledge was one reason Harry Truman had hesitated to accept the nomination for vice president in 1944. The death of David Wallace, who, apparently suffering from depression, shot himself in 1903, devastated Madge Gates Wallace, Bess Truman's mother. Not only had she lost her husband, she had been thrown into despair by what she perceived to be the vast shame of her husband's act.

Bess Wallace is eating watermelon in the backyard of 219 North Delaware circa 1904. Pictured are, from left, brother Fred Wallace, Ethel Noland, Nellie Noland, brother Frank Wallace, Bess Wallace, brother George Wallace, and Will Boger.

The Independence high school graduation class of 1901. Harry Truman is in the last row, fourth from left; Bess Wallace, second row, far right; Charles Ross, class valedictorian and Truman's press secretary, front row, far left.

Her later reliance on her eldest child was clear to many, perhaps including the suitors who came calling.

Margaret Truman, in her biography of her mother, described the decisions facing Bess Wallace in the spring of 1917.

Harry Truman, who had made the quality of his intentions regarding Bess Wallace clear, nevertheless was training with his Missouri guard unit, preparing to fight in World War I. Bess Wallace, meanwhile, was now in her early thirties and – though

Mary Ethel Noland, first cousin to Harry Truman. On how young Harry Truman re-introduced himself to former high school classmate Bess Wallace by returning a Wallace family cake plate from the Noland home:

"Yes, that's one legend that's true. You know there are so many of them that are just absolutely plucked out of thin air, but that is true, that cake plate incident. Mrs. Wallace was very neighborly and she loved to send things. Oh, we did back and forth, you know. She would send over a nice dessert or something, just to share it and here was a plate. Well, we hadn't taken it back, and I said, 'Why don't you take that plate home, it's been around here a few days.'"

"'Well,' he said, 'I certainly will.'"

she cared for her mother – also was considering her own imperatives.

In 1982, the year her mother died, Margaret Truman found a piece of paper in the attic of 219 North Delaware. It was the rough draft of an engagement announcement, including the names of Harry Truman and Elizabeth Virginia Wallace. The handwriting

Formal portrait of Harry Truman about the age of twenty-four, circa 1908.

belonged to the future president.

"Bess knew that it was one of the most important documents in her life," Margaret wrote.

After their 1919 wedding, Harry and Bess Truman knew adversity.

There was the failure of the Truman-Jacobson haberdashery. There also were two miscarriages. So determined was Bess Truman not to tempt fate while pregnant with Margaret that she declined to shop for infant clothes and supplies. When Margaret arrived on February 17, 1924, there was no place to put her, and so she spent her first days in a pulled-out dresser drawer outfitted with blankets.

During Harry Truman's time as Jackson County presiding judge, his wife grew worried about his health. He worked into the night hours and couldn't walk two blocks in either Kansas City or Independence without being approached by a job seeker or a taxpayer with a grievance. Years later, on the night of the 1940 Democratic primary for U.S. Senate, Bess Truman slammed down the telephone when a campaign worker called from St. Louis to congratulate the family.

She had thought it a cruel joke, only to

The wedding party of Harry and Bess Truman included bridesmaids Louise Wells, left, and Helen Wallace. Harry's friend (left) Ted Marks served as best man, and Bess's brother, Frank, gave her away.

ORAL HISTORIES

Ted Marks, fellow artillery officer during World War I, Kansas City tailor, best man at Truman's 1919 wedding. On escorting Truman's mother, Martha Ellen Young Truman, during her son's 1919 marriage to Bess Wallace:

"It was a quiet wedding, didn't take long. I was nervous, holding the ring. Then, after the wedding, I took his mother down to see Harry off. She had me by the arm, you know, and she was a small woman, and I said to her, 'Well, now, Mrs. Truman, you've lost Harry.' And she looked up at me with those little blue eyes and said, 'Indeed I haven't.' And she never did. I can see her face to this day."

Mary Ethel Noland, first cousin to Harry Truman. On Harry Truman's wedding day.

"I remember when Harry came out from the vestry room as bridegrooms do, and stood waiting for the bride, how eager and expectant he looked watching for her to come in, and finally here came the wedding march and she was coming in."

relent when the campaign worker called back. Her husband was winning, he said.

Bess Truman was only weeks shy of her fiftieth birthday when she first arrived in Washington as a senator's wife in 1935. It was a full ten years later when her husband became president, and by then she was not about to sacrifice her privacy to accommodate the curious.

In 1945, Bess Truman was reported to stand five feet four inches tall, and weigh about 130 pounds.

About anything else, reporters could not be certain. In 1947, frustrated by the lack of information, reporters submitted forty questions to Bess Truman through the First Lady's secretaries. Among Mrs. Truman's answers were eleven "No comments." Six other times her full answer was "No."

Those answers that did emerge were abrupt.

Have you ever traveled on a campaign train? "Yes, briefly."

Would you enjoy this experience? "I did enjoy the first trip I made."

Will you go along in 1948 if the travel is by train, if by plane? "Will answer this one in July 1948."

Newsweek published the entire transcript, perhaps as evidence of the First Lady's stiff-arm to the press. But one writer found much to consider in one of Bess Truman's answers. Asked which period of White House history

most interested her, Bess identified the administration of James Monroe.

The assembled press corps shrugged that off. But Truman biographer Jonathan Daniels, writing in 1949, found the remark "a profoundly revealing statement." Elizabeth Monroe, wife of the fifth president, he wrote, was an elegant, cultivated woman who followed Dolley Madison, a flamboyant first lady who had made the White House the social center of Washington. Elizabeth Monroe, however, exhibited a less effusive personal style, and chose to keep the wedding of her daughter Maria a private ceremony.

If Bess Truman decided she could live without press coverage, it's not hard to understand why. Even the authors of friendly articles about Mrs. Truman still felt free to take the occasional shot. "Her modish black hat is slanted too far forward on her forehead, giving her the look of a little Missouri side-wheeler going full steam ahead," wrote Lilian Rixey in *Life* magazine in 1949.

Other critics were less cunning.

Life was owned by Henry Luce, whose wife, Clare Boothe Luce, a Republican congresswoman, once referred to Bess Truman as "payroll Bess."

There was no better way to ensure the enmity of Harry Truman than to publicly attack his wife. Another politician to discover this was U.S. Representative Adam Clayton Powell. The African-American Democrat was disappointed when Bess Truman did not quit the Daughters of the

American Revolution when the organization didn't allow Powell's wife, singer and pianist Hazel Scott, to perform in the DAR-owned Constitution Hall.

Eleanor Roosevelt had resigned from the organization a few years earlier, when it had prevented contralto Marian Anderson from appearing in the facility.

When Bess did not quit the DAR, Powell responded by describing Bess Truman as the "last lady."

Bad idea.

President Truman banned both Powell and Luce from the White House. "The order was issued at the White House and carried out all during his term," Louis Renfrow, assistant White House military aide, said in 1971. Luce and Powell, he said, "could never come inside the gates of the White House, no mattered what happened."

Bess Truman served out her White House time on her terms. Even while living in the White House, she rode to her old beauty shop and continued to pay three dollars for her weekly manicure, shampoo, and set, just as she had while the wife of a senator.

She was jealous of burdens that came between her and her husband, no matter how momentous. After the 1945 atomic bombings of Hiroshima and Nagasaki, Bess Truman was angry. What angered her, Margaret wrote, wasn't necessarily the use of the weapons but how her husband had left her out of the loop, not discussing the crucial decision with her.

After the assassination attempt on Harry Truman in November 1950, Secret Service officers convinced the president to enter and leave Blair House – the residence used by the Trumans during the renovation of the White House - by its rear entrance.

Mrs Truman agreed – but only insofar as her husband was concerned. She continued to leave by the front door.

Her interest in competitive sports continued. While Harry Truman was president, the First Lady would sometimes attend Washington Senators baseball games without him.

Also, even if her husband was president, Bess Truman was determined not to neglect her mother back in Independence. So she spent much time at 219 North Delaware even when her Washington address was 1600 Pennsylvania Avenue.

Both her husband and daughter felt her absences.

"When she's in Missouri, Dad and I realize how bleak it is to have no one around who understands," Margaret once said. "So we often find ourselves picking up the phone, dialing Independence 3690."

Journalists continued to consider the First Lady's mysterious countenance. "Certainly nothing is so characteristic of Bess Truman as the quizzical smile of a woman who expects the incredible but intends, if possible, to be amused by it," wrote Jonathan Daniels in 1949.

During the last weeks of the Truman administration, writers who perhaps had been frustrated by Bess Truman's low profile began admitting their grudging admiration of her. "Why does everyone love Mrs. Truman and Margaret?" asked correspondent Raymond Lonergan. "Because, during all the years they have

Margaret Truman, age two, 1926

been in a worldwide spotlight, they have never permitted position or prestige to go to their heads. They have remained the gracious, simple ladies we like to feel are indigenous to this land of ours."

The *Los Angeles Times* added, in an editorial, that Bess Truman had been "a model First Lady and a loyal and dignified partner to the President during every difficulty that has beset him and the nation."

After the January 1953 inauguration of Dwight Eisenhower, the Trumans rode a train home to Independence. The appearance

of hundreds of Independence residents upon their arrival at the town's small depot touched Bess Truman.

Still, she insisted on maintaining a private life at 219 North Delaware. If Mrs. Truman wanted to keep the public at arms' length, it was something she had learned over many years.

After her husband had became president, souvenir hunters had bent twigs off the Truman trees, and soon had begun snapping off splinters from the home itself. A fence went up around the property, but that didn't discourage the curious who lingered beyond the barricade, waiting for any glimpse.

Even after her White House years, Mrs. Truman often shut herself inside her home rather than endure the attention of those standing outside it. "One day when I went there I said, 'Your flowers in the backyard are just beautiful,' " neighbor Hazel Graham recalled. "She said, 'I wish I could enjoy them.' " After Mrs. Truman explained she was tired of venturing outside only to have sightseers telling her to pose for their cameras, Graham went out and cut some flowers herself.

Not long after the 1963 assassination of President John Kennedy, Congress appropriated funds for the lifetime protection of former presidents. "Mother reacted as if they had just told her she was going to have to spend four more years in the White House," wrote Margaret.

President Lyndon Johnson then called Mrs. Truman and personally asked her to accept the protection.

Bess Truman soon allowed the Secret Service to accompany her husband to and from the Truman Library, but she did not let

A Secret Service agent escorts Mrs. Bess Truman into the Second Baptist Church in Independence, where she attended funeral services for Vietta Garr in January 1974.

First lady Nancy Reagan (left) with former first ladies Rosalynn Carter and Betty Ford attending the graveside services for Bess Truman, October 22, 1982.

the agents into the house or on the property at 219 North Delaware.

Mrs. Truman remained independent after her husband's death in 1972. While agents often would accompany her on errands, they knew better than to take hold of her arm.

That was something, Hazel Graham recalled, she wouldn't allow.

She was loyal to friends and family. One of Bess Truman's last public appearances was at the 1974 funeral of Vietta Garr, the Trumans' longtime cook and helper.

Bess Truman died on October 18, 1982, at ninety-seven years old. Her funeral was held at Trinity Episcopal Church, where she had married Harry Truman sixty-three years earlier, and she was buried alongside her husband in the Truman Museum courtyard. Attending the services were First Lady Nancy Reagan as well as former first ladies Betty Ford and Rosalynn Carter.

In 1947, one of the forty questions submitted to Bess Truman's secretaries had included one she had answered easily.

What would you like to do and have your husband do when he is no longer president?

Bess Wallace Truman's answer: "Return to Independence."

After Bess Wallace Truman's death in 1982, Margaret Truman, as her mother's executor, gave the letters written to her mother by her father to the people of the United States.

The collection was opened in March 1983 at the Truman Museum. Robert Ferrell, the historian who edited the subsequent volume, *Dear Bess: The Letters from Harry to Bess Truman, 1910-1959*, found more than twelve hundred letters written as early as 1910 and ending in 1959. The correspondence represented what Ferrell called a "simply extraordinary account of what a man can do if he puts his mind and will to it."

Harry Truman first met Bess Wallace at Sunday school in 1890. They graduated together from Independence High School in 1901. He started writing regularly to her in 1910.

Students of Truman like to consider his unceasing series of letters to Bess Wallace Truman as the thirty-third president's first campaign. During the courtship's early years, Truman sometimes used greetings such as "My Dear Bessie" that perhaps were too familiar. It was one way, Ferrell noted, that Harry used every possible literary device to get closer to her.

Yet once Truman married Bess Wallace, the letters didn't stop.

JUNE 22, 1911.

In this letter, Harry Truman, twenty-seven-year-old Grandview farmer, proposes to Bess Wallace of Independence.

Speaking of diamonds, would you wear a solitaire on your left hand should I get it? Now that is a rather personal or pointed question provided you take it for all it means. You know, were I an Italian or a poet I would commence and use all the luscious language of two continents. I am not either but only a kind of good-for-nothing American farmer. I've always had a sneakin' notion that some day maybe I'd amount to something.

JULY 12, 1911.

Here, Harry Truman refers to Bess's response.

You know that you turned me down so easy that I am almost happy anyway. I never was fool enough to think that a girl like you could ever care for a fellow like me but I couldn't help telling you how I felt. I have always wanted you to have some fine, rich, good-looking man, but I knew that if I ever got the chance I'd tell you how I felt even if I didn't even get to say another word to you. What

makes me feel real good is that you were good enough to answer me seriously and not make fun of me anyway. You know when a fellow tells a girl all his heart and she makes a joke of it I suppose it would be the awfulest feeling in the world. You see I never had any desire to say such things to anyone else. All my girl friends think I am a cheerful idiot and a confirmed old bach. They really don't know the reason nor ever will. I have been so afraid you were not even going to let me be your good friend. To be even in that class is something.

JULY 16, 1923.

Harry Truman married Bess Wallace in 1919 following his return from World War I. For several summers Truman wrote his wife from reserve officer training camp. In 1923 he wrote from Fort Leavenworth, Kansas.

My Dear Wife: I hesitated somewhat on that word. I wanted to say, honey, sweetheart, Miss Bessie. But the one I used is in the last analysis the finest and loveliest word in the world. When a man has a perfect one as I have, what in life is better?

MAY 7, 1933.

As Jackson County presiding judge, Truman took a moment to take stock of his life.

Tomorrow I'll be forty-nine and for all the good I've done the forty might as well be left off. Take it all together though the experience has been worthwhile; I'd like to do it again. I've been in a railroad, bank, farm, war, politics, love (only once and it still sticks), been busted and still am and yet I have stayed an idealist. I still believe that my sweetheart is the ideal woman and that my daughter is her duplicate.

JUNE 26, 1936.

Harry and Bess Truman were married in Independence on June 28, 1919. In this letter, which pre-dates the couple's anniversary by two days, now U.S. Senator Harry Truman apparently ponders whether he could have made more money by being less honest.

Do you seriously regret that action seventeen years ago when you promised to "love, honor and obey"? I know that you have had a difficult time sometimes, particularly when the income wouldn't and doesn't meet the outgo, and I sometimes wish I'd gone after things like other men in my position would have but I guess I'm still fool enough to like honor more. I hope you believe I'm right.

The only regret I have about today [the twenty-eighth] is that it didn't happen in 1905 instead of 1919. You were, are, and always will be the best, most beautiful and sweetest girl on earth.

JULY 22, 1945.

In postwar Berlin, Truman took time off from the Potsdam conference to discuss the gift he would bring home for his wife with money he won during a poker game. This letter begins with the president mentioning that a letter from Bess had arrived the night before "while I was at Joe's dinner."

The "Joe" referred to is Soviet premier Joseph Stalin.

I bought you a Belgian lace luncheon set – the prettiest thing you ever saw. I'm not going to tell you what it cost – you'd probably have a receiver appointed for me and officially take over the strong box. But I came out a few dollars to the good in the game of chance on the boat, so it's invested in a luxury for you . . .

JUNE 28, 1948.

The president summarizes individual episodes in his young married life in this brief anniversary note. The references to Detroit, Port Huron in Michigan, and the Blackstone Hotel in Chicago were all stops on the couple's 1919 honeymoon.

Detroit, Port Huron, a farm sale, the Blackstone

Hotel, a shirt store, County Judge, a defeat, Margie, Automobile Club membership drive, Presiding Judge, Senator, V.P., now!

You still are on the pedestal where I placed you that day in Sunday school 1890. What an old fool I am.

JUNE 28, 1957.

Perhaps Harry Truman's most famous letter to his wife is the following, in which the former president attaches brief recollections to each year of his marriage.

June 28, 1920. One happy year.
June 28, 1921. Going very well.
June 28, 1922. Broke and in a bad way.
June 28, 1923. Eastern Judge. Eating.
June 28, 1924. Daughter 4 mo. old.
June 28, 1925. Out of a job.
June 28, 1926. Still out of a job.
June 28, 1927. Presiding Judge – eating again.
June 28, 1928. All going well. Piano. Al Smith.
June 28, 1929. Panic, in October.
June 28, 1930. Depression. Still going.
June 28, 1931. Six-year-old daughter.
June 28, 1932. Roads finished.
June 28, 1933. Employment Director.
June 28, 1934. Buildings finished.
*   Ran for the Senate.*
June 28, 1935. U.S. Senator. Gunston.
June 28, 1936. Resolutions Philadelphia.
*   Roosevelt re-elected.*
June 28, 1937. Grand time in Washington.

June 28, 1938. Very happy time. Margie 14.
June 28, 1939. Named legislation.
June 28, 1940. Senate fight coming.
June 28, 1941. Special Senate Committee.
*   Margie wants to sing.*
June 28, 1942. Also a happy time.
June 28, 1943. Lots of work.
June 28, 1944. Talk of V.P. Bad business.
June 28, 1945. V.P. & President. War End.
June 28, 1946. Margie graduate & singer.
*   80th Congress.*
June 28, 1947. Marshall Plan & Greece & Turkey.
*   A grand time 28th Anniversary.*
June 28, 1948. A terrible campaign. Happy day.
June 28, 1949. President again. Another happy
*   day.*
June 28, 1950. Korea – a terrible time.
June 28, 1951. Key West – a very happy day.
June 28, 1952. All happy. Finish, Jan. 20, 1953.
June 28, 1953. Back home. Lots of Roses.
June 28, 1954. A happy 35th.
June 28, 1955. All cut up but still happy.
June 28, 1956. A great day – more elation.
June 28, 1957. Well here we are again, as Harry
*   Jobes would say.*
Only 37 to go for the diamond jubilee!
*   H.S.T.*

Here are some ones & some fives. If it is not enough for a proper show, there will be more coming.

Your no account partner, who loves you more than ever!

BESS TRUMAN'S LETTERS TO HARRY

Bess Wallace Truman's regard for privacy could take even her husband by surprise.
The former president, daughter Margaret Truman Daniel once wrote, was shocked one day during the 1955 Christmas season to come home and discover his wife burning a pile of his letters to her.

"Think of history!" Harry Truman said to his wife. "I *have*," she replied.

Harry Truman wrote more than twelve hundred letters to Bess. Scholar Robert Ferrell has said the correspondence represents the most compelling collection of letters ever written by a president or a man who would become one.

And yet, they only tell one side of the story. Today 180 letters from Bess Wallace Truman to Harry Truman survive. These are held by the Truman Museum for the Trumans' daughter, Margaret, who retains copyright to them.

In 1998 Margaret agreed to a one-time museum exhibit of fifteen letters from Bess to Harry. The letters had never been seen before outside the Truman family. Dating from 1919 through 1942, the letters revealed a warm spouse who shared with her husband moments both intimate and mundane.

"Dear Old Sweetness," Bess began July 17, 1923, when her husband was away at reserve officers camp at Fort Leavenworth., Kansas. Another letter, this time written when her husband was at Fort Riley, Kansas, achieved a similar sentimentality. "My dear, lots and lots of love and please keep on loving me as hard as ever," Bess Truman wrote on July 16, 1925. "You know I just feel as if a large part of me has been gone for the last 10 days."

In a postscript, she added: "There isn't anybody else on earth I'd stop to write at this time of day."

Several letters suggested how even Washington power couples could be occupied by the details of domestic bliss. In 1937, Bess Truman requested that her husband, then a United States senator, bring

home from Washington a supply of hair nets.

"They are 30 cts a doz. cheaper there," Bess Truman wrote November 5.

In 1940 the purchase of seat covers for a family car prompted another report.

"These look very nice and fit nicely – & it's a joy to get into the car now & not have to fight your way across the front seat," she wrote April 8.

Bess knew when to compliment her husband. "Your speech last night was really 'something,' " she wrote July 16, 1942. "I think it was the best radio speech I have heard you make. Your radio 'technique' has improved immensely – [cousin] Ethel [Noland] said your consonants were all pronounced just as her speech teacher had taught her."

She also noted how some events would not be the same without him.

"Louise and Bill Duke are having a cocktail party this evening – their 20th anniversary," Bess wrote November 3, 1937. ". . . think I'll skip it. I might not be able to drive home afterwards."

Finally, when her husband made sure that the correct number of flowers arrived by a certain date, Bess made sure he knew that she appreciated it.

"Thank you very much for the lovely roses – all twenty-three of them – and for the lovelier letter which really arrived when it should have," she wrote June 28, 1942, the Trumans' twenty-third anniversary.

MARY PAXTON KEELEY

She was Bess Truman's best friend.

But Mary Paxton Keeley also was a journalist who never submitted her best story. Maybe that's one reason Bess, who so valued her privacy, loved her as much as she did.

The life of Keeley, who was born in Independence, Missouri, in 1886 and who died in Columbia, Missouri, one hundred years later, constitutes a Missouri epic.

In an era when women were not expected to have careers, Keeley carved out several as a journalist, educator, playwright, artist, and photographer.

A tea given by a nineteen-year-old Mary Paxton in 1905 merited the front page of the Jackson *Examiner*, which listed hostesses that included "Bessie" Wallace. But such genteel pursuits would not hold Keeley's interest. Her mother, Mary Gentry Paxton, had been an early graduate of the University of Missouri, and her

father, John G. Paxton, an Independence lawyer, encouraged his daughter's newspaper ambitions. When Keeley arrived at the University of Missouri School of Journalism, she brought a gift from her father: a used Remington typewriter.

She was the school's only student with such technology.

In 1910 she was the journalism school's first female graduate. Days after receiving her degree, she became probably the first woman newspaper reporter in Kansas City, joining *The Kansas City Post*, which Keeley herself called the "yellowest newspaper in the country, next to the Hearst publications."

In big-city muckraker mode, Keeley investigated Kansas City's red light district and a reform school for troubled girls in Chillicothe, Missouri.

During World War I, she served in Europe for ten months with the Y.M.C.A. canteen service.

After the war, she married a Virginia farmer, Edmund Burke Keeley. When he died in 1926, Keeley became a single mother, rearing their son, John Paxton Keeley, born in 1921. Keeley worked as a home extension agent in Holt County, Missouri, and then as a correspondent for the *Atchison County Mail* in Rock Port, Missouri. She earned a master's degree from the Missouri journalism school in 1928 and began teaching at Christian (now Columbia) College in Columbia that same year. She retired in 1952.

Her personal life included unrequited love and tragedy. She broke off a relationship with fellow journalist (and former Harry Truman high school classmate) Charlie Ross some thirty years before he would become President Truman's press secretary. Keeley carried a torch for Ross for years, writing letters to Ross that she never mailed.

In the early 1970s, her son died of the same kidney ailment that had killed his father.

However sweeping Keeley's life, it also commands interest because her long correspondence with Bess Truman serves as an open window into the former first lady's thoughts. Keeley saved the letters that Bess Truman wrote to her over several decades. Margaret Truman, Keeley's goddaughter, excerpted several of them in her 1986 book, *Bess W. Truman.*

One exchange in 1945 was prompted by a condescending dispatch by Duke Shoop, *Kansas City Star* Washington correspondent, who depicted Vice President Harry Truman and wife as rubes dazzled while attending a party of Washington A-list hostess Evalyn Walsh McLean.

"I know it is all right to go to that dame's dinner," Keeley wrote Bess. "But it shouldn't get in the paper as if Harry was a wide-eyed country boy who had left the plow handles to eat off the gold plate."

Bess agreed, with feeling. "We have eaten off the 'gold plate' once or twice a month (or have been asked to – we don't always go) for the last four or five years,"

Mary Paxton Keeley continued to write at age eighty-two, but she never wrote at length about her friends Bess and Harry Truman.

she wrote. "But D. S. is never there so he wouldn't know."

After Franklin Roosevelt's death elevated Truman to president, Keeley's letter to Bess was one of consolation, not congratulation.

"Yours is the hardest job I have ever known any woman to undertake but I have never known you to do anything that you did not do well," Keeley wrote.

Bess, in her reply, described her husband's new job as the cross that fate had given her to bear. "I think you have sized up the situation pretty well," she wrote. "We are not any of us happy to be where we are but there's nothing to be done about it except to do our best – and forget about the sacrifices and the many unpleasant things that bob up."

Bess also took Keeley's advice that Harry needed a good press secretary. She suggested that Charlie Ross take the job, which he did.

Keeley never wrote at length about Bess and Harry Truman.

"I promised Bess I would never write about her," Keeley said in a 1975 interview, "and I value her friendship more than any rewards

I might get from a book."

Keeley did leave a manuscript, "Back in Independence," which she stipulated could only be published after her death. Upon its appearance in the early 1990s, readers found that while the book contained a few unflattering references to a few long-deceased Independence residents, it only mentioned the Trumans in passing.

She could have written plenty. Keeley was there in 1903, when Bess's father, David Wallace, shot and killed himself. Keeley never wrote of that day, but Margaret Truman did in her biography of her mother. "The two young women, already best friends and now united by a searing bond of sorrow, walked back and forth together, saying nothing. What was there to say?"

When Harry Truman lay dying in a Kansas City hospital room in 1972, Keeley, then eighty-six years old, talked her way past the Secret Service to Truman's room, where she found Bess.

Margaret Truman quotes Keeley's last letter to Bess. "No one could take your place in my life," she wrote.

When Bess died at age ninety-seven in 1982, Keeley sent a single yellow rose to the funeral service.

The Mary Paxton Study Class, organized by Keeley's mother, Mary Gentry Paxton, near the beginning of the twentieth century, was still convening in 2003. The group of about fifty women meets regularly from the fall through the spring in the Whistlestop Room at the Truman Museum in Independence.

Captain Harry Truman in Brittany, France, summer of 1918.

CHAPTER 4

WORLD WAR I

In 1917, a U.S. Army recruiting office in Kansas City hung a sign bearing a promise outside its front door. JOIN THE ARTILLERY AND RIDE.

At least some future members of Battery D of the 129th Field Artillery thought it sounded like a good way to spend the war declared on Germany by the United States in April. They enlisted. About a year later they would think twice about that advertisement as they walked all night over dark and pitted roads in France, wearing sixty-pound packs in the rain.

Another member of the battery had his own romantic ideal of what service in the U.S. Army during World War I would be like.

I felt that I was a Galahad after the Grail, and I'll never forget how my love cried on my shoulder when I told her I was going. That was worth a lifetime on this earth.

Harry Truman, who wrote the above in a memoir some twenty years after the war ended, knew well the distance between the ideal he harbored when he rejoined the Missouri National Guard in the spring of 1917 and the reality of the experience he had endured when he returned from France to Kansas City two years later, in May 1919.

There was little about the war that had resembled Galahad's quest.

As captain of Battery D, Truman often rode a horse. But horses were a constant problem. Each artillery battery required 164 horses: 116 draft animals and 48 riding horses. Six horses were needed to pull each field gun; still others were needed to pull

the ammunition-bearing caissons. The six-horse field gun teams were minded by three drivers riding the horses; other battery members rode on caissons or the limbers, the two-wheeled towing vehicles to which each field gun was attached.

At least, that was the plan.

But Battery D didn't enter the fray until August 1918, and after several years of war, the horse population of France had been thinned. Often the horses of Battery D grew exhausted during its all-night marches, suffering the effects of gas, sometimes wan-

Harry Truman's American Expeditionary Forces identity card, identifying him as a captain in the 129th Field Artillery.

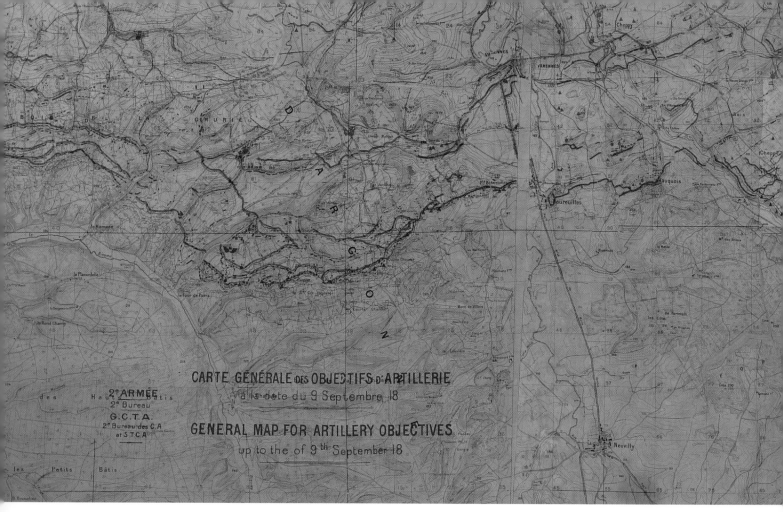

CARTE GÉNÉRALE DES OBJECTIFS D'ARTILLERIE
à la date du 9 Septembre 18

GENERAL MAP FOR ARTILLERY OBJECTIVES
up to the of 9th September 18

Captain Harry S. Truman used this French artillery objective map during combat in the Meuse-Argonne offensive, September 26 – October 2, 1918. Following his first taste of battle four weeks earlier, Truman wrote his sweetheart Bess, "I am in a most beautiful country and it seems like a shame that we must spread shells over it."

dering off over sheer cliffs or sometimes just falling down on the trail and having to be destroyed.

On the battery's long night marches to the Meuse-Argonne offensive that September, most members walked so as not to add to the burdens of the battery's horses. This the infantry found amusing, since they only had their packs and weapons to account for, and so were often trucked to the front.

"Join the artillery and ride," they yelled as they swept by the batteries.

In dealing with their horses, and in every other way, Battery D knew that sometimes little about the Great War was great.

In moving forward in the first hours of the Meuse-Argonne offensive, the battery crossed territory that its own shells had churned up. Writing in 1938, one battery sergeant, Eddie Meisburger, remembered it this way: "On that journey, we rode over the destruction that had been wrought by our guns. It looked like humans, dirt, rock, trees and steel had been turned up by one plow."

Later in the same battle the battery came upon the bodies of Americans soldiers killed by machine-gun fire, and still others who had been shot in the back.

The battery contemplated the sight of "a pile of American soldiers in all sorts of ghastly positions, shot by enemy machine gunners," Truman wrote in a thirty-four-page memoir he composed while a U.S. senator in the late 1930s. "There were seventeen of them and nearly a dozen more lying head to heel down the road shot in the back after they'd gone by. The Battery had been chattering and carrying on as they usually did when on a road march and when they saw this spectacle everything became as quiet as a church and a hard-boiled sergeant remarked, 'Now you so and sos, I guess you'll believe you're in a war.' "

In November, the battery found itself in position near Verdun, site of the 1916 battle in which hundreds of thousands of French and Germans had died. "The outlook I have now is a rather dreary one," Truman wrote Bess Wallace on November 1, 1918. "There are Frenchmen buried in my front yard and Huns in the back yard and both litter up the landscape as far as you can see. Every time a Boche shell hits in a field over west of here it digs up a piece of someone."

And yet, as grim as it sometimes was,

Truman's military career was also arguably the defining experience of his life. He once said his entire political career was based on his "war service and war associates." A historian who visited the White House in 1949 to discuss Truman's artillery career watched as the president took a small key and unlocked the top left drawer of his desk.

The drawer contained just three items: A small black notebook containing the names of all of his Battery D comrades; a copy of *The Artilleryman*, a 1920 history of the 129th Field Artillery; and a program from the June 14, 1905, celebration of the organization of a battery in the Missouri National Guard.

Listed as a member was Corporal Harry S. Truman.

"He studied drill regulations and read President Wilson's speeches and if ever Sir Galahad was moved by higher motives it is not so recorded," Truman later wrote of himself. "Our young man was a true patriot." He had, Truman wrote, "joined the Artillery (to ride?) and wanted really to fight for his country."

As a young man, Truman's favorite books were about soldiers and statesmen. He had read of Alexander, Hannibal, Napoleon, Robert E. Lee, and Stonewall Jackson. As a teenager, he had played war games. During the Spanish-American War, Truman and his Independence friends had assembled a "junior brigade," in which members armed themselves with .22-caliber rifles and conducted drills. "He made up

Truman carried this photograph of Bess Wallace with him across France.

his mind that he would be a military man," Truman later wrote, "although he was afraid of a gun and would rather run than fight."

In 1905, Truman joined a Kansas City artillery battery that was part of the Missouri National Guard. But his duties at the Truman family farm in Grandview proved too demanding, and Truman ultimately left the guard in 1911. Then the United States declared war on Germany, and Truman

As soon as Truman arrived in France, he was issued this steel helmet and gas mask. While in the front lines, American troops had standing orders to wear helmets and carry gas masks at the "ready position" on their chests. Note the stenciled insignia of the 129th Field Artillery, 35th Division.

soon re-enlisted, despite turning thirty-three years old in May 1917.

There was no way, he decided, that he was going to miss the war. But there were consequences. Truman's father had died in 1914, and Truman's decision to leave the Grandview farm in the care of his aging mother and his young sister – as his younger brother, Vivian, had married and left the farm – may not have been a popular one.

And then there was Bess Wallace, whom he had courted for several years.

"It seems that I have caused you to be unhappy by my over-enthusiastic action in getting myself into the war," Truman wrote Bess in July 1917 from the National Guard's training site in Kansas City.

"In six months she would be thirty-three years old," daughter Margaret Truman wrote in her 1986 biography of her mother. "Many people were predicting that the war would last at least four years. She might be too old to have a child when Harry Truman came back – if he came back."

men in Battery D who found much about Truman that was Galahad-like.

The last Battery D member died in 1998. But in the decades that followed Armistice Day, the battery maintained an oral tradition about Truman's wartime service. The stories told over the decades concerned a handful of specific incidents, each one of which, they believed, illustrated Truman's capacity for bravery, loyalty, and fairness.

Some battery members, nevertheless, enjoyed recalling Truman's first appearance before the battery as its captain in July 1918. One battery member, Eddie McKim, insisted that Truman's knees were knocking together.

Others were equally underwhelmed.

"He gave the impression of a professor more than he did an artillery officer," one member, Floyd Ricketts, recalled more than fifty years later.

That night, several members staged a mock stampede of the battery horses. Later, four members were taken to the infirmary following a brawl.

Edward D. McKim, Kansas City resident who served as a private in Battery D; longtime Truman friend and political aide. On seeing Truman the morning in 1918 when he took command of Battery D in France:

"He took command of the battery on a cold, frosty morning at Camp Coetquidan, which was an artillery training center, and my recollection of him was that his knees were knocking together."

Still, Truman left. And during the two years that followed, many of the qualities that so endeared Truman to political and personal associates in the coming decades – courage, loyalty, common horse sense – emerged while he was in uniform. These qualities were apparent to the 194 enlisted

The battery's attitude toward its new captain may well have been casual. Before Truman, it had gone through several other commanders. Also, it considered itself a unique unit. More than fifty years later, two members, Meisburger and Eugene Donnelly, recalled just how rugged a bunch Battery D was. They insisted it could draw from its ranks baseball and football teams that could hold their own against squads drawn from much larger units. One battery member, Thomas Murphy, had been an amateur lightweight boxing champion in 1917.

The battery was heavily Catholic, many members having grown up on the streets of a Kansas City not too many years removed from its frontier origins. "They were the wild Irish and German Catholics from Rockhurst Academy in Kansas City," Truman wrote in a memoir. "They had had four commanders before me. I wasn't a Catholic, I was a thirty-second-degree Mason. I could just see my hide on the fence when I tried to run that outfit."

Even before they went to training in Oklahoma in September 1917, many members were picking fights downtown outside of Convention Hall, where they trained.

Named to command them in July 1918, meanwhile, was Truman, about ten years their senior, wearing glasses and coming not from the streets of Kansas City but from a farm in eastern Jackson County.

"He was so badly scared he couldn't say a word and he could feel the battery sizing him up and wondering how much they could put one over on him," Truman later wrote, referring to himself.

Still, the morning after the brawl and the fake horse stampede, the battery found posted a list of about half of the battery's noncommissioned officers, as well as most of the first-class privates. All had been reduced in rank.

Truman then instructed the remaining noncoms that it was their duty, not his, to keep the men in line.

"And then we knew that we had a different 'cat' to do business with than we had up to that time," Vere Leigh, a battery member, recalled in 1970. "He didn't hesitate at all. The very next morning [the posting] was on the board. He must have sat up all

night, you know."

Another surprise awaited battery members the next month, when the battery was assigned to fire its first rounds against the enemy in the Vosges Mountains district of France, on the night of August 29, 1918. During an answering barrage from German artillery, several battery members panicked and started to flee.

Over the ensuing decades, the incident was referred to by battery members as the Battle of Who Run. But little about it was amusing at the time.

Again, horses were involved. Battery D had received orders to shell opposing German positions. To ensure that the battery's horses were not spooked by the firing, Truman told a sergeant to take the horses to a distant point, and then return with them ninety minutes after the battery's

Military stopwatches were considered precision fire control instruments and were carefully protected. Truman personally identified this as the "D Battery stopwatch used for firing barrages in the Big War."

49

Officers of the 129th Field Artillery, including Harry Truman (third from right) in front of a chateau in Montigny sur Aube, France, May 1918.

shelling began. This way, the battery could fire its rounds and then hitch up their guns and leave the area before the Germans returned fire.

The shelling began, with the battery firing five hundred gas shells.

But the horses were a half-hour late. By the time they arrived, panic was settling in. Then the Germans answered, with high explosive and shrapnel shells. Some fell just beyond the battery's position, others just short.

The sergeant who was late with the horses lost his head. "Run, boys, they got a bracket on us," he yelled, according to many who recalled the incident.

It's unclear how many battery members ran. Truman later said everyone ran but himself and six or seven privates. The oral histories of some battery members, on file at the Truman Museum, don't contain descriptions of any such mass exit.

But what is clear in all the recollections was Truman's reaction. After freeing himself from his horse, which had fallen into a shell hole, Truman instructed the battery to return – in vivid vernacular.

"I explained a few things to them in language that they could understand," Truman said in an interview in the 1960s.

In any case, his choice of words so startled the battery members that many calmed down almost out of curiosity. None of the men were injured in the shelling. The battery also had to abandon two field guns mired in

mud, only to have to retrace its steps in the morning and bring them back.

Regardless, battery members had new respect for their allegedly professorial captain. Truman, meanwhile, didn't let on about his own wish to flee.

"My greatest satisfaction is that my legs didn't succeed in carrying me away, although they were very anxious to do it," he wrote Bess Wallace a few days later.

The Battle of Who Run might be the principal Battery D legend. But there are other stories that members often repeated to demonstrate Truman's regard for his men. A prominent example concerned Truman's decision to disobey a higher officer's order to discipline exhausted battery members.

In September, the 35th Division received orders to move almost one hundred miles to new positions for the upcoming Meuse-Argonne offensive. Over twelve days, Battery D undertook a series of long night marches. The marches would have been

rugged enough in good conditions. But the small roads of France were so crowded sometimes that the battery could travel only three or four miles in six hours.

For good measure, it rained.

"It was march all night and part of the day, grab a few hours' sleep, and march some more," Truman later wrote. "On every night march they had to walk and carry packs weighing from sixty to eighty pounds, depending on the number of souvenirs in each pack."

One much-repeated story detailed how the colonel in command of the 129th Field Artillery, a West Point graduate, had come upon the battery after it had been slogging over rough roads for several nights.

"And there was an order out that we cannoneers who were walking and following the guns were not to hold on to any part of the gun or the caissons so as not to put any more burden on the horses," battery member Floyd Ricketts said in 1970. "But walking

along almost dead on your feet, you could hardly resist grabbing a hold of the caisson to help you along."

On this one night, the colonel noticed several battery members doing just that.

"He came fluttering down the highway and complained about Battery D sort of straggling, and talked to Captain Truman," said Meisburger in a 1975 interview. "I don't know what the words were between them, but anyway, the colonel gave the order, 'Call these men in and double-time them up this hill.'"

Truman listened to the command.

Then Truman ordered the battery not to double-time up the hill, but instead to deploy off the road into the woods and rest.

"We think it was a pretty fine act on the part of Truman not to do it," Ricketts said.

"From then," Meisburger remembered, "Battery D would have let [Truman] walk over them. They adored him."

Just how Truman finessed his decision

Within days of arriving at Camp Doniphan in Oklahoma, Truman was named the regimental canteen officer. He operated the canteen with Kansas City friend Eddie Jacobson, with whom he would start a haberdashery after the war. Some scholars believe that Truman stands fifth from right, while Jacobson strikes a jaunty post with hand on hip.

51

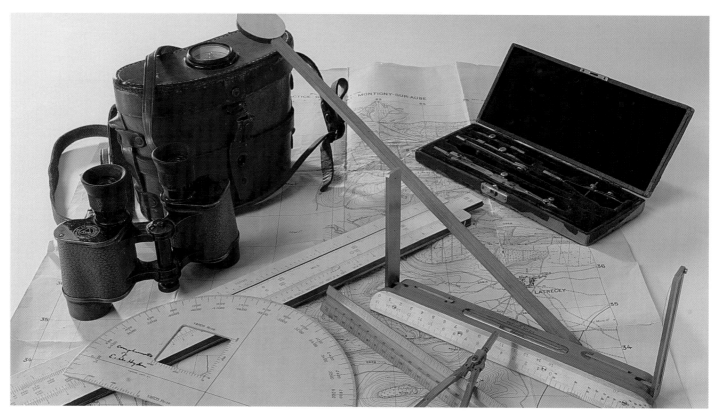

Captain Truman used a wide variety of tools to accurately target fire from Battery D. With these field glasses, he observed and destroyed several German artillery positions. For indirect fire missions, he used maps and instruments such as this slide rule, alidade, protractor, and engineer's scale.

to disobey the order remained a mystery to battery members. But the episode revealed something else that the battery's 194 enlisted men noticed immediately: Truman didn't carry himself like many officers.

"Well, my impression was he wasn't a military character, especially," Meisburger said. "He was just sort of like a man getting his family around a table and telling them what the score was and what he could expect of everybody."

What battery members didn't know, and what Truman didn't reveal until many years later, was that he thought very little of some fellow officers. "Some men let authority make fools of them," Truman wrote.

This attitude was years in the making.

As a twenty-one-year-old member of the Missouri National Guard in 1905, Truman was thrilled when a captain called him into his tent and asked his help in removing his boots. "The young man was glad to help and felt very much pleased that so high an officer should notice him," Truman later wrote.

Twelve years later, when the thirty-three-year-old Truman was helping to operate a canteen at Fort Sill in Oklahoma, a small incident prompted Truman to revise his regard for some officers.

"I was alone in the canteen one day," Eddie Jacobson, Truman's canteen partner, recalled in 1946, "when a general came in, looked around, and wanted to know where Lieutenant Truman was. I told him he was down on the picket line with the horses. 'Go get him,' the general snapped.

"It was a good quarter of a mile down to that picket line where we kept all the horses, and I ran all the way, meanwhile wondering what was up. So did Truman when I told him. We double-timed all the way back. When we got in the canteen Truman stood at attention and gave the general a salute. Then the general took a quarter from his pocket, laid it on the counter and said, 'Give me two packages of Piedmonts, Lieutenant.' When Truman gave him the cigarettes, the general left the place without saying a word. And was Truman mad. When he got mad in those days he was really mad."

Truman also resented the stigma sometimes associated with National Guard troops and the disdain that the artillery regiment's colonel treated them with.

"He had German ideas about discipline and a superiority complex because of his education and his wife's money," Truman wrote. "He'd never associated with volunteer troops and didn't understand that nearly all of them were from good families, a number were college graduates and nearly all had high school training."

Truman didn't come easily to some officer responsibilities.

"It very nearly breaks my heart sometimes to have to be mean as the dickens to some nice boy who has been a model soldier on the front and whose mail I've probably censored and I know he's plum crazy about some nice girl at home but that makes no difference," Truman wrote in a letter to cousin Mary Ethel Noland.

"I have to make 'em walk the chalk. You'd never recognize me when I'm acting Bty Commander."

But, in fact, Truman often passed up opportunities to dress down enlisted men. Vere Leigh told how, during one long battery march, he and several others had grown impatient with the battery's slow pace and had gone on ahead to the town it was scheduled to spend the night in.

When the battery finally showed up, Leigh and his colleagues slipped into the battery's rear. But an officer spotted them, and directed that their names be given to Truman. This was a court martial offense, Leigh said, "and I mean they could make it kind of nasty for you, and our names were turned over to Captain Truman. The next morning we were all ready to be summoned up there and court martialed, but nothing happened."

This service coat was purchased by Harry S. Truman in June 1917, taken to France and worn by him in combat. An American officer was distinguished by braid on both cuffs and by his collar ornaments. Rank insignia was worn on the shoulder straps. The 35th Division shoulder sleeve insignia and the six months overseas service chevron were applied shortly after the Armistice.

Wristwatches were practical and popular accessories for the doughboys in France. Many, like this Elgin watch worn by Harry S. Truman, were actually small pocket watches fitted into special wrist straps. Period catalogs referred to them as "wrist bracelets."

During WWI, American officers traveling overseas were authorized to take one bedding roll, one clothing roll, and one trunk locker measuring 31.5"x18"x13.5" 35th Division baggage was stenciled with the Sante Fe cross so that it could be easily recognized during debarkation.

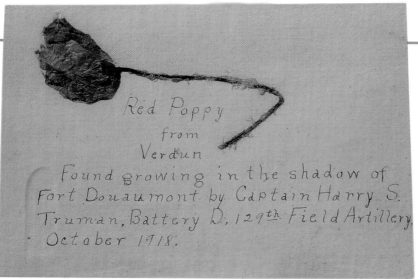

Red Poppy
from
Verdun
Found growing in the shadow of
Fort Douaumont by Captain Harry S.
Truman, Battery D, 129th Field Artillery,
October 1918.

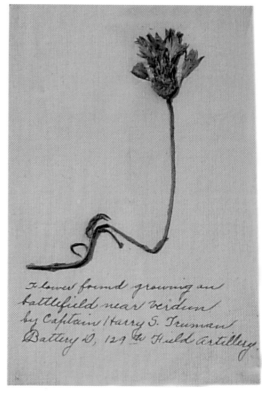

A flower found growing on
battlefield near Verdun
by Captain Harry S. Truman
Battery D, 129th Field Artillery.

Just days before the war's end, Truman found these flowers and enclosed them in a letter home to Independence. "I walked right out to the observation post the other day to pick an adjusting point and I found two little flowers alongside the trench blooming right in the rock."

Not long after that, Leigh approached Truman, who merely told him not to do it again.

"But I think that was just . . . that was understanding," Leigh said, "and I know that every one of us tried a little harder after that, you see, because that's one way to make believers out of kid soldiers."

There were other instances in which Truman tried to look the other way.

Battery member Ora Goosey in 1946 remembered how Truman routinely gave him the benefit of the doubt. "I was AWOL four times," he said. "Not AWOL when there was any fighting going on, you understand. I just took off from rear areas. But not one of those AWOLS is on my service record. The captain just had me dig up half of France making garbage pits and latrines."

Floyd Ricketts recalled how, just after the war ended, several battery members, himself included, gave in to the temptation of hoarding souvenirs. His job on one of the battery's four field guns had been to pull the gun's lanyard, firing it. But the guns belonged to the French government, and soon the battery was ordered to turn them in.

Before they did, Ricketts helped himself to the gun's lanyard, which was a small wooden knob and cord.

"Then I thought, 'Well, I'll take the firing pin,' and I took the firing pin off, and that led to another piece."

Before he was through, Ricketts had filled a small bag full of field gun parts and kept them hidden. Weeks later, however, the French government insisted the missing parts be returned.

"I suppose some of the other fellows had taken souvenirs also," Ricketts said. "So one evening Captain Truman asked us if we had any of these parts and to turn them in. Well, there was complete silence and none was turned in." On a subsequent morning, Truman decided to have the battery drill while he had individual beds searched, with all mattresses being turned over.

Under Ricketts' mattress, Truman found the soldier's small bag of field gun parts.

Truman ordered Meisburger to empty the bag onto the mattress. "My God, he's got everything but the barrel," Meisburger remembered Truman saying.

"But I'll tell you this, nothing was ever said to me, I wasn't disciplined," Ricketts said.

There also were moments when Truman revealed his sheer pleasure at being where he was and who he was with.

The night before the battery joined the vast artillery barrage that opened the Meuse-Argonne offensive on September 26, 1918, the atmosphere was solemn. Meisburger remembered a line of the battery's Catholic members waiting to go to confession with a Catholic priest assigned to the artillery regiment.

On the same night, Truman gathered together several of his battery members. "I want to tell you this, too, fellows," he said, according to one account. "Right tonight I'm where I want to be – in command of this battery. I'd rather be right here than be president of the United States. You boys are my kind."

It was the kind of sentiment that Truman usually was only comfortable sharing with intimates like Bess Wallace of Independence.

In late October, Battery D was moved to a position near Verdun. On October 31, 1918, Truman found some tiny flowers blooming near a trench. Truman enclosed the flowers in a letter he wrote the next day to Bess, but not without a note of almost-cynical bravado, lest anyone think him too sentimental.

"The sob sisters would say that they came from the battle-scarred field of Verdun," he wrote that day. "They were in sight and short range of Heinie and were not far from the two most famous forts in his line of defense. You can keep them or throw them away but I thought they'd be something."

Truman sent the tiny blossoms home to Independence, where today they are still held by the Truman Museum.

So is the loving cup bearing Truman's name and presented to him by the members of his battery. According to battery legend, the cup was paid for with the proceeds of a craps game played while on the ship back from France. But if the money came from a low pursuit, the trophy's inscription to Truman invokes only honorable qualities.

"Presented by the Members of Battery D," it reads, "in appreciation of his justice, ability and leadership."

After the war, members of Truman's artillery battery pooled money to buy this loving cup for their captain. The cup later was displayed at the Truman & Jacobson haberdashery in Kansas City.

"BACK FROM FRANCE" BATTERY D 129th FIELD

BATTERY D

Harry Truman's artillery battery served in combat for less than three months in the summer and fall of 1918.

For the next sixty years, the men of Battery D held reunions and basked in the attention generated by their captain, who became president in 1945. After Truman's move to the White House, the battery's reunions became newsworthy, often attended by journalists.

One result was that battery members began issuing membership cards, signed by the president, vouching that the bearer was indeed an authentic battery member – as opposed to the hundreds who apparently claimed to have served in the unit after Truman became president.

A second consequence, over the ensuing decades, was the lingering suggestion that Battery D's chief legacy was years of reunions and parties, highlighted by its trip to

Washington in January 1949 to march in their former captain's inaugural parade.

But whatever notoriety Battery D enjoyed after Truman became president, its members had no need to apologize for the service they had rendered during the war.

"Truman's battery was frequently employed well forward," wrote D. M. Giangreco, an editor

RY April 1919.

The members of Truman's artillery battery posed for a photographer after their return from France.

at *Military Review*, published at the U.S. Army Command and General Staff College at Fort Leavenworth, Kansas, in a paper delivered at the 2002 annual meeting of the Society for Military History.

Truman's Battery D served in the Vosges Mountains in August 1918 and the next month was held in reserve during the St. Mihiel campaign. During the subsequent Meuse-Argonne offensive in late September, Truman's battery was credited with either wiping out or forcing the abandonment of two opposing artillery batteries, as well as clearing out a German observation post.

One of the German artillery batteries destroyed under Truman's direction was, in fact, out of his artillery battery's "sector," or approved zone of fire. Yet

Truman, sensing the danger it posed to American troops, ordered it shelled by his battery anyway and endured the angry complaints of his commanding officer.

By the time the armistice arrived on November 11, 1918, Truman's battery had lost only a handful of members. While records indicate that four members of Battery D died in France, Truman often said that no Battery D soldiers had died in action. This was remarkable, given the casualties suffered by the 35th Division just during the Meuse-Argonne campaign. The division, made up of perhaps 27,000 men formed by National Guard units from Missouri and Kansas, lost almost 7,300 soldiers during several days of fighting. Of that number, 1,126 were killed or died from wounds, and

4,877 were severely wounded. The balance were soldiers either slightly wounded or suffering from combat fatigue who returned to duty. The casualties, wrote Giangreco, represented the highest four-day loss rate for any U.S. division during the war, and virtually all of these casualties occurred within two to three miles of Truman's artillery battery.

Nobody was thinking about this kind of thing on April 6, 1917, when the United States declared war on Germany.

Truman soon re-enlisted in the Missouri National Guard, with which he first had signed up in 1905. He joined a newly formed field artillery battery and, in a

Harry Truman had his first taste of the military in the Missouri National Guard, which he joined in 1905.

day when National Guard troops elected their officers, was elected a lieutenant.

President Woodrow Wilson called the National Guard into federal service in July 1917, and the 2nd Missouri Field Artillery was mobilized the next month. On September 26, it left Kansas City for training at Camp Doniphan, Fort Sill, Oklahoma.

In March 1918, Truman was one of perhaps a dozen officers selected for early transfer to France with the advance overseas detail of the 35th Division. He landed in April and attended artillery school. Following six weeks of study Truman graduated and rejoined his regiment, where he learned he had been promoted to captain.

On July 11, he took command of Battery D.

The battery's first assignment was the Vosges Mountains, in the Alsace region of France. The region was somewhat removed from the main battlefields, and so was considered a good place to break in new units. Battery D went into position on August 23. At about eight P.M. on August 29, it fired five hundred shells of gas upon enemy artillery in ninety minutes. The panic that followed when the Germans began to fire back became known as the "Battle of Who Run" among battery members.

"That was our first time we were under fire," said battery member Vere Leigh in a 1970 interview. "And we were firing away and having a hell of a good time doing it until they began to fire back."

Following the successful completion of the St. Mihiel offensive, the 129th received new orders to proceed to the Meuse-Argonne region. They made night marches of twelve, eighteen, twenty-two, and twenty-five miles.

The Meuse-Argonne offensive began for Battery D on September 26, 1918, one year after Truman and his Kansas City and Independence area colleagues left Kansas City for Fort Sill, Oklahoma.

The battery helped open one of the great artillery preparations of World War I.

"The sky was one lurid glare," Truman later wrote.

"It just looked like the world was afire," McKinley Wooden, the battery's chief mechanic, recalled in a 1995 interview.

After the initial firing, Battery D was ordered to produce a rolling barrage, gradually increasing the distance of its shells in support of advancing 35th Division infantry. Soon, the battery itself began moving forward.

It was at six P.M. the next day that Truman, situated in a forward observation post, saw a German artillery battery positioning itself to fire on the advancing infantry of the 35th Division.

Although the Germans were not in his "sector," Truman ordered them shelled. Battery D

At one point, as American troops began to fall back, Battery D members were reminded of their orders that, if they had to retreat, they should take the artillery firing pins with them, so the field guns could not be turned against them.

In mid-October, the battery moved to a new position near Verdun, the site of the battle that had lasted for most of 1916, causing hundreds of thousands of German and French casualties.

20, 1918, Easter Sunday, in New York. On May 3, Battery D paraded in Kansas City. The battery was mustered out of service at Fort Riley, Kansas, three days later.

Some historians exploring Truman's decision to deploy atomic weapons against Japan in 1945 have found it difficult to resist speculating over just how Truman's brief but vivid combat experience influenced his decision to use them.

Edgar Hinde, fellow artillery veteran of World War I. On how Harry Truman found the Folies-Bergere distasteful after seeing it in Paris:

"Oh yeah – the show was a little risqué, I'd say. And he never did care much for that stuff. Just like – you read so much about Harry drinking bourbon, you know, during that campaign – why, he can make a highball last longer than anybody I ever saw. I've seen him take one highball, and – all evening that would be all he'd take, but he'd drink with everybody that'd come in. That always amused me – how much Harry Truman drank. Well, he didn't. I never saw him when he was anywhere near under the influence of liquor and I never saw him drink very much."

poured in forty-nine rounds in two minutes.

The following day Truman spotted an enemy observation post and cleared it out with artillery fire that he directed. An hour or two later he saw a second German battery and directed more than forty shells toward it in two minutes. It resulted in six abandoned guns and several German dead.

Some 26,000 Americans died in the Meuse-Argonne offensive. And though the Germans were ultimately defeated, that result was far from obvious at the time.

"Every time a shell lights it blows up a piece of someone," Truman wrote in a letter to his cousins, the Noland sisters.

On November 11, Battery D sent over its last barrage at 10:45 A.M. In a 1960s interview, Truman remembered allowing the battery's cooks to pull the lanyards, firing the last shots.

By the end of the war, Truman's battery had fired more than ten thousand shells from its 75mm field guns into the German lines.

The battery boarded ship to return home and arrived on April

Giangreco, in his 2002 paper, chose instead to focus on the decision facing Truman before the atomic bomb became a realistic option: an invasion of Japan.

The man, Giangreco wrote, "who later ordered the invasion of Japan in the face of massive casualty estimates knew exactly what he was asking of our soldiers, sailors and marines, and he understood it at a level that most Americans today would find unfathomable."

THE LAST OF BATTERY D

McKinley Wooden outlived them all.

There were around two hundred members of Battery D of the 129th Field Artillery of the 35th Division when it was on the ground in France during World War I. In March 1995, when he turned one hundred years old, Wooden was the battery's final survivor.

"There's no doubt about it," the centenarian said one day that year in his efficiency apartment in a Lee's Summit, Missouri, retirement community. "I'm still here, and all the boys ain't."

Wooden had enlisted in June 1917. He had served as Battery D's chief mechanic, and as such saw much of the world beyond Walker and Nevada, in west central Missouri, where Wooden grew up.

In his last years, the world came to him. A British Broadcasting Corporation documentary team interviewed him, as did another group producing a Harry Truman documentary for the Arts & Entertainment cable television

network. In 1998 the French government informed Wooden that he had been named Chevalier of the National Order of the Legion of Honor.

Wooden received the decoration during Veterans Day ceremonies at Kansas City's Liberty Memorial that November. He was dead within a month, and the obituaries noted how Wooden's passing meant that all Captain Harry's boys now had passed on.

The charting of the battery's mortality had been observed for years by its own members. At some battery reunions, especially those held in the 1970s, time was

sometimes set aside for reading aloud every name of those battery members who were deceased.

Wooden was a fixture at these later reunions.

Members always had taken their reunions seriously. As an artillery unit, it had seen perhaps three months of action during World War I. For the next sixty years, into the late 1970s and early 1980s, battery members organized reunions, compiled mailing lists, and – following Truman's death on December 26, 1972 – honored their former captain's memory.

Usually two reunions were

A 1920 Battery D reunion photograph included former battery captain Harry Truman, in foreground, holding his glasses instead of wearing them.

McKinley Wooden, then considered the "last" member of Truman's artillery battery, laughed in 1995 at the memory of some of his war adventures.
Right: Wooden during World War I.

held each year, one near Armistice Day and the other, in recognition of the battery's significant Irish contingent, on St. Patrick's Day. The battery's first St. Patrick's Day party had occurred in 1918, in a mess hall at Camp Doniphan, at Fort Sill, Oklahoma, where the outfit had trained before leaving for overseas.

Some of the ensuing reunions were more memorable than others.

A 1920 gathering at Kansas City's Hotel Muehlebach was documented by a group photograph that contains one of the few images of an adult Harry Truman not wearing his glasses. In the photo about fifty of the battery's young men sit composed and calm, apparently awaiting their dinner entrees.

The next year, the entrees barely had time to arrive.

It was the 1921 St. Patrick's Day party at a Kansas City Elks Club that established the battery's reputation. Oral histories of battery members on file at the Truman Museum detail how the event

Third Annual Banquet Battery D, 129th Field Artillery

escalated into a small riot with members hurling dishes and glassware.

The Truman Library archives also contain the letter written a few days later by the Elks Club secretary, detailing the damage.

Eight coffee cups: $2.24
Nine saucers: $2.03
Ten tumblers: $1.35
Twelve punch cups: $2.40

The secretary assessed an additional $4 "special charge," as battery members, not content with merely destroying the dining room, had entered the kitchen to throw dishes and glassware at the Elks Club cooks. The total bill for the evening: $167.80.

"The reason for this breakage was due to some of the members of the party who seemed to have taken it for granted that

If Truman wasn't responsible, battery legend nevertheless has it that he picked up the tab, at about the same time his Kansas City haberdashery was struggling.

Yet that wasn't all. It was in 1921, some accounts insist, that Truman was approached by the Pendergast family to run for Jackson County eastern judge the following year.

The battery's St. Patrick's Day riot could have provided opportunity for any opposing candidate to embarrass Truman, given how dry eastern Jackson County had become upon the arrival of Prohibition across the country in January 1920.

The event's invitation, also in the Truman Library archives, directed battery members to R.S.V.P. to the Truman-Jacobson

But the riot never emerged as a campaign issue, and the battery members made themselves heard at several of their former captain's election appearances across Jackson County in 1922.

"He [Truman] was awful proud of the battery," Wooden said in 1995. "I don't see why. Because [it] embarrassed him once in a while."

Kansas City's Muehlebach Hotel was the official site of many Battery D reunions. After Truman became president in 1945, the Muehlebach became Truman's hotel of choice while visiting Kansas City. That's why, Wooden said, the battery sometimes chose to descend upon the Hotel President, two blocks south of the Muehlebach, so as

Edgar Hinde, fellow artillery veteran of World War I. On rowdy veterans during the 1921 American Legion convention in Kansas City:

"They were full of pep, you know, and they tore that whole town up. They had the Hotel Baltimore there at Twelfth and Baltimore right catty-cornered from the Muehlebach over there on the northeast corner. Some of those boys went down [to] the stockyards and they got a steer and brought him up to Baltimore Hotel and put him on an elevator and took him up to the fifth or sixth floor. They paraded around up there – that was the roughest thing you ever saw in your life. Why, they turned cars over and the darnedest things – they were just full of pep."

they could stage an 'uproarious' time,' " the secretary wrote Truman. "We regret very much the occurance [sic] of that evening, and realize that the officers were not responsible for the acts of the individuals."

haberdashery at 104 W. 12th Street. It also advised members to "bring your own 'iron rations' in the old hip pocket," adding that members could "use your own judgment and pay your own bond."

not to embarrass the president.

After Truman became president, the battery informed him that the White House would be the site of a Battery D reunion.

That never occurred.

Truman did remember the

Edward D. McKim, Kansas City resident who served as a private in Battery D; longtime Truman friend and political aide. About the infamous 1921 Battery D reunion in Kansas City:

"Everything was going along fine until a little brawl started. Somebody asked somebody else to pass the soup and he airlined it. And then they started throwing rolls and pretty soon they were throwing dishes, and I know about that time I went under the table. They were flying my way, too. I was doing fine until somebody skipped a sugar bowl down this tile floor. I ducked that one. But it ended up in quite a brawl. Somebody sent a riot call to the police and they sent down two policemen, and one of them happened to be George Brice, who had been in the battery. They proceeded to practically undress him. . . . Well, I remember Mr. Truman had to pay the bill right afterwards, not that night but the next day. I don't remember what the bill was. It ran up into important money, a couple of hundred dollars as I recall, for the damage done."

battery, however, after he was elected president in 1948. Truman invited the entire battery to march in his inaugural parade the following January, and 79 of the then 138 surviving members attended.

The editors of *Life* magazine, charmed by the battery, assigned a writer to accompany many of the by-then middle-aged men on their train from Kansas City to Washington. The battery converted one rail car's men's room into a bar. In the adjoining car, a craps game began. But time had taken its toll and by midnight, most members had drifted off to their berths.

Upon arrival in Washington, many battery members went immediately to mass. "In the old days, we'd land somewhere, get in a fist fight, and *then* we'd go

to mass," one member told *Life*. On inauguration day, the members met the president for a seven A.M. breakfast at the Mayflower Hotel. "After one o'clock and about twenty-five minutes," Truman said, "I don't care what you do. But I want you to stay sober until that time."

So directed, battery members saw their captain sworn in as president and then formed an honor guard marching alongside Truman's limousine in the inaugural parade.

Truman, meanwhile, picked up the check for the inauguration breakfast.

Battery members behaved themselves in Washington and most of the time thereafter. Still, when twenty-five members showed up at the Muehlebach in March 1968, almost fifty years after

Armistice Day, one member – not identified by *The Kansas City Star* reporter who covered the event – tied two napkins across the top of his suit to approximate a reasonable facsimile of a women's brassiere.

That November, the battery observed the fiftieth anniversary of the war's end with a reunion which included an invitation to the Truman home in Independence. It was the last time many of the battery members saw their former captain.

In November 1970, twenty-five members of the battery's seventy survivors attended a reunion at the Muehlebach. In November 1972, fourteen members reported to the Muehlebach, out of the fifty-eight who survived.

On St. Patrick's Day in 1973, the battery held their first reunion since Harry Truman's death the previous December. Sixteen members gathered at Truman's grave in the Truman Museum's courtyard. Eugene Donnelly, longtime battery association president, placed a wreath at the president's grave, saying, "Captain, Battery D is present or accounted for."

Then they went back to the Muehlebach.

In November 1974, ten of the forty-eight surviving members attended the Muehlebach reunion.

In March 1978, fifteen of thirty-two surviving battery members reported to the Golden Ox Restaurant in Kansas City's stockyards district. In November 1980, six of twenty-three surviving members met at the same location.

Seven members gathered in 1980; five in 1981.

In 1984, Wooden and one other battery member presented a check for $409, the battery association's bank balance, to the Truman Museum.

Members of Battery D passing out identifying armbands for the 1949 inauguration.

In November 1975, nine of forty-four surviving members appeared.

In 1989, Wooden was honored by the Kansas City-based Harry S. Truman Good Neighbor Award Foundation as Battery D's last living member. That brought a good-natured protest from

Floyd Ricketts, then ninety-two and living in California. He had been told of Wooden's award by relatives in Kansas City.

"I'm still breathing," Ricketts told *The Star*.

In 1995, when the hundred-year-old Wooden received the Harry S. Truman Public Service Award, sponsored by the city of Independence, nobody challenged the honor.

Wooden was an uncharacteristic last living Battery D member. Though many battery members were Catholic, Wooden was not, nor was he a member of any particular church. He wasn't from Kansas City, as were so many battery members, but from rural Missouri. And in an outfit of ardent Democrats, Wooden, born in 1895, had been named for William McKinley, several years before the Republican governor of Ohio became president.

In Battery D, the word *Republican* was used as a pejorative by its captain. "Harry said half of them was Irish and the rest were Republicans," Wooden said in 1995.

To those who visited him upon his hundredth birthday, Wooden detailed how he had left his job as a farmhand in west central Missouri and ridden a train to Kansas City in 1917 to enlist in World War I. On June 11, he signed up with the 2nd Missouri Field Artillery when he encountered a recruiting booth in Kansas City's old Convention Hall.

After enlisting, Wooden joined about fifty other field artillery members chasing the men of a local taxi cab company who had harassed a fellow artillery member. The next day, when an officer ordered the battery into ranks and then asked who had participated in the affair, everyone – Wooden included – stepped forward.

"They all stood together," Wooden said in 1995. "What one done, they all done. What one stole, they all stole."

Though his formal education had ended in the eighth grade, Wooden had developed a repu-

responsible for caring for the battery's four French 75mm field guns.

"We had run three captains off," Wooden said. "The first time [Truman] addressed the battery he said, 'I didn't come here to get along with you fellows. You're going to get along with me.'

"I said to an Irishman, 'Mike, what do you think of the new captain?' He said, 'Ninety days. Ninety days.' "

As a soldier, Wooden's stiff

Independence. "His name is McKinley Wooden," Truman wrote his future wife on September 15, 1918, "and he is the straightest, stiffest soldier I have. It almost hurts me when he stands at attention to talk to me."

Wooden died in December 1998. He had no surviving relatives, so members of Battery D of the Missouri National Guard's 129th Field Battalion carried his casket to a grave in a Nevada, Missouri, cemetery.

A 1979 Battery D reunion attracted McKinley Wooden, left.

tation for being able to fix machinery. Captain Truman, who took command of the battery in July 1918, recognized that, and promoted him to chief mechanic,

military bearing sufficiently impressed Captain Truman that he bestowed upon Wooden his ultimate accolade – a mention in a letter to Bess Wallace of

Harry Truman received five medals for his service as an artillery battery captain during World War I – the U.S. World War I Victory Medal, the Missouri Medal for the War with Germany (for those Missouri soldiers who served), and the Verdun, St. Mihiel, and Argonne medals, semiofficial decorations issued by those individual communities for troops that saw action in those respective areas.

But there was another medal that Truman apparently kept close to him during the last nineteen years of his life. The decoration was not one Truman earned personally but one that was sent to him by the father of an American soldier killed during the Korean War.

Truman received the medal, a Purple Heart, in 1953, along with an accompanying letter.

"Mr. Truman," the note read, "As you have been directly responsible for the loss of our son's life in Korea, you might just as well keep this emblem on display in your trophy room, as a memory of one of your historic deeds.

"Our major regret at this time is that your daughter was not there to receive the same treatment as our son received in Korea."

The note was signed by William Banning of New Canaan, Connecticut, the father of George C. Banning, one of the more than 36,000 Americans who died during the Korean War.

Today the father's bitter wish that his son's medal be displayed

has come true. The Purple Heart, along with the accompanying letter, is included in the Truman Museum exhibit devoted to Truman's decision to respond after the 1950 invasion of South Korea by North Korea.

The Purple Heart is a combat decoration awarded to members of the United States armed forces wounded or killed in action. The Truman Library staff found the Banning Purple Heart and letter in the former president's library desk after his death in December 1972.

Staff members found no accompanying note explaining why Truman kept the Banning decoration and letter within such easy reach.

George Banning died in Korea on May 11, 1953, several months after Truman left the White House. The Korean War ended just over two months later.

The Banning Purple Heart was not unique. In all, five Purple Hearts were returned to Truman. The medals often arrived with angry letters or telegrams. A.W. Simmons of Eldred, Pennsylvania, wrote after the 1951 death of his

son, Albert, "I lose a son because you order him to his death. . . . You start a blundering useless war that you may dictate in Korea instead of Stalin. . . . Then drag it out so that our munitions makers make millions and the poor lose their sons. . . ."

Newspaper accounts of returned Purple Hearts, however, prompted still other bereaved parents to write letters of encouragement to Truman.

"One of the most unpatriotic gestures any true American could make would be to return a Purple Heart or any medal of honor awarded to a man or woman who [has] given their lives for their country," wrote Faye Becker of Kalamazoo, Michigan, whose son James also died in Korea in 1951.

To those who returned Purple Hearts, Truman did not respond directly. Two parents who returned medals received identical three-page letters on Department of the Army stationery, stating that the medals were being held for the families if they ever reconsidered.

The Banning Purple Heart

went on display at the Truman Museum in 1991, during the opening weeks of the Persian Gulf War. Though its display was planned well before the Gulf War began, its timely exhibition suggested the wartime burdens borne by presidents, not to mention the parents and friends of those Americans lost during combat.

But the medal's display prompted still other theories among Truman historians. Truman often was thought to have suffered few inner doubts about wartime decisions he made as chief executive, including the use of the atomic bomb in 1945 and his decision to intervene in Korea in 1950. The presence of the Banning Purple Heart in his desk, however, suggested a more contemplative side.

Then again, it's possible that the Purple Heart merely reflected Truman's historical sympathy with the individual soldier. During his time as World War I artillery battery captain, Truman resented some higher officers and occasionally shrugged off orders that he felt slighted his battery's enlisted men. Also, four of the approximately two hundred men who served in Truman's artillery battery died in France.

Ultimately, the medal's presence in his library desk suggests that he knew the consequences of ordering soldiers into harm's way.

In late 1952, just weeks before leaving office, Truman extended eligibility for the Purple Heart medal to the Navy, Marine Corps, and Coast Guard retroactive to April 5, 1917, the day before the United States declared war on Germany.

NURSERY RD
NEW CANAAN
CONN.

MR. TRUMAN

AS YOU HAVE BEEN DIRECTLY RESPONSIBLE FOR THE LOSS OF OUR SONS LIFE IN KOREA, YOU MIGHT JUST AS WELL KEEP THIS EMBLEM ON DISPLAY IN YOUR TROPHY ROOM, AS A MEMORY OF ONE OF YOUR HISTORIC DEEDS.

OUR MAJOR REGRET AT THIS TIME IS THAT YOUR DAUGHTER WAS NOT THERE TO RECEIVE THE SAME TREATMENT AS OUR SON RECEIVED IN KOREA.

SINGED
William Banning

Harry S. Truman served as
Jackson County presiding judge
for eight years, then left for the
United States Senate in 1935.

CHAPTER 5

JACKSON COUNTY

Those looking for a reliable sighting of Harry Truman's Jackson County could perhaps begin at the intersection of Missouri 291 and U.S. 24, in Independence, only a few miles east of the Truman Presidential Museum & Library.

The roads meet at a high spot in the county's northeast district. Once there, visitors can turn to the south and southeast and train their eyes on the horizon, noting the color of the distant hills.

It's a subtle but undeniable blue.

The sight is likely similar to what some of Jackson County's first Anglo arrivals noticed when they climbed up and over the Missouri River bluffs after heading south from the river landings. These settlers, many arriving in the early nineteenth century from Kentucky and Tennessee, were said to have remarked on the similarities between this new Jackson County and the look of the horizons back home.

"These splendid blue-grass pastures of forest and field in Jackson County will be compared with the best range in Illinois or Kentucky," reads an 1881 county history.

The county's vistas and wooded districts also delighted the new arrivals, who preferred to clear timber in forested areas for their farms. Visitors from the east coast also were impressed. Washington Irving, writing from Independence in September of 1832, insisted to his sister that a deer hunt he had joined the day before "led me through some scenery that only wanted a castle, or a gentleman's seat here and there

interspersed, to have equaled some of the most celebrated park scenery of England. The fertility of this western country is truly astonishing. The soil is like that of a garden, and the luxuriance and beauty of the forests exceed any that I have seen."

Before Jackson County was founded on December 15, 1826, the district was known as "Blue" county. Near the Blue River eventually would be founded the political township named Blue: the site of Independence, Harry Truman's hometown and the biggest city in the county's eastern district.

It's impossible to summarize Jackson County without noting Truman's storied effect upon it, and it upon him. In his time as well as now, Jackson County covered about six hundred square miles, and Truman acquired an intimate knowledge of the sheer range of experience that acreage offered.

Kansas City dominated the county's western half. Between 1880 and 1890, Kansas City grew faster than St. Louis, more than doubling its population from 55,000 to 132,000. In 1885, one year after Truman was born, the city's first cable car line opened. By the time Truman was riding streetcars into Kansas City to take piano lessons as a teenager, the city's concert halls were attracting the world's finest artists, among them classical pianist Paderewski, whom Truman heard at a downtown theater in 1900.

But Kansas City offered other attractions. At one vaudeville theater, Truman signed on as an usher. Later, courting Bess Wallace, Truman treated her to a Jerome Kern musical at another downtown theater. Half a century later, when then-president Truman was on his way to meet General Douglas MacArthur at Wake Island during the Korean War, Truman visited with Harpo Marx and told him how he, as a young man, enjoyed several Kansas City performances given by him and his brothers.

After high school Truman lived in Kansas City, working in banks as well as – briefly – at *The Kansas City Star* mailroom. After World War I he became a downtown businessman. He helped operate a haberdashery on 12th Street and became a member of the Kansas City Club. Finally, in the 1930s, he would transform the city's skyline with a new three-hundred-foot art deco downtown county courthouse.

And yet it was the county's eastern, or rural, district that Truman probably knew even better. For several months after graduating from high school in 1901, he worked as a construction timekeeper on the Santa Fe rail line through the county.

"There were three construction camps about five miles apart," Truman wrote in one memoir. "It was my job to check the men at each of these camps twice daily. I was furnished with a tricycle car. Its power was by hand and I furnished the power."

Before World War I, Truman worked for several years as a farmer in Grandview, in southern Jackson County. After his father's death in 1914, Truman took over his father's position as county road overseer for the southern half of the county's Washington Township, which included Grandview. He also was appointed Grandview postmaster. During his 1922 campaign for eastern Jackson County judge, Truman visited every county town and township.

But it was in Independence that Truman grew up, was educated, took his first real job at an Independence Square drugstore, married, and fathered a child. Returning after the presidency, Truman lived in Independence for almost twenty years until his 1972 death.

The rise of Independence, the county seat, was the result of geography and circumstance.

One of Jefferson's instructions to Meriwether Lewis and William Clark was to note advantageous sites for forts. In late June 1804, as the party inched into what is now Jackson County, the two noted high bluffs on the Missouri River's south bank. Four years later, in 1808, William Clark returned to supervise the construction of Fort Osage, named for the Indian tribe which in 1825 ceded much of the land that became Jackson County.

Though the Chouteau family of fur traders had established a trading post nearby, on the north side of the Missouri River, that site washed away in an 1826 flood. That same high water prompted other entrepreneurs to seek the relative safety of Independence, founded in 1827.

That year, the county's founders ordered a log courthouse be built. Today what is known as the 1827 Log Courthouse still stands on a block south of Independence Square. In 1932 and 1933, Jackson County Presiding Judge Harry Truman convened meetings of the county court there while the county's Independence courthouse was being renovated.

That same log courthouse was built with the labor of several slaves. The Missouri Compromise of 1820 allowed Missouri into the union the following year without any restrictions on slavery.

It's another reason the Kentucky and Tennessee emigrants felt comfortable in Jackson County and why many of those emigrants brought their slaves with them.

Jackson County included 193 African-American slaves in 1830, the number rising to 1,361 in 1840, and 2,969 by 1850 and close to 4,000 by 1860. In those years, Jackson County was a leading hemp-producing district, and slaves often were assigned the tedious task of processing the plant used to produce rope.

Slave owning in Jackson County was rarely on the plantation scale; the vast majority of owners held only a few. Still, such was the sentiment of Jackson County; both of Harry Truman's grandfathers owned slaves. In his letters as a young man, Truman used the occasional racial slur. But decades later, as president, he emerged as the chief executive who did the most on behalf of African Americans since Abraham Lincoln had signed the Emancipation Proclamation in 1863.

That change of heart began during Truman's time as a Jackson County judge, when he courted the black vote, placed a significant number of African Americans on the county payroll, and took care to fund homes for African-American youths and elderly.

That was of no small significance in Jackson County, which in the nineteenth century witnessed more than its share of intolerance.

In the early 1830s the early settlers of Jackson County banded together to drive out the followers of Joseph Smith Jr. who had begun to gather and buy property in Jackson County. Two years after the first group of Mormons arrived in 1831, their number had swelled to about twelve hundred, at a time when the total population of the entire county was perhaps five thousand. In 1838, Missouri Governor Lilburn Boggs, an Independence resident, issued a Mormon extermination order. It was not rescinded until 1976, by Missouri Governor Christopher "Kit" Bond.

Despite the turmoil of the early nine-teenth century, both the Church of Jesus Christ of Latter-day Saints (the Mormons, based in Utah) and the Reorganized Church of Jesus Christ of Latter Day Saints (based in Independence) were well established in Independence during Truman's rise to power. Truman's relationship with both church communities was cordial. In 1949 he was presented a Book of Mormon signed by LDS leader Ezra Taft Benson, later agriculture secretary under President Dwight Eisenhower.

Truman's first Kansas City area speech after becoming president in 1945 was held at the RLDS auditorium in Independence.

In 2000, Independence city officials joined members of the Mormon and RLDS (today known as the Community of Christ) churches to dedicate a walking tour of Independence that detailed the exact spots where particular instances of intolerance occurred. Only about twenty-five years before, during plans for the bicentennial, a city heritage commission had tabled a similar plan, saying that recalling those unfortunate times would be too divisive. But as of 2000, the Missouri Mormon Walking Trail consisted of plaques set into sidewalks marking the exact spots in Independence

Before World War I, Truman worked for more than ten years as a farmer in Grandview. This view of the old Grandview farm shows sheep grazing in the yard. Today, the farm is surrounded by commercial development.

where, for instance, a Mormon store was sacked, a Mormon newspaper office was demolished, and two Mormon church members were tarred and feathered.

As bitter as the Mormon War had been in Jackson County, it didn't compare to the Civil War, which rendered the bulk of Jackson County into a vast "burnt over" district. During the great unpleasantness, few places were more unpleasant than Jackson County, Missouri, which was fouled by bitter border warfare among Confederate sympathizers in Missouri and free state advocates in Kansas.

Members of both camps routinely committed outrages. Into her old age Truman's mother, Martha Ellen Young Truman, told how her farm was regularly pillaged by marauding Union troops. In 1863, after guerrilla leader William Quantrill's murderous raid on Lawrence, Kansas, Union Brigadier General Thomas Ewing Jr. ordered Jackson County depopulated in an attempt to root out those aiding such guerrillas. Union troops evicted most of the county's population from their homes before burning many of the dwellings.

To Truman, the Civil War was never ancient history. In January 1930, area resident Kate King, once thought to have been married to Quantrill, died in the Jackson County Home for the Aged. At the time, the home was one of several county institutions administered by Truman, Jackson County's presiding judge.

Another example of how Truman's life and Jackson County's legacy often intertwined was the overland trails migration of the 1820s through the 1850s. The traffic transformed Independence into a vast staging area for those traveling over the Santa Fe, California, and Oregon trails. Truman's maternal grandfather, Solomon Young, led wagon trains from Independence and Westport to Utah and California from the 1840s through the 1860s. About sixty years after that, in

between terms on the Jackson County Court, Truman worked for the National Old Trails Road Association, which sought to correct the random numbering of the nation's highways and to encourage states west of Missouri to pave the historic trails. Even as late as 1955, during a flight to San Francisco, Truman found occasion to recall his grandfather and the challenges he faced in pioneer Jackson County.

"As we flew along I couldn't help but think of my old Grandfather Young who'd driven wagon trains from the home farm in Jackson County, Missouri, to Colorado, Utah and California from 1846 to 1860," Truman wrote in a diary excerpt. "We'd left home at seven A.M. and at 11 A.M. were well past the high mountains. Grandpa would have left home at what is now Grandview at four A.M. and in all probability would have been ten or twelve miles west of the Missouri line."

Today, Independence's trails legacy is one of four "pillars" of the city's tourism initiative – the others being Harry Truman, the city's Mormon history, and Independence Square. The square was the commercial and retail center of eastern Jackson County from the overland trails days through the 1970s. At the height of the trails era, Independence Square represented one of the most diverse communities in Missouri, if not the entire American West.

The trails traffic rendered Independence an authentic international trade center. Apparel manufactured as far away as England came through Independence on its way to Santa Fe, which was then in Mexico. In Independence ethnic groups not always known to trust one another worked together in the trails trade, and made money. Anglo-American entrepreneurs learned to write and speak Spanish and married into Hispanic families. One of the city's wealthiest residents was Hiram Young, a free black who throughout the 1850s manufactured and

Martha Ellen Truman in 1934. Into her old age, Truman's mother spoke of how her family's farm was routinely pillaged by marauding Union troops during the Civil War.

sold some of the town's most well-regarded wagons and oxen yokes. In the decade before the Civil War, Young's company was among the largest in Independence.

And yet, some trails-era Independence merchants hedged their bets. After New York entrepreneur Lewis Tappan established the Mercantile Agency, a credit reporting firm, in 1841, many Independence merchants discovered a new way of monitoring the practices of their competitors. Summaries filed by credit reporters who circulated among Independence businessmen noted the drinking habits of merchants, or whether a particular merchant was Jewish, female, or a free black.

Some sixty years later, the square was the site of Clinton's drugstore, where a teenaged Truman took his first job and happened to learn how some of the more pious of the town's Sabbath worshipers satisfied their alcohol cravings.

"In a little closet under the prescription case, which faced the front and shut off the view of the back end of the store, was an assortment of whiskey bottles," Truman wrote decades later. "Early in the morning, sometimes before Mr. Clinton arrived, the good church members and Anti-Saloon Leaguers would come in for their early morning drink behind the prescription case at ten cents an ounce. They would wipe their mouths, peep through the observation hole in front of the case, and depart."

Today Harry Truman might not recognize much of his Jackson County. His Grandview farm is surrounded by development. Independence Square, once the center of gravity in eastern Jackson County, is struggling to re-emerge as a boutique district with restaurants and specialty shops. In the 1970s the square was almost deserted as shopping malls to the south and east emptied the district of shoppers.

In both of these matters, though, Truman arguably played a role.

In the 1930s, Truman supervised the construction of hundreds of miles of new and improved roads. As promised, these roads brought farmers closer to their markets. It also had another effect, not so advertised, but just as profound: It brought the market closer to the farm, turning rural acreage into suburbs of Kansas City.

In this regard, Truman can be considered a godfather of Jackson County sprawl. Just between 1940 and 1950 the population of Independence more than doubled, increasing from 16,066 to 36,963. Much of that increase was due to the installation of the Lake City Ammunition Plant. One ironic result: The eastern Jackson County towns of Blue Springs and Lee's Summit, rural hamlets when Truman was first running for office in 1922, had by the arrival of the twenty-first century evolved into large suburban municipalities – and Republican strongholds.

Upon his return to Independence from the White House in the early 1950s, Truman made Independence Square a familiar sight across the country, as news reporters and photographers often accompanied him on his frequent walks from his North Delaware Street home to the square and back. In 1976, President Gerald Ford dedicated a statue of a walking Harry Truman on the square's east side.

"My home town, Independence, the County Seat of Jackson County, Missouri, is in my opinion the best place for a retired Missouri farmer to live," Truman wrote in a 1962 diary excerpt. "The state has had three 'notorious' characters – Mark Twain, Jesse James and myself. The other two are shoveling coal for Pluto and I'm all that's left to appear for them."

A s a businessman, young Harry Truman made a good farmer.

Before and after World War I, his family had one principal asset: the farm in Grandview. But while Truman worked at the farm for years, it couldn't hold his attention. He tried lead mining, oil drilling, and men's shirt-selling.

All were failures. The oil business went through money belonging to Truman, Truman's mother, and – perhaps worse – Bess Wallace.

But the failure of the haberdashery was a bigger disaster. Truman lost money he had generated by selling assets, such as livestock, from the Truman farm.

Some observers had thought the haberdashery only the latest in a line of whims indulged in by a restless young man. But Truman had resolved to win Bess Wallace, who apparently had proved cool to the notion of being a farmer's wife. Seen in that context, Truman's various schemes testify to the urgency he brought to the task of marrying her.

"I am going to start in real earnest now to get some of the dirty pelf," Harry wrote Bess in 1911, not long after their courtship began. *Pelf* was a term denoting money perhaps acquired dishonestly.

If Truman's various ventures were honest, they were also high-

risk. The lead and zinc mine, near Commerce, Oklahoma, near the southwest Missouri border, was an example. "I became interested in a mining deal along with a neighbor and a promoter from Harrisonville," Truman wrote in a 1954 memo. "I learned a lot about hard rock mining and received a lot [of] experience but made no money." The mine was played out.

He returned to the family farm in Grandview, but when he met entrepreneur David H. Morgan, he soon invested in the Morgan & Company Oil Investments. The company issued stock, and shares sold fast enough that Truman sometimes had to stay late in the company office to count it all. Money, he wrote Bess, "is coming in by the basketful." Bess Wallace soon was writing friends about a possible wedding.

But the United States declared war on Germany in the spring of 1917, and the value of Morgan oil stock sank. A wartime manpower shortage was one factor that forced the company to shut down.

Truman felt the failure in his stomach.

"I seem to have a grand and admirable ability for calling tails when heads come up," he wrote

Bess. "My luck should surely change. Sometime I should win. I have tried to stick. Worked, really did, like thunder for ten years to get that old farm in line for some big production. Have it in shape and have a crop failure every year. Thought I'd change my luck, got a mine, and see what I did get. Tried again in the other long chance, oil."

Perhaps he was conscious of his father's experience: Shortly after the turn of the century, John Truman had lost virtually all of his family's assets in grain speculation.

By the summer of 1917, Truman had rejoined the Missouri National Guard and had decided to join the war effort, this time leaving the farm to his mother and sister.

While training as an artillery officer in Oklahoma, Truman finally got lucky – though it didn't appear so at the time. He was assigned to be the regimental canteen officer. He set up a small store in which soldiers could purchase items the U.S. Army didn't issue. The canteen was a success. One reason was the tenacity Truman brought to the task. He modified his prized Stafford automobile, turning it into a small truck and bringing a variety of

HOSIERY GLOVES BELTS HATS

TRUMAN JACOBSON

The Truman-Jacobson haberdashery at 104 W. 12th in Kansas City. After the war Truman and his army buddy, Eddie Jacobson, set up the store across the street from the Muehlebach Hotel. It flourished for more than a year before the crash of 1921 forced them to close.

These paper blotters doubled as advertisers for Truman-Jacobson Haberdashers.

Harry Truman, left, in the haberdashery.

merchandise in from surrounding towns.

The biggest reason for the canteen's success, however, may have been Truman's partnership with Eddie Jacobson, whom Truman had met years before while working as a clerk at the National Bank of Commerce in downtown Kansas City. Jacobson had ten years of experience in the retail clothing business. After the war, Truman and Jacobson resolved to open another store, this one back in downtown Kansas City.

The haberdashery represented an option to working on the Truman farm. "Returned to the farm but could not settle down on it," wrote Truman in the 1954

75

Truman in front of an oil well derrick. His investment in the oil business went through money belonging to Truman, his mother, and – perhaps worse – Bess Wallace.

memo. Truman sold the equity in his farm to his mother and sister, and went into the shirt-selling business.

The Truman & Jacobson haberdashery, which opened on November, 28, 1919, sold shirts as well as ties, underwear, gloves, belts, and hats. The store, just across from the Muehlebach Hotel, attracted former members of Truman's artillery battery, as well as other alums of the 129th Field Artillery and 35th Division.

While the store prospered its first year, a nationwide economic recession in 1921 and 1922 lowered prices of farm produce and manufactured goods. Truman often attributed the problem to Andrew Mellon, Warren Harding's treasury secretary, who, Truman believed, had encouraged prices to fall. In any case, inventories dropped in value while sales went down. Times were hard, and the same battery members who bought Truman and Jacobson's shirts and collars in 1920 now did not.

"They just did without, and they did without real good around Truman's store," Vere Leigh, a

former Battery D member, recalled in 1970.

The haberdashery's cash flow stopped. In this context, the invitation from the Pendergast family to consider running for Jackson County eastern judge held obvious appeal. "He was an unsuccessful civilian going back and forth from his insolvent store on Twelfth Street to his mother-in-law's house in Independence," Jonathan Daniels wrote in his 1950 Truman biography, *The Man of Independence.*

Truman and Jacobson held a going-out-of-business sale in September 1922. Two months later Truman was elected Jackson County eastern judge. While Jacobson declared bankruptcy in 1925, Truman never did, in part because, after he was elected, he was a public official and his salary could not be garnished.

It would take him about twelve years, when Truman was a U.S. senator, before his haberdashery obligations were resolved.

That didn't stop him, however, from investing his time in helping to run a community bank. In the fall of 1925, after losing his re-election bid as Jackson County

eastern judge, Truman formed a partnership with two business associates. Together they operated Community Savings and Loan in Independence. Truman withdrew from the partnership in 1931, while serving as Jackson County presiding judge. One of his partners eventually was convicted of bank fraud for misrepresenting the assets of the savings and loan.

Truman apparently lost no money in the savings and loan. But he frequently considered his financial condition perilous, telling one friend in 1944 that one reason he didn't want to run for vice president was that he was still in debt, and couldn't afford another campaign.

Eventually, he ran anyway.

"Obviously Truman had some of the characteristics of the gambler in him," Truman biographer Jonathan Daniels said in 1963. "If he hadn't, he wouldn't have been in the oil stock business, the speculation in lead mines. When he ran for the Senate, it was a great wild speculation that he would be elected to the Senate of the United States."

BOSS TOM

When he died on January 26, 1945, Tom Pendergast was a broken and disgraced man, not long out of the federal penitentiary at Leavenworth, Kansas.

But you would not have known that from his funeral.

The Quirk and Tobin funeral chapel of Kansas City soon was awash in 209 wreaths and sprays from a wide range of Kansas City residents, from members of Bartenders Local 420, which sent white gladioli, to the R. Crosby Kemper banking family, which forwarded white, red, and pink carnations.

The line of mourners paying homage stretched out the door beyond Linwood Boulevard and Main Street. Fifty years later, some close relatives of Pendergast still could recall the many admirers of Tom Pendergast who approached them.

"A few came up to me and wondered which Pendergast I was," Bob Pendergast, a nephew of Pendergast and one of eight pallbearers at the machine boss's funeral, said in 1995. "Quite a few gave me the same story. Their father died in such and such a year, and Mr. Pendergast had given their father a job at the city."

Such admirers were presumably not among those who had called the home of Bob Pendergast in 1939, soon after Tom Pendergast had reported to Leavenworth federal penitentiary after pleading guilty to income tax evasion.

"When he was sentenced and sent to Leavenworth, only two of us happened to have our telephones listed, Jim [Bob's brother] and myself," Bob Pendergast

In May 1939, Tom Pendergast was sentenced to fifteen months at the federal penitentiary in Leavenworth, Kansas.

said. "We would get calls at two or three in the morning.

"People would say, 'How do you think the old SOB likes it now?'"

The most familiar face at the Pendergast funeral belonged to Harry Truman, who only days before had been sworn in as vice president of the United States.

Any discussion of Truman's rise to political power would have to include prominent mention of Tom Pendergast, without whom Truman may never have become a candidate of any kind.

And, just as Bob Pendergast encountered those who either revered or reviled Tom Pendergast, there is more than one way to perceive the machine boss who is arguably Kansas City's most vivid historical figure.

The Jackson Democratic Club during the Pendergast era. Pendergast built the building at 1908 Main Street in 1924 and maintained an office on the second floor.

Perhaps scholars should deride the corpulent, spats-wearing crook who disgraced Kansas City, joining forces with gamblers and transforming its very name into a definition of early twentieth-century urban corruption.

Or maybe they should defend the urban patriarch whose organization, beginning back in the 1890s, assumed the burden of Kansas City public assistance after the town's elite shrugged off the task.

Truman himself had to reconcile his personal integrity with the corrupt political machine that first helped elect him to public office in the 1920s and – with fraudulent vote totals out of Kansas City – put him in the U.S. Senate in 1934.

In that year's Democratic primary for senator, Truman defeated U.S. Representative John Cochran of St. Louis by 120,180 votes to 1,221 votes in Kansas City, and 17,349 to 304 in the rest of Jackson County. That gave Truman a total Jackson County margin of about 136,000 votes. As pointed out by Truman historian Robert Ferrell, Cochran carried the rest of Missouri by 95,259, so Truman's ultimate margin was more than 40,000 votes.

"The work of the Kansas City machine was heroic," Ferrell wrote.

In his "Pickwick Papers," or memoirs that Truman wrote in Kansas City's Pickwick Hotel while escaping the pressures of Jackson County politics, the future president bemoaned the corruption that plagued the county. But in a 1939 letter to a friend, Truman – at the time a U.S. senator – defended his use of Pendergast machine votes.

"Any man would have been very foolish to turn down the support of the organization which at that time controlled 100,000 votes, and I acted just as every other candidate would have done," he wrote.

None of the Pendergast machine outrages unveiled during its collapse in the late 1930s was ever connected to Truman. In fact, the former Jackson County presiding judge apparently was shocked at the scale of the graft and the greed attributed to machine leaders. Various audits revealed that $11 million in funds for the retirement of Kansas City water revenue bonds was unlawfully diverted to other purposes. Another $2.6 million also had been diverted to unauthorized uses.

"Looks like everybody in Jackson County got rich but us," Truman wrote his wife, Bess, during the revelations.

By 1940, when Truman resolved to run for re-election to the U.S. Senate, his connection with Pendergast had become a liability. In a 1940 speech, Missouri Governor Lloyd Stark, campaigning hard for Truman's senate seat, announced that the "decent, honest God-fearing law-abiding citizens of Missouri know [Truman] for what he is – a fraudulent United States senator, elected by ghost votes . . . "

And yet Truman won. In a field of three candidates in the Democratic primary, Truman prevailed by less than 8,000 votes out of about 665,000 cast.

He returned to Washington much more his own man, and not the "senator from Pendergast," as he had been derided upon his arrival in Washington in 1935. Yet, without Tom Pendergast, Truman never would have been a senator from a border state, an attractive option for Democrats considering a running mate for President Franklin Roosevelt in 1944.

The 1890 city directory listed Tom Pendergast as a clerk, rooming at 501 Walnut Street in Kansas City.

That year he followed his older brother James down from St. Joseph. Since 1881 James had operated hotels and saloons in the city's West Bottoms, also known as the city's First Ward. Voters there elected James Pendergast alderman in 1892, and he directed political life in the district through 1910.

Over time, followers of the Pendergast machine came to be called "Goats," ostensibly for the goats kept by some of the residents of the steep bluffs overlooking the First Ward. Through the years they battled for political dominance with a rival Democratic machine known as the "Rabbits," a nickname given in tribute to their quickness and tenacity in seizing political opportunity.

There was opportunity for Kansas City political gangs when the Commercial Club, a forerunner of today's Greater Kansas City Chamber of Commerce, decided that welfare work was not among its responsibilities following the financial panic of 1893.

Back then, Kansas City had no public welfare system. The subsequent bag of coal, holiday meal, or job that the Pendergast machine awarded gave voters a

name to remember on election day.

In 1900, Tom Pendergast was named Kansas City's superintendent of streets, taking the position seriously enough to get out from behind his desk and sweat along with his charges. The department employed more than two hundred workers — more than any other city office except the mayor's.

This experience had several

Senator-Elect Harry S. Truman in his judge's office in November 1934. His connections to machine boss Tom Pendergast caused Truman to be sometimes called "the senator from Pendergast."

rewards for the future proprietor of the Ready Mixed Concrete Company. Pendergast learned about the possibilities for personal enrichment through lucrative heavy construction contracts. He

The Rural Jackson County Democratic Club met at several locations in the 1920s; one of its locations is thought to have been at 211 West Lexington Street, Independence. The eastern Jackson County branch of Tom Pendergast's organization, it was headed by Tom's brother, Mike, in the early and mid-twenties. *Photo by Ray Geselbracht*

council, part of its recently approved charter government.

Truman's election as Jackson County presiding judge the next year gave Pendergast control of county patronage.

By then the Pendergast machine had a known street address. In 1924, Pendergast had purchased the Monroe Hotel at 1904 Main Street. The same year he built a two-story building next door at 1908 Main Street, which served as Pendergast's office.

Throughout the 1930s, during the height of the Pendergast machine's power, the two buildings came to be known as the unofficial capitol of Missouri. Pendergast's Jackson Democratic Club occupied the second floor of 1908 Main Street, and throughout the 1930s the sidewalk routinely spilled over with supplicants seeking an audience with the Boss.

Though Truman first was elected as a Goat candidate in 1922, as Jackson County eastern judge, scholars believe Truman didn't visit Pendergast at 1908 Main Street until several years later.

Truman's first encounter with the Pendergast machine likely occurred in 1921. That year, Truman was visited at his 12th Street haberdashery by Jim Pendergast and his father, Mike Pendergast.

Truman had known Jim Pendergast during the war. Mike Pendergast was Tom's brother and head of the Pendergast machine's eastern Jackson County operation. The

Pendergasts proposed that Truman run for eastern Jackson County judge.

The proposal was attractive for both parties. Truman's haberdashery, of course, was failing and it would close the next year. But the Pendergast machine may have needed Truman more. Tom Pendergast had controlled the county court off and on, but now had lost his influence in the county's rural districts. To the Pendergasts, Truman seemed the ideal candidate. He had been a farmer, was a Mason and a Baptist, and was a member of a large and established Jackson County family with bases in Independence and Grandview.

Truman was elected Jackson County eastern judge in 1922 as Pendergast machine officials worked hard to soft-pedal Truman's connection to the organization. Two years later, Truman lost his post during a feud between Goat and Rabbit factions. In 1926, Truman won the post of Jackson County presiding judge, and worked hard to establish himself as an honest office-holder. Voters approved two bond issues to build roads and Truman angered longtime Jackson County contractors by insisting on accepting the lowest bids for road work.

Contractors who came to 1908 Main Street to complain to Pendergast received no sympathy from the Boss. "T.J. turned to his friends and said, `I told you that he's the contrariest man in the county. Get out of here,' " Truman wrote in a memoir. "When they were gone he said to me, `You carry out your commitments to the voters.' I did just that."

If Truman didn't mind anger-

also noticed how voters would ignore the most brazen City Hall scandal as long as the city's potholes were filled in a timely manner.

After James Pendergast's death in 1911, Tom Pendergast took control of the political machine and expanded its influence. In 1914, Pendergast's Goat operation, together with rival Rabbits, joined with Republican business interests. As one they passed a revision of the franchise agreement enjoyed by the Kansas City Metropolitan Street Railway Company. In 1925, Pendergast consolidated power in Kansas City by winning a majority of seats on the new city

ing Pendergast road contractors, he was careful to dole out patronage jobs to Pendergast appointees. From its infancy, the Pendergast machine proved popular among immigrant families because, not only did the machine offer food and coal for families, it also offered jobs.

When Mike Pendergast died in 1929, Tom Pendergast asked Truman to take over leadership of the machine's eastern county organization.

After serving two terms as presiding judge, Truman thought he was out of political options. But then there was an open seat in the U.S. Senate in 1934.

Pendergast had to be talked into naming Truman, but eventually he agreed. Few were excited.

"It's hard to believe, in this eastern end of Missouri, that boss Pendergast really means it when he comes out for a candidate for the United States Senate whose only experience in public life has been to sit ten years as a member of the Jackson county court," the *St. Louis Star-Times* announced in May 1934.

Even Pendergast machine officers in Kansas City were underwhelmed. Secret recordings of the telephone conversations of Pendergast machine officials, which surfaced in the 1990s, cap-

tured prominent Democrats consoling one another on Truman's candidacy.

Machine insiders knew that, by the 1930s, Pendergast ward workers could deliver 100,000 votes. But during the March 1934 city election, four persons died in violence at the polls. Thugs beat up dozens of others, and chased one *Kansas City Star* reporter back to the newspaper's door. That July a Pendergast ally, Johnny Lazia, was gunned down. The Union Station Massacre, which had occurred the previous year, led others to consider Kansas City a terrorized community. "An irresponsible political machine, concerned with spoils, is in full, terrifying control," the *St. Louis Post-Dispatch* insisted in a December 1934 editorial.

In 1936, the sheer scale of the Pendergast machine vote frauds was embarrassing. The size of election majorities, merely suspicious in previous years, grew ridiculous. In one ward a Pendergast candidate won a primary for state office, outpolling his opponent 19,201 to 13.

Researchers Lawrence Larsen and Nancy Hulston, in preparing their 1997 book *Pendergast!*, found a letter written by Tom Pendergast Jr. that was meant for but apparently never mailed to Margaret Truman, who in the 1970s had published a biography of her father. In the letter, the younger Pendergast admitted that machine precinct workers "got carried away and voted the sick, the dying and the dead."

During the Depression, it was not hard to find residents willing to sell their votes to the machine, Pendergast officials conceded years later. "Some people were dependent upon the election for their bread and butter," Matt Devoe, a former Pendergast machine precinct worker, said in 1996. "You handed them a ballot and a dollar."

A federal grand jury convened within weeks of the 1936 election, with the first indictments arriving the following spring. Throughout 1937 and

1938, juries brought in guilty verdicts on 259 out of 278 persons indicted. As a result of the investigations, some sixty thousand bogus names were stricken from Kansas City voter registration lists.

While such activities clipped the wings of the Pendergast political machine, it didn't put the Boss himself in prison. Pendergast's gambling debts, and a subsequent insurance company payoff, would do that. In 1935 and 1936, Pendergast accepted $440,000 from insurance companies eager to settle a long-litigated rate case in Missouri.

The gross indiscretion may have been out of character. In previous years, Pendergast had proved careful. During Prohibition, he had shut down his family's wholesale liquor company, warehousing his inventory and even refusing to unload the liquor to bootleggers.

But by the 1930s, Pendergast was into horse-racing bookmakers for hundreds of thousands of dollars. The bookies had nicknamed Pendergast "Sucker."

Pendergast was indicted for income tax evasion in the spring of 1939.

Truman did his best to show his loyalty. "Tom Pendergast has always been my friend and I don't desert a sinking ship," he told reporters after the indictment.

In February 1940, Truman filed for re-election to the U.S. Senate. Pendergast was newly deposited at the federal penitentiary in Leavenworth, and few seemed eager to donate to Truman's campaign. Three days before the primary in August, Truman's Sedalia headquarters

reported $53.16 on hand.

The end of Tom Pendergast was swift.

Part of the problem was his health. There had been a heart attack in 1936. Doctors diagnosed a bowel obstruction and performed a colostomy. Not long after, *The Kansas City Star* noted that an opening had been made in the common wall between the Monroe Hotel at 1904 Main Street and the Jackson Democratic Club at 1908 Main Street. Pendergast, arriving at the hotel, would ride the elevator to the second floor and then walk into his office next door.

It was there, in his office, that Pendergast's mania for betting on horse-racing across the country was indulged. After seeing visitors during the morning, Pendergast cut off all visits in the afternoon while he listened to horse-race results. Tom Evans, a Truman friend, recalled visiting the Pendergast office at 1908 Main Street during one afternoon and seeing Pendergast sitting on the edge of his chair, looking out the window and listening to the description of a faraway horse race.

"So I waited," Evans said, "and in a few minutes, he said, 'Come on in.' I walked in and he said, 'Well, you've caught me at my one and only vice.'

"I said, 'Is that so; what's that?' I didn't know what he was talking about.

"And he said, 'I'm gambling on horses; I just won. You brought me good luck.' "

The good luck didn't last. Federal government figures showed that Pendergast lost $600,000 in

Pendergast's Jackson Democratic Club building as it looks today.
Photo by Tammy Ljungblad

Scowling, T. J. Pendergast (right) looks back at John G. Madden (left), his attorney, and nephew Jim Pendergast as the three enter a car after he was sentenced to prison.

1935 on horse-racing bets.

"He was like a man on dope," wrote Tom Pendergast Jr. in his unsent letter to Margaret Truman. "He needed a fix. A fix for him was each race."

It was the gambling losses, many believe, that led Pendergast to take the bribe money for helping negotiate the insurance settlement.

After Pendergast pleaded guilty to income tax evasion, workers closed the common doorway between the Monroe Hotel and the Jackson Democratic Club.

Pendergast suffered a heart attack a few days after entering the Leavenworth prison. Still another heart attack followed a few months later.

Pendergast was paroled from Leavenworth after serving one year and one day. Under the terms of his parole, Pendergast was forbidden to visit his old office at 1908 Main Street, or to leave Kansas City except for medical reasons.

When he died some five years later, at age seventy-two in Kansas City's Menorah Hospital, the official cause of death was

coronary disease.

Writing in his letter almost thirty years later, Tom Pendergast Jr. had a different diagnosis.

"My father died of a broken heart," he wrote.

Truman's decision to attend the Pendergast funeral at Visitation Catholic Church reminded everyone of his connection to the Pendergast political machine. Many considered it a brave act of

loyalty on Truman's part.

Tom Pendergast Jr. didn't see it that way, arguing in his unsent letter to Margaret Truman that Truman had abandoned his father upon the fall of his machine.

Today the Pendergast leg-

Tom Pendergast leans over the desk of Charles H. Thompson, U.S. commissioner, and signs the bond. Behind him are Thomas McGee, area Democratic leader, and Tom Pendergast Jr.

end in Kansas City is becoming gentrified.

A statue of James Pendergast can be found in Kansas City's Case Park, which occupies a high spot overlooking the confluence of the Missouri and Kansas rivers. The Pendergast statue, which had been dedicated in 1913 and vandalized over several decades, was refurbished in 1990 and moved to Case Park, where the seated bronze figure now looks over the West Bottoms, Kansas City's old First Ward, the seat of Pendergast's power.

The Kansas City Board of Parks and Recreation Commissioners, usually reluctant to move statues, agreed to move the James Pendergast statue after a request by Tom Pendergast Jr. in 1990.

The younger Pendergast's request was unusual. In 1965, 1967, and 1980, he had filed lawsuits to prevent entrepreneurs from opening bars and restaurants that tried to exploit the Pendergast name.

In 1978, he argued against a city plan to place the Pendergast headquarters at 1908 Main Street on the National Register of Historic Places.

He died in1990, only a few weeks before his uncle's statue was re-dedicated before several hundred spectators.

In 1996, Robert Altman, filmmaker and Kansas City native, released the film *Kansas City*, a movie set in the Pendergast era which features an actor portraying the historical character of Tom Pendergast. Still another film, *Truman*, made for the HBO television network, chronicled the rise of the politician, and featured yet another actor playing the machine boss.

By the summer of 2003, plans were in place to turn the Monroe Hotel at 1904 Main Street, which had been closed since the late 1970s, into several loft condominiums.

And on summer weekends, one of the many rock bands available to clubgoers in Kansas City's Westport entertainment district was named Pendergast.

Top Tom Pendergast's 1945 funeral was held at Kansas City's Visitation Catholic Church. Here the crowd is leaving the church after the ceremony.

Left Vice-President Harry Truman shakes the hand of Jim Pendergast during the Kansas City funeral of Tom Pendergast in January 1945.

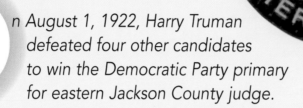

THE 1922 ELECTION

On August 1, 1922, Harry Truman defeated four other candidates to win the Democratic Party primary for eastern Jackson County judge.

Years later, Truman described the campaign as a "hot affair." It was all of that and more.

The race was fierce, as the two principal Democratic factions, the Pendergast "Goats" and the Shannon "Rabbits" battled over the judge's seat and the patronage jobs it controlled. In the primary Truman prevailed by 279 votes out of some 12,000 cast and might have lost the race if an attempt by Shannon forces to seize a ballot box at a rural polling station had not been thwarted.

"It was the hottest primary fight in the history of the county," the *Examiner* of Independence reported August 2.

It was hot literally. By mid-summer, the *Examiner* reported that trees, for lack of water, were dying across Jackson County. The heat may have gotten to Truman in mid-July, when he arrived at perhaps the county's biggest summer picnic, at Oak

Campaign button used during Harry S. Truman's first bid for elected office in 1922.

Grove, by biplane.

Truman, with a former World War I pilot, had circled the site dropping brochures to the estimated four thousand residents below, many of whom watched as the candidate – once the plane had landed – climbed from his seat and threw up.

"Our candidate got out . . . and gave forth with a lot of

ORAL HISTORIES

Edward D. McKim, Kansas City resident who served as a private in Battery D; longtime Truman friend and political aide. On his arrangement for a pilot to fly Truman to an important political picnic during the 1922 race for Jackson County eastern judge:

"There was a fellow named Clarence England [who] ran a garage about 14th and McGee Street. I think that Clarence had been a flyer in World War I. Anyway, he had one of those old jenny planes that was held together with bailing wire, and at Truman's suggestion, I made a deal with Clarence to take Truman up and drop some leaflets over a picnic at Oak Grove, Missouri. Well, we got them started off and got the leaflets loaded in, took off from the pasture, and circled around this picnic at Oak Grove. Then they were to come down in a pasture right next to the picnic grounds. They came down all right, but Clarence had a little trouble stopping the plane and it ended up about three feet from a barbed-wire fence. Our candidate got out and draped himself over this barbed-wire fence and gave forth with a lot of things I know he didn't eat. He was as green as grass. I think it was his first flight, but he mounted the rostrum and made a speech."

things I know he didn't eat," said Truman friend Eddie McKim, responsible for arranging for the airplane. "He was as green as grass. I think it was his first flight, but he mounted the rostrum and made a speech."

The 1922 campaign, Truman's first, is remembered for the poor speeches Truman made. Thirty years later, in a diary entry, Truman admitted as much. "I had stage fright so badly that all I could say was 'I hope you'll vote and work for me in the primary' in a trembling voice and then I sat down," he wrote, describing a speech at a March 7 rally in a Lee's Summit American Legion hall.

Other early speeches were not much better.

"I never will forget the first speech he made – that I ever heard him make – was down at Sugar Creek one night," Edgar Hinde, a longtime friend, said in 1962. "Boy, it was about the poorest effort of a speech I ever heard in my life; I suffered for him."

But Truman soon found his voice. Today, the candidate's appearance at the Oak Grove picnic is remembered not only for his lost lunch but also for his firm and steadfast address. He stated his specific plans for the county's roads, a principal concern for the many farmers in the audience. He also defended his political support of John Miles, a Jackson County marshal – and Republican – whom Truman had come to know and admire in combat during World War I.

The Pendergast organization had approached Truman to consider running for eastern Jackson County judge.

There was no blare of trumpets at this development and Truman himself seemed somewhat sheepish about his plans. Edgar Hinde, who in 1922 was running a car dealership in Independence, remembered Truman coming by and sitting down. As Hinde recalled it, Truman "kind of grinned" at him.

"What would you think if I told you I was going to run for eastern judge?" Truman asked Hinde.

"Well," Hinde said, "I'd think you're crazy."

"Well, I got to eat," Truman replied.

Much was at stake, for both Truman and the Pendergast operation. For Truman, the timing could not have been better. His Kansas City haberdashery was failing.

The Pendergast machine, meanwhile, was eyeing control of the eastern county judge's seat, an administrative position, and one of three county judges, or executives.

The county government controlled some nine hundred jobs, and the control of those jobs rested in the county court. Just in the eastern part of the county lived about sixty road overseers, themselves overseen by the eastern Jackson County judge.

The eastern judge enjoyed about as much power as the other two judges, even though about 400,000 people lived in Kansas City and only about seventy thousand lived in eastern Jackson County. Of those, about eight thousand lived in Independence – Truman's hometown.

In one memoir, Truman said the machine approached him in July or August 1921. Truman's

name appeared in print as a possible candidate in the *Examiner* in January 1922. "Among the younger men Harry Truman is talked of," the paper reported. Of the five eventual candidates, Truman at thirty-eight years old was the youngest. Not that Truman thought that an asset. "So it was a busted merchant, an ex-soldier and farmer who had no political experience against four good men," Truman wrote in a 1952 diary entry.

His first public appearance as a candidate came at the March 1922 rally in Lee's Summit, where he appeared before three hundred roaring former servicemen.

"The hall was filled and many stood back of the seats," reported the *Examiner* on March 8.

Truman was not the only attraction. There were free cigars as well as a wrestling match, a boxing match, and then another wrestling match, this time pitting two brothers, ages eight and nine, against one another. Then Truman spoke briefly. Then there was more boxing. Ethel Lee Buxton, a vocalist who had entertained troops in France during World War I, sang "When Irish Eyes Are Smiling." After a comedy sketch, Mrs. Buxton returned to sing "Mother Machree."

In April, Truman's name was put forth officially at a meeting of the Rural Jackson County Democratic Club. Mike Pendergast, a brother of Tom's who was in charge of the Pendergast machine operations in eastern Jackson County, announced Truman's name to the assembled club members.

"We've decided that Harry Truman's going to be the candi-

Independence politician Robert L. Hood and Judge Harry S. Truman in 1924.

date for eastern judge," Edgar Hinde recalled Pendergast announcing.

Truman's rivals were formidable, especially the Rabbit candidate, E. E. Montgomery, a Blue Springs banker. But in the race, Truman benefited from several circumstances. First, there was the women's vote, still a novelty in Missouri after the recent arrival of women's suffrage. Women had first voted in Missouri in the summer of 1920, just days after the nineteenth amendment had been certified.

"They are turning out to the meetings and listening to the speeches," the *Examiner* said of the county's women on June 22.

Several women, including a former teacher of Truman's, knocked on doors for him. Harry Abbott, a Pendergast machine canvasser in the Fairmount district, near Kansas City, did his best to exploit the female vote by taking care to go door-to-

door during the day.

"You bet I did," Abbott, then ninety-six, recalled in a 1990 Truman Library oral history. "And most of the time there was nobody home in the daytime but the wives. I had them thoroughly convinced." Later, he added, "There's nobody any better than a wife to influence the husband to vote. You learn that early."

Then there was the veterans angle.

Of the five candidates in the Democratic primary, Truman alone could claim to have served in World War I. The loud reception for Truman at Lee's Summit in March had prompted the *Lee's Summit Journal* to comment upon the significance of the new "army" vote.

Truman himself later agreed. "The soldier stuff and the soldier boys won for me," he said.

Truman leaned hard on his military career. Often, when he drove to a town to speak,

Truman brought along a Boy Scout bugler, who would walk the town playing military calls. A second scout carried a sandwich board announcing the time and place of Truman's appearance.

If history sometimes pivots on small, crucial moments, then August 1, 1922, qualifies. On election day a Rabbit worker tipped off the Truman forces that Shannon thugs were planning to visit a rural polling station to steal the ballot box. Two deputy marshals dispatched by County Marshal John Miles – the same Republican whom Truman admitted supporting during his Oak Grove speech – arrived before the gang. The deputies saved the ballots, and likely Truman's thin margin of 279 votes, and probably the beginning of his political career.

Yet the election still was not over. Several days after the voting

Rufus Burrus, Independence lawyer and longtime Truman friend. On how Truman, attending the Kansas City School of Law while eastern Jackson County judge in the early 1920s, had to hide in Rufus Burrus' law office to get his studying done at night:

"You know he used the library at the courthouse in Independence for his work that he had to do for the school. People would see a light up there and the folks knew that he was up there and they'd come in the courthouse and bother him, and he couldn't get his work done. They would just harass him to the point he couldn't get the homework done. I said to him one day, 'Here's a key to our office; come across the street and use our library over there, my dad's and mine. Nobody will know you're over there and you can get the same books and you can work on it and get it done over there.' And he did. Then it got to the place where he couldn't go over there without people coming over and bothering him."

the two principal candidates convened at the election board and watched as the votes from each of the fifty-eight precincts were counted again.

"Mr. Montgomery and Mr. Truman sat on the same side of the table with a commissioner and a clerk between them," the *Examiner* reported.

In the end, Truman prevailed. In the November election, Truman prevailed over his Republican opponent by a comfortable margin.

In 1956, thirty-four years after the summer of 1922, Truman attended the Jackson County Fair and Western Horse Show in Lee's Summit, where his career had begun with wrestling matches.

"I will tell you now," he said, "that I was more scared then than I was at any time later, even when I was on the front in the first world war in France."

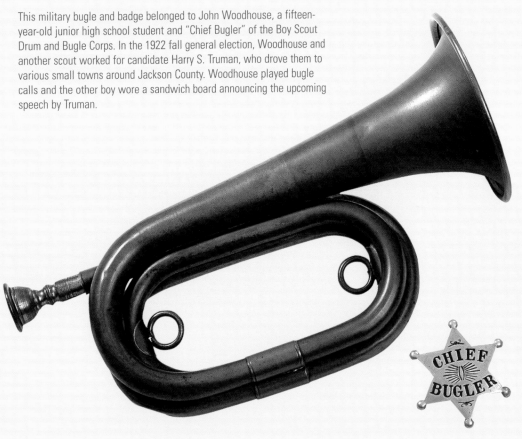

This military bugle and badge belonged to John Woodhouse, a fifteen-year-old junior high school student and "Chief Bugler" of the Boy Scout Drum and Bugle Corps. In the 1922 fall general election, Woodhouse and another scout worked for candidate Harry S. Truman, who drove them to various small towns around Jackson County. Woodhouse played bugle calls and the other boy wore a sandwich board announcing the upcoming speech by Truman.

On Saturday, July 15, 1922, some four thousand Jackson County residents turned up for a picnic in Oak Grove.

All five candidates for the position of eastern Jackson County judge addressed the crowd. In a day when campaign oratory was a principal source of summer weekend entertainment, the chief topic for most of the candidates was roads and their maintenance.

George W. Shaw was known by all as a longtime Jackson County road builder. He said that the county spent from three to six times more than it needed to spend on its roads.

Thomas W. Parrent was a county road overseer, and president of the Road Overseers Association. His discussion, the *Examiner* of Independence reported, included "especial attention to the roads of the County."

E.E. Montgomery, a Blue Springs banker, declared himself in favor of oiled roads. The statement, the *Examiner* declared, "made a decided hit with the crowd."

James V. Compton, a former eastern county judge, apparently did not mention roads at the Oak Grove picnic, but a political advertisement he placed in the *Examiner* two days later did – at length.

"I measured Woodland Avenue after I became judge and found it short and the contractor was ordered back to complete the road," the advertisement read. "I also measured every road that was completed while a member of the county court."

Then there was Harry Truman. He, too, was in favor of oiled roads, he told the crowd in Oak Grove.

And there was more, much more, about roads.

For all the low gamesmanship that marked the 1922 Democratic primary for eastern Jackson County judge – such as the attempted theft of a ballot box on election day – all the candidates spoke like engineers, as their campaign speeches routinely included technical lectures on the challenges and rewards of Jackson County road building.

Anybody who lived and worked in eastern Jackson County before and during the 1920s was hostage to the conditions of the roads, which often flooded or fell apart in poor weather.

Jackson County residents had built some of their first roads with a saloon tax. By 1904 there were 225 miles of macadam rock roads. By the 1920s, building and maintaining roads was among the principal concerns of the Jackson County Court, and anyone who deemed himself a candidate for eastern judge had to have an intimate knowledge of the topic.

Truman did. His father, John Truman, had received the patronage position of road overseer in Grandview when Robert Mize was elected eastern judge in 1912.

"It was quite a job," the younger Truman wrote of his father's post in one memoir. "He had to fix bridges and culverts, fill up mudholes and try to help everyone in the neighborhood get to and away from his farm in bad weather."

There were only a few miles of macadam road in Washington Township, Truman added. "All the rest were dirt."

As road overseer, the elder Truman seriously injured himself maintaining Jackson County roads when he attempted to move a large boulder, causing a hernia and a subsequent intestinal blockage.

When John Truman died in November 1914, Mize appointed son Harry to succeed his father.

After Mize died in December 1915, Truman soon lost the position.

"Of all county officials, road overseers had the greatest impact on the daily lives of rural residents," wrote Truman biographer Richard Lawrence Miller. In the early part of the twentieth century, he added, county roads were "miracles providing ties to civilization and breaking profound isolation."

The specific maintenance of particular roads, as discussed at sessions of the county court, received regular coverage in the *Examiner*. Only through continual maintenance could some county roads remain passable in poor weather.

Jackson County residents were used to shoddy road construction. A 1921 county investigation revealed that one road that was supposed to have a base of crushed rock had stretches of either uncrushed rocks or no rock at all, crushed or uncrushed.

In 1924, some road work was done by chain gangs, comprising county prisoners serving terms less than one year. But much more often, the work was done by laborers who had political connections. Road overseers were political positions, named by the county judges. Each overseer, in turn, hired men and teams, and so could then reward political allies with county road money.

When Truman made his political debut in March 1922 in Lee's Summit, the *Examiner* noted the large number of road overseers from several districts in attendance. The following February, about one month after taking office, Truman and Henry F. McElroy, eastern and western Jackson

County judges, and both affiliated with the Pendergast Goats, selected thirty-six road overseers. One of them was Vivian Truman, Truman's younger brother.

On roads, Truman proved a confident and informed speaker.

"Jackson County's roads were built before autos became so cheap and so numerous," Truman said in one speech. "Those roads were built for two-ton traffic going three miles per hour and for horse-drawn pleasure vehicles weighing 500 pounds moving about five miles per hour. Now you have five to fifteen tons moving from twelve to twenty-five miles per hour and 2,000- to 5,000-pound pleasure cars moving from twenty-five to sixty miles an hour."

Those who worked the roads, meanwhile, represented the backbone of the work done for the county, and Truman, in his Oak Grove speech that July, appealed to that ethic. "I want men for road overseers who know roads and who want work – men who will do a day's work for a day's pay," he said. "I would rather have forty road men for overseers who are willing to work than to have sixty politicians who care nothing about work."

Truman took office as Jackson County presiding judge on January 1, 1927. His first task upon taking office was organizing and promoting a bond issue for new roads.

An inventory of Jackson County roads soon found 350 miles of roads the report described as "piecrust roads," or roads that would

give like pastry to a fork after bad weather.

"County judges had known little about engineering," wrote Robert Ferrell, Truman scholar. "As a result, in 1927, many roads were of water-bound macadam, improperly arranged at curves and turns, undrained and repaired by piling a little surface material on worn places."

The maintenance of such roads, Truman said, cost the county $900,000 a year. It was a better idea, he said, to build new

This road sign, held by the Truman Museum, is a remnant of the early Jackson County road system, which was dramatically improved by Truman during his tenure as eastern Jackson County judge. This example from Sni-A-Bar Road refers to a creek that runs through eastern Jackson County. The creek was explored by a frontiersman by the name of Abar who first thought that he had found a slough or "sni."

Hazel Graham, 1989, first executive director, Jackson County Historical Society; neighbor of Harry and Bess Truman. On the 1859 Jail, Marshal's Home and Museum in Independence — restored and reopened in 1959 by the Jackson County Historical Society - and its role in Truman's political career:

"But finally I said to him, 'You know, Mr. Truman, I don't believe you'd have ever gotten into the White House if it hadn't been for the old jail.' He said, 'What do you mean?' I said, 'Well, didn't you gain your first fame in politics for building such a wonderful hard-road system in Jackson County?' Everybody knew when they got to the county line because the roads got better. 'Weren't you responsible to a great extent for that hard-road system?' He said, 'Well, I guess so.' And I said, 'Well, who did the labor on those roads? Was it not the chain gang out of the old jail?' He said 'You're right.' "

roads. With the support of two prominent engineers – one Democrat, the other Republican – Truman proposed in 1927 hundreds of miles of new roads, placed so that no farm resident would be more than two and a half miles from a paved road.

Truman proposed that a $6.5 million bond issue be submitted to Jackson County voters. Boss Tom Pendergast told Truman that county residents would never approve such a plan, out of the quite reasonable fear that much of the money would be stolen or wasted.But Truman staked his reputation to its passage, insisting that contracts would be let to the lowest bidders. As it happened, when Truman traveled from town to town campaigning for the bond issue, it was in the wet spring, when the need for paved roads was the most obvious.

On May 8, 1928 – Truman's forty-fourth birthday – the road measure passed by a three-to-one margin.

Local contractors soon learned that Truman meant what he said about awarding contracts to the lowest bidders. The first group of new roads was completed so efficiently that $75,000 was left over. Truman used some of that to commission a new statue of Andrew Jackson. The rest he devoted to a huge county barbecue to which everyone was invited.

In 1931, voters approved another $3.5 million for more roads.

By September 1933, a 312-mile road system was complete. The result was clear to everyone. In part to trumpet his accomplishment but also just to document the sheer beauty of the county that the new road system had made more accessible, Truman published a book entitled *Results of County Planning* and distributed it across the state.

Its pages were filled with many pastoral rural scenes, all of them having in common a new county road. In a cover letter, Truman insisted that even for those who had spent their lives in Jackson County, the new road system "has opened up new wonders, new beauty and new farm values as we had not in the beginning anticipated."

Years later, Ardelia Palmer, Truman's high school Latin teacher, said her former student had helped bring Jackson County residents into a new age. Jackson County, she said, "was about the muddiest county anywhere and by the time Harry got through with that program . . . he [had] pulled Jackson County out of the mud."

This 1923 road map of Jackson County was heavily annotated by Truman while planning his road bond issue. His handwritten notes included: "look at road," "no good - oil," "oil if possible," and "go and see it."

I n his first race for re-election to political office in 1924, Truman lost.

He managed the distinction of losing to a Republican in the November general election, a unique accomplishment for a Democrat in Jackson County. His rival, Henry Rummel, became only the second Republican to win the seat of eastern Jackson County judge since the Civil War.

But there were reasons for this. In his two years in office Truman had managed to alienate several groups: Republicans, two separate Democratic political factions, the National Association for the Advancement of Colored People, and even the Ku Klux Klan.

The Republicans disliked Truman because he was a Democrat. But they also resented him because, almost immediately after taking office in January 1923, he and western judge Henry F. McElroy – a fellow Pendergast Goat – harassed Leo Koehler, the county's head road engineer and Republican. The two Pendergast Goats sold Koehler's fleet of cars.

They also cut his $8,000 salary by $2,000, in open court. On display in this episode, wrote Truman biographer Richard Lawrence Miller, was "a new malevolence in Truman. The happy Harry of Grandview farm days disappeared in World War I. That

Harry would never have enjoyed summarily reducing a man's livelihood by $2,000, grinning while the victim squirmed."

Truman and McElroy also resolved to make life difficult for Elihu Hayes, the Jackson County presiding judge, and member of the Shannon Rabbit Democratic faction. They voted to take away his county car and fire his driver. That wasn't all. In June, they announced that the county's purchasing agent, also a Rabbit, was fired and then they named a Goat to take his place.

Hayes protested, saying the purchasing agent had been his only patronage employee. The purchasing agent himself said more. Standing before McElroy, he said, "Politically, I don't care a damn for you and personally I think you could stand flatfooted and kiss a gnat."

Accounts of this remark differ, with some saying the sentence ended with a portion of the gnat's anatomy.

The second Democratic faction alienated by Truman was that headed by Miles Bulger, the county's presiding judge for the previous eight years and the head of his own machine. Truman and McElroy ordered an audit of county finances under

Bulger. The audit revealed that Bulger had come into office with a $117 deficit and had left eight years later with a $1.2 million deficit. Truman and McElroy also had investigated a county home built by Bulger for young African-American men.

Truman and McElroy were not opposed to such a home. But they found the building, with its fine appointments and plaque on the façade bearing Bulger's name and likeness, represented an outrageous expenditure that Bulger apparently authorized largely as a monument to himself.

That subtlety, however, was lost on the local NAACP, which resented Truman and McElroy for making the home an issue.

Finally, the Ku Klux Klan, which met openly in western Missouri throughout the 1920s, had little use for Truman, given his allegiance to the Pendergast political machine, dominated by Catholics.

In November, Rummel received 8,791 votes to Truman's 7,932. Across the county, Republicans romped. MACHINE SMASHED, read the headline in *The Kansas City Star*.

In contemporary parlance, the Rabbit Democrats had knifed

Truman and McElroy by aligning with the Republicans.

It would be the last political campaign Truman would lose.

For a person so given to introspection on paper, Truman did not appear to dwell on the 1924 race. "Public service was a secondary matter if the political factions could get the jobs they wanted," Truman wrote in one memoir.

But he clearly remembered the defeat.

Decades later Keith Wilson, a former Independence city manager, showed a Truman Museum researcher a letter that Truman had written to a Catholic priest inviting him to the dedication of the Memorial Building in Independence. Apparently Truman never mailed the letter and ultimately used it as scratch paper. On the letter's reverse side were figures – vote totals from Truman's 1922 victory over Republican Arthur Wilson, Keith Wilson's grandfather – and his 1924 defeat to Henry Rummel.

Even two years after his election loss, Truman was still chewing over the vote totals from 1924 and his interest wasn't an idle one. The city's Memorial Building was dedicated in 1926 and Truman, after two years of forced exile from Jackson County politics, was now running for the office of county presiding judge.

ORAL HISTORIES

Henry Chiles, Rabbit election worker who in 1924, following faction orders, worked to elect Republican Henry Rummel over incumbent Jackson County eastern judge Harry Truman.

"So the next morning after election – I was as ashamed of it as I could be, but I stuck to my job (they would have fired me if I hadn't of stayed with them, of course) – I saw Harry coming and I said, 'Well, I didn't want to see him this morning.'

"So I crossed over the street and then, just down from the square, he saw me and called me over there, stuck out his hand, and said, 'Now I want you to understand there's no hard feelings.'

"I said, 'Harry, yesterday was the hardest day I've ever had of any kind, let alone in politics – many more of that and I'm going to quit. I had to go out and fight you yesterday and I hated to do it, and I'm ashamed of it now, but I did it.`

"He said, 'Don't worry about it, there's no hard feelings. You did what your gang told you and I did what my gang told me.' He said, 'There's no hard feelings,' and shook hands and said, 'Now let's forget all about it.' "

Harry S. Truman (center), presiding judge of the Jackson County Court, Robert W. Barr (left), eastern district judge, and Howard Vrooman, western district judge.

THE 1926 ELECTION

Jackson County voters elected Harry Truman in 1926 to serve as presiding judge. Over the course of two consecutive four-year terms in that position Truman supervised the construction of hundreds of miles of roads, as well as the renovation of one courthouse and the building of a second.

It all would not have happened, however, if not for two events.

First, in November 1924, not long after that year's election, Democratic Party faction leaders Tom Pendergast and Joseph Shannon encountered one another on a Kansas City street. The Goat and Rabbit factions had quarreled that year, and when Shannon had thrown the support of his Rabbits to Republican candidates, Pendergast's candidates, Truman included, had lost their races.

On this the two argued at length, drawing a growing crowd. They both finally decided to hold their fire and convene later at a safe remove from the sidewalk. There they settled their differences, agreeing to share in any patronage jobs and other spoils resulting

from future political victories.

Second, Truman finally met Tom Pendergast.

In was early in 1926, scholars agree, that the two first sat down together. Until then Truman had been content to work through Mike Pendergast, the Boss's brother and head of the Pendergast machine's eastern Jackson County operations.

Truman brought a request to Tom Pendergast: He wanted to run for the office of Jackson County collector. The collector received commissions on taxes extracted from deadbeats, and Truman thought he could do well enough to earn $25,000.

But Pendergast had promised the collector's position to someone else and, instead,

offered Truman the position of presiding judge. Truman was disappointed, as was Mike Pendergast, who later offered to throw the support of his eastern Jackson County operation behind Truman if he insisted upon going after the collector's post.

But having watched the Democrats divide in 1924, Truman didn't want to cause a new split in 1926.

Truman ran unopposed in the Democratic primary and in November defeated Republican candidate L. L. Adams by a wide margin.

Compared to his 1922 campaign, Truman's 1926 race was a vacation. Four years earlier Truman had flogged himself back

Rufus Burrus, Independence lawyer and longtime Truman friend. On how Truman named him assistant counselor of the Jackson County court after Truman's election as presiding judge in 1926:

"I went over and he was just a few steps ahead of me, and he saw me and said 'Come on, join us.' There was some gentleman with him that I didn't know, a stranger to me. He went over to the table that was set up for him, and he hadn't anymore got set down and I got set down, and the gentleman with him got set down, that he turned to this man with him and said, 'Fred [Boxley], you're going to be my county counselor. That's a Rabbit job, and you're my kind of Rabbit, and I want you to be the county counselor.'

"Well, I afterwards learned that he had been a great friend of Truman's in the National Guard and in other ways, and he said, 'Burrus is going to be *the* assistant counselor. That's a Goat job, and he's my kind of Goat.' "

and forth across Jackson County making speeches and courting voters before the 1922 Democratic primary for eastern county judge.

But in the summer of 1926, since he had no primary opponents, he left the county entirely, attending Army reserve camp at Fort Riley, Kansas. When Bess wrote him that July and included a favorable mention of Truman as presiding judge candidate by William Southern, publisher of the *Examiner* of Independence, Truman shrugged.

"Mr. Southern seems to be taking some active interest in politics," Truman wrote back. "He usually does where there is nothing to fight about."

Even in July, Truman believed the title of presiding judge already was his. In November, the voters proved him right.

Presiding Judge Harry S. Truman at the swearing in ceremony in 1931. He is flanked by Eugene P. Purcell, eastern district judge, and William O. Beeman, western district judge.

Harry Truman had a habit of disappearing.

The most famous instance would occur on election night in November 1948 when, on the verge of the twentieth century's most remarkable political upset, the president fled the press vigil surrounding his Independence home by spiriting himself and a few aides up to an Excelsior Springs hotel for the night.

But perhaps he perfected the ritual of such escapes in the early 1930s, when he was running Jackson County, Missouri. Then, when he disappeared, it was often to the Pickwick Hotel.

In 1930, the ten-story hotel opened at Tenth and McGee streets, in downtown Kansas City. Not long after, the county's chief public executive began making arrangements with its ownership.

He would check in without signing the registration book. He would enter one of the hotel's 450 rooms alone and stay there for several hours, sometimes overnight. For anyone else, not to mention Jackson County's presiding judge, the behavior would seem odd or suspicious. Yet what Truman was doing there would have disappointed the scandal-minded. He was sitting at a hotel desk, indulging in an interior monologue, or conducting a personal inquiry of his political ethics, or venting against brazen crooks looting the county's general revenue – all in longhand, on hotel stationery.

The earliest such document dates from December 1930; the last to May 1934. Today the ninety-two surviving pages comprise a document today known as the Pickwick Narratives, or Pickwick Papers.

Some excerpts suggest the self-referential drama with which Truman perceived his public life. The entry for May 14, 1934, the last of the Pickwick papers, describes his state of excitement as he prepared to announce his candidacy for the U.S. Senate.

"Tomorrow, today, rather, it is 4 A.M. I have to make the most momentous announcement of my life," he wrote. "I have come to the place where all men strive to be, at my age and I thought two weeks ago that retirement on a virtual pension in some minor county office was all that was in store for me."

Much more of the dialogue details Truman's frustration in attempting to operate a reasonably honest local government within the context of a political machine headed by Tom Pendergast, who is referred to in the Pickwick Papers as the "Boss."

One of Truman's signature accomplishments as presiding judge likely was the passage of $10 million worth of bond issues to construct over three hundred miles of new roads across Jackson County. Truman staked his reputation on the project, and when voters approved the two separate bond issues bankrolling the construction, Truman resolved to see the low bidders, not the machine's friends, receive the contracts.

Truman's memoirs, published in the 1950s, include Truman's now-familiar description of how Pendergast, faced with angry contractors wanting their share of the road work, backed Truman. But the memoirs do not mention the recollections preserved on Pickwick Hotel stationery some twenty-five years before. Those papers surfaced later, and they suggest that Jackson County road-building during the Depression was more complicated than Truman had let on.

Apparently Truman, while seeing the roads built, had decided to look the other way as various officials helped themselves to not-so-petty amounts of cash from the county's accounts.

Truman averted his eyes, he wrote, "to keep the crooks from getting a million or more out of the bond issue. Was I right or did I compound a felony? I don't know."

In another passage, Truman wrote, "At the same time I gave away about a million in general revenue to satisfy the politicians. But if I hadn't done that the crooks would have had half the seven million." The $7 million was about the amount the first bond issue generated.

The Pickwick Papers vary in tone and pitch.

Some passages on random topics have not aged well. "Some day we'll awake," Truman wrote on one occasion, "have a reformation of the heart, teach our kids honor and kill a few sex psychologists, put boys in high schools to themselves with men teachers (not sissies), close all the girls finishing schools, shoot all the efficiency experts, and become a nation of God's people once more."

Truman made no secret of his sanctuary, at least to his family. "I have to go and hide," he wrote Bess in an April 1933 letter. "I am now on the seventh floor of the

The Pickwick Hotel during the period Harry Truman escaped to one of its rooms for privacy.

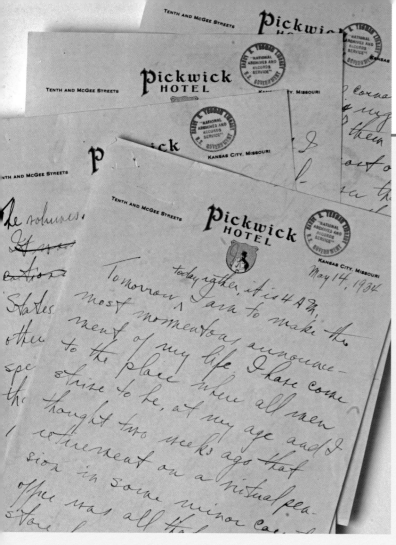

A few of the surviving ninety-two handwritten pages on hotel stationery by Harry Truman known as the Pickwick Papers. The earliest is dated December 1930 and the last May 1934, the year that Truman entered the race for the United States Senate.

Pickwick hotel. The manager gave me a room without registering so no job holder who wants to stay on can see or phone me."

In another document, Truman indulges in a measure of self-pity. "I always believed in Santa Claus I guess," he wrote. "It was my opinion . . . that most men had a sense of honor. Now I don't know."

But other passages – such as the following, only two paragraphs down from his Christmas reference – grab the reader by the collar. "Who is to blame for present conditions," he wrote, "but swindling church members who weep on Sunday, play with whores on Monday, drink on Tuesday, sell out to the [Big] Boss on Wednesday, repent about Friday, and start over on Sunday. I think

maybe the boss is nearer heaven than the swindlers."

In other entries, Truman names names, including Joseph Shannon, head of the Rabbits, the Democratic faction that usually served as rival to the Pendergast Goats, and Casimir Welch, a Democrat who controlled his own Kansas City fiefdom.

"What chance is there for a clean, honest administration of the city and county when a bunch [of] vultures sit on the sidelines and puke on the field . . . " Truman wrote. "If we only had Tom to deal with, the public might have a chance, but Tom can't operate without Joe [Shannon] & Cass [Welch]. Cass is a thug and a crook of the worst water; he should have been in the pen twenty years ago. Joe hasn't got an honest appointee on his payroll."

However conflicted Truman may have felt about public life, he left the Pickwick Hotel on May 14, 1934, to begin his campaign for the U.S. Senate. He won, and left Jackson County for Washington. If Truman ever spent another night in the Pickwick, no page of hotel stationery has been discovered describing his state of mind at the time.

He did, much later, return to the Pickwick at least once. In January 1953, Truman sat down in the Pickwick's grill for a lunch of pig hocks, sauerkraut, and potatoes, for which he paid 75

cents. The event was recorded in detail by the St. Louis Post-Dispatch, as Truman had just returned to Independence after leaving the White House, having served as president for nearly eight years. Truman, now the private citizen, was renting a three-room office in the nearby Federal Reserve building, and apparently knew of a good place to find lunch not far away.

The Pickwick still stands. In 1973, officials re-dedicated the building, then renamed Royal Towers, as subsidized housing. In 2003, the building was known as the Pickwick Plaza Apartments.

The former Pickwick Hotel at 10th and McGee is currently known as the Pickwick Plaza Apartments. *Photo by Ray Geselbracht.*

THE ANDREW JACKSON STATUE

When it came to sculpture, Harry Truman knew what he liked when he saw it.

In the early 1930s Truman, then Jackson County presiding judge, wanted to set aside money to pay for a statue of Andrew Jackson to complement the new Kansas City Jackson County courthouse, then under construction. At some point he had seen and admired a statue of Confederate commander Thomas Jonathan "Stonewall" Jackson, dedicated in 1921 in a Charlottesville, Virginia, park.

Truman commissioned the sculptor of the Stonewall Jackson statue, Charles Keck, to produce a statue of Andrew Jackson, the namesake of Jackson County. In January 1934 Truman traveled to Keck's New York City studio to examine various models the sculptor had prepared.

"We took Andy all apart and put one man on one horse and then tried him on another until there was a combination that will

be unbeatable," Truman wrote Bess and Margaret from Washington on January 2.

"Then I caught a taxi and my train and here I am back in politics," he added. "From the height of the esthetic to the basement of the practical, and I confess I like them both."

The three-ton statue cost $35,000. Truman initially imagined that the sculpture could stand atop the roof of the three-hundred-foot-tall courthouse. Instead the statue was installed on a pedestal on the north lawn of the courthouse, where it still stands today.

Margaret Truman, ten years old, unveiled the statue on December 27, 1934, the same day the new courthouse was dedicated.

In 1949, almost fifteen years later to the day, Margaret performed the same service during the Independence dedication of a half-sized version of the same statue presented by Keck to Truman, who in turn presented it to Jackson County. Today the sculpture stands on the west side of the Independence Square courthouse.

A third, miniature version of the statue, also presented by Keck to Truman, stood on Truman's Oval Office desk during his White House years. The statue would play an unexpected role in Truman's decision in 1948 to approve de facto recognition of the infant state of Israel.

This statue of Andrew Jackson, which stands on the north lawn of Kansas City's Jackson County courthouse, was commissioned by Truman.

Though Harry Truman built hundreds of miles of roads in Jackson County, he was not content with that. He also left his signature on the Kansas City skyline with a new Jackson County courthouse, three hundred feet tall and completed in 1934.

Principal funds came from a citizen-approved bond program backed by the Pendergast machine and supported by the governments of Kansas City and Jackson County. Approved by the voters in 1931, the $40 million "Ten Year Plan" helped employ hundreds of Kansas City area workers.

The plan included $200,000 for a renovation of the Jackson County courthouse in Independence and $4 million for a new courthouse in downtown Kansas City.

The new courthouse project gripped Truman's imagination. Truman wrote in a 1952 memo that he took "my private car – not a county one – and drove to Shreveport, Denver, Houston, Racine, Milwaukee, Buffalo, Brooklyn, Lincoln, Baton Rouge and several other places." It was in Shreveport, Louisiana, where he saw and admired the Caddo Parish Courthouse, designed by architect Edward Neild.

Truman arranged a meeting with Neild and his partner, Dewey Somdal. Truman ultimately selected three Kansas City architecture firms for the Jackson County courthouse project, but also hired Neild and Somdal as design and plan consultants.

The resulting Kansas City courthouse occupied an entire city block between 12th and 13th streets and between Oak and Locust streets. The finished building was sheathed in some 100,000 cubic feet of limestone. Though the building stood three hundred feet high, it had but fourteen floors, as a two-story ground-floor lobby and two-story courtrooms lowered the number of levels. The design included a jail and an execution chamber.

Dedication ceremonies took place on December 27, 1934. Film of the event, donated to the Western Historical Manuscript Collection at the University of Missouri-Kansas City in 1995 by the Swenson Construction Company of Kansas City, depicted Truman pouring a clear liquid over a small model of the courthouse.

Contemporary accounts of the ceremony detail how Truman sprinkled corn over the courthouse model, and also poured small amounts of wine and oil. Corn, wine, and oil are symbols recognized by the members of Masonic orders as the wages in which the builders of King Solomon's temple were paid.

Once Truman became president, researchers grew interested in his career as a builder. Writer John Hersey once noted that Truman's career in the Masons, the fraternal order that also uses the tools of the building crafts as symbols, may have prompted his interest in architecture.

As president, Truman advocated a complete renovation of the White House and Neild was among the group of experts who made a detailed examination of the historic structure.

On May 8, 1976, President Gerald Ford, while dedicating a statue of Truman outside the Independence Square Courthouse, described how he was among several skeptical Republican members of Congress who once received a personal tour of the White House by President Truman. Not long after the tour ended, Ford said, the delegation went back to Capitol Hill and approved the appropriation that Truman wanted to fund the renovation of the building.

In the early 1930s, however, it was the Jackson County courthouse project that dominated Truman's thoughts. "When I get that job done I can probably retire to a quiet job and enjoy life a little bit with my family," he wrote to his wife, Bess, on May 11, 1933.

It didn't happen. Truman's appearance at the courthouse's dedication was his final appearance in Kansas City as Jackson County presiding judge. The next day he left for Washington and his new career as U.S. senator from Missouri, a post to which he had been elected the month before.

County Judge Truman got approval for a new $4 million Jackson County Courthouse in Kansas City. It was dedicated in December 1934.

THE JACKSON COUNTY COURTHOUSE IN INDEPENDENCE

Those who today visit the old Jackson County Courthouse on Independence Square can see it as it appeared in the 1930s – both inside and outside.

Inside, the courthouse includes the courtroom and judge's office used by Truman when he served as Jackson County presiding judge restored to its 1930s appearance. Halfway through his second term as presiding judge, Truman moved into the office when an east wing addition to the courtroom was completed in 1932.

As for the outside, a renovation of the courthouse exterior was completed in January 2003. The makeover left the red brick Georgian colonial courthouse appearing much as it did when Truman dedicated it on September 5, 1933.

The building whose renovation Truman supervised was the sixth incarnation of the county courthouse which had occupied the same space on Independence Square since 1836.

Organizers of Jackson County named Independence its county seat in 1827. But population in the county's western districts boomed in the years after the Civil War, and Kansas City

The old Jackson County courthouse on Independence Square held the offices of Truman when he was presiding judge. *Photo by Ray Geselbracht.*

received its own county courthouse in 1872.

A bond issue often called the Ten Year Plan that financed several large Kansas City construction projects in the 1930s included $4 million for a new Kansas City courthouse and $200,000 for a renovated Independence courthouse. For the Independence project, Truman hired his brother-in-law, Fred Wallace, as architect.

Inside the Jackson County Courthouse in Independence, the courtroom and judge's office used by Truman when he was Jackson County presiding judge have been restored to their appearance in the 1920s and 1930s.
Photo by Tammy Ljungblad

I n October 1944, the Hearst newspaper chain reported that Harry Truman, then a candidate for vice president, had been a member of the Ku Klux Klan in the 1920s.

Truman denied the charge and didn't seem too concerned about it. "Mr. Hearst has been having a grand time accusing me of being a Ku Kluxer," he wrote Bess a few days later, adding he should sue for libel.

"Be nice to tour South America at his expense, wouldn't it?" he wrote.

Kansas City friends of Truman were not amused. A 1944 advertisement in the *Kansas City Jewish Chronicle* included testimonials from Rabbi Samuel S. Mayerberg and Eddie Jacobson, Truman's former haberdashery partner.

The charge never stuck.

Though historians believe Truman was never a member of the Klan, it appears that he did at least flirt briefly with it in 1922 while running for eastern Jackson County judge. But after meeting with a Klan organizer, Truman apparently turned down Klan support after learning that, in exchange for it, Truman would have to promise not to give any patronage jobs to Catholics.

Truman's political sponsor, Tom Pendergast, was Catholic, as were many members of Truman's World War I artillery battery.

Truman's record on civil rights as president later documented his regard for equality and social justice. Ultimately, the story of Truman's brush with the Klan says less about Truman than it does about the realities of Jackson County politics in the 1920s.

Klan membership across the United States soared from 100,000 in 1921 to 5 million in 1924. Klan rallies, with attendant cross burnings, were considered news. In covering one rally, the *Examiner* of Independence found it appropriate to report that the particular cross burned that evening had stood forty feet high and had required six barrels of oil to properly ignite.

Over in Kansas City the Klan met just as openly. In advance of the 1922 general election, Klan organizers rallied in Kansas City's Convention Hall. There, Klan speakers identified their principal target as Kansas City's largely Catholic Democratic political factions and instructed those attending in a campaign song.

"The town is full of KKK," the Klan members sang, "the only thing that they will say, is good-bye Tom and goodbye Joe, the crooked gang has got to go." The "Tom" and "Joe" were Catholics Pendergast and Joseph Shannon, Kansas City Democratic Party faction leaders.

Perhaps, as a candidate, Truman decided he had to acknowledge the Klan's presence. Perhaps that is why when Independence car dealer Edgar Hinde approached Truman, saying the local Klan had asked to meet him, Truman agreed.

Hinde was a member.

"Some of us had joined to see what it was, to see what was going on, you know," Hinde said in 1962. "So they got after me to get Truman to join the Klan."

Hinde delivered the ten-dollar Klan membership fee to a local barber, and Truman went down to the Baltimore Hotel in downtown Kansas City to meet with a Klan organizer. The two apparently agreed that their differences were just too great, and Truman left without Klan support.

"So, that was it," Hinde said. "And they gave me the ten dollars back."

Other encounters with the Klan were not so gentlemanly. Hinde recalled a local Klan meeting when a speaker from Atlanta claimed Harry Truman was not 100 percent American.

"Anybody who says Harry Truman's not 100 percent American is a liar," Hinde said he shouted in reply. "And they jumped up and hollered, 'Throw him out.' Boy, they commenced to mill about there."

Fisticuffs were averted, but soon Hinde quit the Klan. The Sunday before the 1922 election, Klan members stood before the doors of several Protestant churches in Independence and handed out sample ballots. Next to Truman's name were the words "Church affiliation protestant, endorsed by Tom and Joe."

Truman won. But the elec-

mism for the Klan.

Hoffman had his own agenda regarding Truman. In 1920 he had been defeated for Jackson County marshal by John Miles, Truman's Republican friend from World War I.

Though Hoffman promised five thousand Klan votes, Truman shrugged it off. But apparently the Klan wouldn't take no for an answer.

"They threatened to kill me,"

member of the Klan. Hoffman was one of them.

Truman was elected vice president anyway. Still, what Truman might have been thinking twenty years earlier is hard to figure.

"How he thought Klan support might offset the devastating effect such an alliance would have on the Pendergasts . . . is difficult to imagine," Truman biographer David McCullough wrote. Only a year before, McCullough added, Truman had supported a Masonic effort to suppress the Klan in St Louis. "He had to have known what the Klan was about."

Independence car dealer Edgar Hinde approached Truman, saying the local Klan had asked to meet him, Truman agreed.

Hinde was a member.

"Some of us had joined to see what it was, to see what was going on, you know," Hinde said in 1962. "So they got after me to get Truman to join the Klan."

Hinde delivered the ten-dollar Klan membership fee to a local barber, and Truman went down to the Baltimore Hotel in downtown Kansas City to meet with a Klan organizer. The two apparently agreed that their differences were just too great, and Truman left without Klan support.

"So, that was it," Hinde said. "And they gave me the ten dollars back."

---

tion's one identified Klan candidate, running for the county circuit court, received 3,004 votes in eastern Jackson County, or 21 percent of the vote.

In 1924, feelings were just as high. That February Harry Hoffman, a former Jackson County marshal, said in a Kansas City speech that local "independent" Democratic clubs had been formed in six of the city's sixteen wards and claimed a membership of 4,159. Pendergast factional leaders, in turn, insisted that the word *independent* was a euphe-

Truman once said.

"And I went out to one of their meetings and dared them to try." Then, Truman said, he walked through the Klan rally to his car. "There I met my gang with a load of shotguns in a car. It was a good thing they did not come earlier. If they had met, there would have been trouble."

Hoffman would hold a grudge. Twenty years later, when the Hearst chain trumpeted the Klan charge, it reported that several former acquaintances of Truman had sworn that he was a

A few days before Election Day in November 1988, Olive Truman, the eighty-nine-year-old widow of Ralph Truman, a cousin of Harry Truman, summoned the press to her apartment at the Grandview Manor Care Center, south of Kansas City.

On Mrs. Truman's mind: what President Ronald Reagan recently had said down in Springfield, Missouri.

While making a campaign appearance a few days before at the Springfield airport, Reagan had announced that the Democratic Party that Harry Truman knew no longer existed.

"Harry Truman's party is the Republican Party," Reagan, himself a former Democrat, had said.

Reagan had come to Independence in 1985. Standing in front of the Truman statue that stands on Independence Square, Reagan had campaigned for tax reform and ended his remarks with the statement, "I think Harry would be pleased."

The president had been well received in Independence.

While some local Democratic Party officeholders were careful to remark afterward that Harry Truman might not have admired some aspects of the Reagan tax plan, everyone had remembered their manners.

But now such a statement, days before Election Day, could not be allowed to pass.

A coalition of local Democrats purchased a full-page ad in The Kansas City Times, reading, in part, "Harry Truman a

Republican? Rubbish!" Margaret Truman Daniel sent word to the office of U.S. Representative Alan Wheat of Kansas City, saying she found the president's statement "stupid," adding that it made her "furious."

But it was Olive Truman who explained why Harry Truman would never have joined the Republican Party. "His mother would have disowned him if he'd been for a Republican," she said.

Some might have thought Olive Truman's assertion a mild, heat-of-the-campaign exaggeration.

It wasn't. Harry Truman loved his mother. And Harry Truman's mother had disliked Republicans, for several reasons.

For one, she was a longtime resident of Jackson County, where Democratic Party candidates had routinely prevailed. It had much to do with how many of the county's earliest settlers, including all four of Harry Truman's grandparents, came from Kentucky and were admirers of Tennessee favorite son Andrew Jackson, seventh president, war hero, and the Democrat for whom the county was named.

It involved how both of Truman's grandfathers, while liv-

ing in Missouri, a slave state before the Civil War, owned small numbers of slaves. They may not have appreciated abolitionist talk or how the opening in 1854 of the Kansas territory – right on Jackson County's western border – could tempt their slaves if all the Republican free-soilers from Massachusetts then coming to Kansas prevailed in keeping slavery from becoming established in the new state.

But it also involved how many Jackson County residents had suffered during the Civil War. Those residents included Harriet Louisa Young, Harry Truman's maternal grandmother.

Harriet Louisa Young, Truman's maternal grandmother, who filed a claim against the United States government for damages suffered during the Civil War.

More than once during the Civil War, Union troops stopped at the Jackson County property of Solomon and Harriet Young and helped themselves to whatever property they believed needed liberating. In 1862, Solomon Young had signed an oath swearing loyalty to the United States. But that didn't stop Union troops, who took advantage of Young's frequent absences while hauling freight west.

On one occasion, Harriet often said, the family silver disappeared. And there were other raids. In a claim filed years after the war, Harriet said Union troops had taken fifteen horses, fifteen mules, 150 cattle, forty-four hogs, and much more, in total worth $21,442.

Then came August 1863, when Union Brigadier General Thomas Ewing Jr. issued General Order Number 11.

Following the raid a few days earlier on Lawrence, Kansas, by guerrilla leader William Quantrill, and in an effort to remove sources of comfort for Southern-sympathizing irregulars, Ewing ordered all those who could not prove their loyalty to the Union to leave several western Missouri border counties, including Jackson County.

The county soon was rendered a vast "burnt-over" district, as Union troops drove families from their homes and often torched them. If Union troops did not burn homes, they abused them, in some cases spurring their horses up and down staircases. And if some Union officers considered General Order Number 11 an outrage, that was a subtlety lost on those western Missouri residents forced to flee their properties.

That included Harriet Louisa and her daughter Martha Ellen.

In 1906, the U.S. Court of Claims ruled that the federal government owed Harriet Louisa Gregg Young $3,800 for property seized during the Civil War. At about that same time, her grandson Harry, who had joined the Missouri National Guard, made the mistake of visiting her home while wearing the guard's dark blue uniform.

"She looked me over and I knew I was going to catch it," Truman wrote in a memoir. "She said 'Harry, this is the first time since 1863 that a blue uniform has been in this house. Don't bring it here again.' I didn't."

In those days, Jackson County Republicans who admitted to their sentiments were considered newsworthy. In 1912 the *Examiner* of Independence published a profile of P. N. Grinter, a ninety-two-year-old pioneer who had come to Jackson County from Kentucky in 1849. "It is an interesting fact," the *Examiner* reported, "that Mr. Grinter cast the only vote in Independence for Abraham Lincoln in 1860 and in relating the circumstances said that he was greatly censured by his neighbors."

Martha Ellen, meanwhile, felt the Republican Party complicit in the unpleasantness she endured as a girl during the Civil War, and her thoughts regarding Republicans endured into her final years. In 1945 while visiting her son, the new president, in the White House, she declined a joking invitation to sleep in the Lincoln bedroom. In 1947, a few days before President Truman became the first chief executive to address the National Association for the Advancement of Colored People, the president wrote his mother, warning her.

He would be quoting Abraham Lincoln, he said.

But if Martha Ellen Young Truman was an ardent Democrat, she was more than matched by her husband, John Truman, whom she had married in 1881. John Truman's enthusiasm for the Democratic Party was such that in 1892, when Grover Cleveland won his second term as president, Truman climbed to the top of his roof to tie an American flag to the weathervane. That night, he rode in the Cleveland victory parade in Independence.

In 1900, John Truman attended the Democratic National Convention in Kansas City's old Convention Hall. Son Harry, sixteen years old, accompanied him. Years later, the elder Truman owed part of his livelihood to an eastern Jackson County judge, a Democrat, who named him a Jackson County road overseer, a patronage position.

As Democrats largely ran Jackson County, it would be pleasant to say that they conducted themselves in a mature manner, tolerating one another's strengths and sharing the wealth. Pleasant – but not true. The legacy of Democratic machine politics and its often brawling nature endures today. Jackson County, alone among all Missouri counties, has two separate election boards – one in Kansas City, the other in eastern Jackson County –

specifically because of the excesses of Democratic machine politics before World War I.

The 1916 elections prompt-

In Sugar Creek, the small Standard Oil refinery town that was home to many laborers, the

Abbott found out, however, that such thinking made some Democratic Party bosses queasy. They dismissed Abbott after they

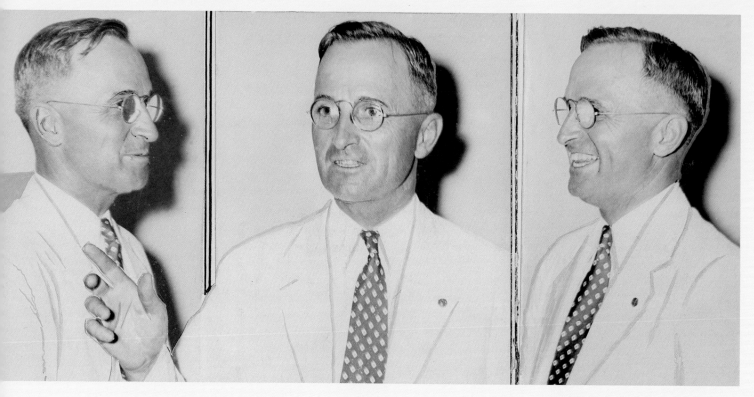

Judge Harry Truman after the announcement that he would be the Democratic senatorial candidate in 1934.

ed pitched battles between Jackson County Democratic machine bosses Tom Pendergast and Joseph Shannon – heads of rival camps known as the Goats and Rabbits, respectively. In one low episode during that year's February Democratic primary in Kansas City, fisticuffs followed after Goat and Rabbit election captains lined up opposing ranks of transients to cast fraudulent votes at the same polling place.

Eastern Jackson County had its own indiscretions. In 1916 officials with the Jackson County court, which administered elections in the county's rural districts, changed the locations of some polling places to spots

new polling place was a smoke-filled room known as Mike Bine's Pool Hall.

All of it combined to prompt the state legislature to act, and the separate Jackson County election board was born.

In 1922, when Truman ran as the Pendergast candidate for Jackson County eastern judge, the only election that mattered was the Democratic primary in August. Running one precinct near Independence was a Standard Oil employee named Harry Abbott. His job was to convince the precinct's residents to vote for Truman.

He didn't care if the voters were Democratic or Republican.

learned that he was using a car supplied by the Pendergast machine to shuttle voters – any voters, not just Democrats – to the polls on election day.

For this offense, Abbott was fired and paid off with seven dollars. To give a Republican a ride in a Democratic car was to put a smell on it. Even as late as 1990, almost seventy years after the election, Abbott – then ninety-six – resented his dismissal.

"But they didn't want Republicans riding in a Democratic car," Abbott said in a Truman Museum oral history.

But even Truman in 1922 had to answer a charge about consorting with Republicans. During the campaign a rumor spread that Truman, in 1920, had voted for Jackson County Marshal John Miles, a friend from the war who also happened to be a Republican.

"It was the worst his opponents had been able to come up with, and given the spirit of Jackson County politics, it was a serious charge," David McCullough wrote in his 1992 biography, *Truman*.

According to McCullough, Truman confessed. "I'll plead guilty," Truman said during a summer picnic in Oak Grove, "along with five thousand other ex-soldiers. I was closer to John Miles than a brother. I have seen him in places that would make hell look like a play-ground."

At that moment, McCullough wrote, "for many who were listening, the primary election for eastern judge was over, and Harry Truman had won."

Once the Democratic primary was over, the entire election was over, as Truman later recalled in a memoir. "The election in the fall went off without incident because eastern Jackson County is as Democratic as Mississippi or South Carolina," he wrote.

Republicans weren't motivated in 1922. County GOP leaders asked Arthur Wilson, an Independence lumberyard operator, to run against Truman. Wilson's appeal was that he was, like Truman, a World War I veteran. But Wilson agreed to run only if he didn't have to campaign.

During the election, he went fishing, and finished some 2,700 votes behind Truman.

In 1924, Republicans again had to search for a candidate, as no one had filed for eastern judge. This time they asked Henry Rummel, an Independence harness maker. He agreed to run, but didn't exert himself. And yet he won, ben-efiting from a bitter Democratic Party squabble which ended when the Rabbit faction decided to throw their support to the Republicans.

"The fact of the matter is, Henry Rummel didn't make much of a campaign," Henry Chiles, an Independence Rabbit precinct worker, remembered in 1961. "We made it for him."

When Rummel won, he repre-sented only the second Republican elected to represent the court's eastern district since the Civil War.

But Truman won election as the county's presiding judge in 1926 and served two four-year terms, leaving Jackson County in January 1935 to begin his career in the U.S. Senate.

Even as president, Truman stayed current on Jackson County voting trends. Days after Truman's 1948 election as president, he received a vote breakdown of Sugar Creek's two precincts from the town's mayor R. J. "Rudy" Roper. In Sugar Creek, Roper reported, Truman had received 814 votes to Tom Dewey's 143.

"It sure is good to lead the ticket in one of the home precincts," Truman wrote in his reply.

After leaving the White House, Truman continued to be active in national Democratic Party activities. Truman wrote to Sam Rayburn, speaker of the U.S.

House of Representatives, in 1959, complaining about the direction of the Democratic Party. "I've no ax to grind," he said, "only the welfare of the United States of America and the Democratic Party. They are synonymous."

Meanwhile, Abraham Lincoln's stature in Jackson County had not improved.

Hazel Graham, Truman neigh-bor and first executive director of the Jackson County Historical Society, once recalled a day in the early 1960s when a young man from the South had visited the society's restored 1859 Jail, Marshal's Home and Museum near Independence Square. He had purchased a postcard and had then asked to buy a stamp. The society didn't sell postage stamps, but Graham offered the visitor a spare stamp of hers.

The stamp happened to bear the face of Abraham Lincoln. The young man gave the stamp back, saying he wouldn't lick a Lincoln stamp.

Graham found this funny, and repeated the incident to jail volunteers, some of whom were members of local chapter of the United Daughters of the Confederacy.

The volunteers heard nothing remarkable in Graham's story.

"One of them said, 'Well, you don't need to think I would lick a Lincoln stamp,' " Graham later recalled.

TRUMAN AND FREEMASONRY

In late 1908, a cousin of Harry Truman's mother visited the Truman family farm to inspect some livestock.

The twenty-four-year-old Truman noticed the Masonic pin on his cousin's coat.

After Truman inquired after the organization, the cousin soon returned with an application form. Truman petitioned the Belton Lodge 450 in December, and received his first degree the following winter.

"That spring and summer I spent teaching the plow horses all the Masonic lectures," Truman wrote in a memoir.

Truman ultimately was associated with Freemasonry for sixty-three years. Brother Truman, as his Masonic colleagues called him, believed the principles of Freemasonry guided him throughout his life.

"Freemasonry is a system of morals which makes it easier to live with your fellow man, whether he understands it or not," he once wrote.

In 1911, Truman led the effort to organize a separate lodge in Grandview, and rose within Missouri Masonic circles.

"From the very start of his Masonic career, he was a pro-found student of the ritual and immediately rose to prominence in the fraternity because of his proficiency," read one account of Truman's lodge history.

Masonic membership was powerful in early twentieth-century Missouri. "In Truman's day," wrote Truman historian Richard Lawrence Miller, "community leaders still tended to belong to Masonic lodges, a fact that attracted ambitious young men

Truman wearing a Masonic pin in his lapel around 1908.

hoping to lubricate business and political careers through lodge fellowship."

All that was true with young Harry Truman. While training for World War I artillery duty in Oklahoma, Harry urged two of his superior officers to join the Masons. Both did. In the 1920s, one partner of Truman's in the Community Savings and Loan of Independence was a Kansas City official of DeMolay, the young men's Masonic organization.

Freemasonry organizations usually attempted to exist apart from the hostilities of partisan politics. At the 1930 gathering of the Grand Lodge of Missouri, held in Kansas City, three grand lodge officers – all Republicans – appointed Truman to the progressive line of the grand lodge. "This meant that eventually with no mishaps I'd be Grand Master," Truman later wrote.

Truman's status in Masonic circles benefited him. Among the many attractive constituencies that Truman the candidate appealed to – veterans, farmers, Independence insiders – were the thousands of Masons who lived in Missouri. Truman biographer Robert Ferrell has noted that by his 1934 race for senator, Truman had been attending Masonic meetings in Missouri for twenty-five years, and that it "gradually became clear that Truman possessed a base in the 'outstate' or country counties that his opponents had not counted on."

A few Missouri Masonic members apparently did not admire Truman.

In his 1938 lodge election to senior grand warden, a high state office, Truman prevailed by only a slim margin. Two years later, while engaged in a rugged campaign to be re-elected to the U.S. Senate following the demise of the Pendergast machine, Truman also was up for election as Missouri grand master.

Nine days before the grand lodge vote, an anonymous letter arrived at Masonic lodges in Missouri. The letter discouraged any member from voting a man who "through the power of crooked votes was elected to the U.S. Senate by the champion of all racketeers, Tom Pendergast."

Truman, however, coasted to victory, receiving 2,708 votes compared to 689 tallied for other candidates. At the end of the two-day meeting, Truman was installed in office by William R. Gentry, a past grand master and one of the three Republicans who had appointed him to the grand lodge line in 1930.

Truman served as Missouri grand master from 1940 through 1941. He later was criticized for saying that his election was the highest honor that ever came to him. His explanation was that the office of grand master came to him unsolicited, and that he did not campaign for it.

In the early 1940s, Truman perceived the rise of fascism in Europe from a Freemasonry context. "The Masonic Fraternity on the European Continent has been suppressed," he told a St. Louis lodge audience in the fall of 1941. "It has been suppressed because it stands for freedom of thought and freedom of expression."

President Harry Truman received the 33rd Degree of the Scottish Rite in October 1945. About three months after the end of World War II, he authorized a European Freemasonry committee to travel to Europe. In 1950, Harry and Bess Truman attended a Masonic graveside service in Arlington National Cemetery for Leslie Coffelt, a White House police officer killed in the assassination attempt that year on the president.

As president, Truman did not make a show of his Masonic membership. One night in November 1947, Truman walked up Pennsylvania Avenue trailed only by a Secret Service guard keeping a discreet distance. The president walked the three blocks from the White House to a nearby Masonic temple and once inside, donned the traditional apron.

The occasion: an assistant White House physician was taking the lodge's third degree.

During his 1948 whistlestop campaign, Truman slipped away from reporters after an Indianapolis speech to ride to nearby Beech Grove, where he witnessed a master Mason degree being conferred upon a sailor serving on the Williamsburg, the presidential yacht.

But Truman didn't ignore the

> "Freemasonry is a system of morals which makes it easier to live with your fellow man, whether he understands it or not," Truman once wrote.

Left In 1948, artist Greta Kempton painted the portrait shown at left. Kempton commented that "he really enjoyed wearing his Masonic regalia and apron for each sitting." *Collection of the Masonic Grand Lodge of Missouri.*

Top In 1911, Harry Truman helped organize Grandview Lodge No.618, and over the years, assisted other area lodges whenever he could. On January 16, 1914, he received this jewel from Coldwater Lodge No.485 in Drexel, Missouri, as a token of appreciation.

Top Right Harry S. Truman received the master Mason degree on March 9, 1909, in Belton Lodge No.450, A.F.&F.M., Belton, Missouri. This was his "Blue Lodge" jewel.

Bottom Right Masonic apron of a past grand master of the Missouri Grand Lodge, A.F.&A.M. Truman received this apron in 1941 and wore it often for Masonic ceremonies.

favorable press that that his Masonic membership, occasionally displayed, could yield.

In 1949, Truman flew to Chicago to speak before fifty thousand Shriners in Soldier Field. It wasn't a whim that brought the president to Chicago as much as shrewd appeals to Truman the Democrat. "There will not be a similar opportunity for several years of achieving this kind of demonstration," Frank Land, Kansas City founder of the DeMolay organization, wrote Truman before the Chicago convention. Land added that the president's appearance would be helpful in the 1950 congressional elections.

During the 1960 campaign of Democratic presidential candidate John Kennedy, party strategists sent Truman on a speaking tour through several southern states. In his speeches, Truman often referred to his status as a Baptist and Freemason who saw no problem in voting for a Catholic for president.

Truman expressed the same sentiments in private. In 1960, when a Scottish Rite Mason in North Dakota wrote Truman asking how a Scottish Rite Mason could vote for a Catholic for president, Truman grew agitated. He wrote back, telling the correspondent that tolerance represented "one of the most important things under the Constitution of the U.S." He added: "If in the campaign of 1948 any Catholic priest had arisen and said no Catholic should vote for me because I happen to be a Baptist and a member of the Masonic Fraternity, I certainly would have blown the roof off."

During the July 1957 dedication of the Truman Presidential Museum & Library in Independence, a large parade of Freemasons preceded the laying of the museum cornerstone.

Among those presiding at the late president's December 1972 memorial service at the Truman Museum was W. Hugh McLaughlin, then grand master of Missouri. "He was our brother by adoption," McLaughlin said of Truman. "He was our companion by choice."

TRUMAN MEDICAL CENTER LAKEWOOD

Truman Medical Center Hospital Hill, south of downtown Kansas City, bears the name of the thirty-third president.

But Truman Medical Center Lakewood, which stands about sixteen miles southeast of downtown Kansas City and which Harry Truman helped build as Jackson County presiding judge, bears the man's mark.

The same president who long campaigned for national health insurance for senior citizens showed his interest in health care issues early in his political career.

He resolved to build a county hospital after being elected presiding judge in 1926.

The hospital's original site served as the farm of Henry Washington Younger, whose son, Cole, became a prominent associate of outlaws Frank and Jesse James. Jackson County later purchased the Younger farm in the nineteenth century and for years the location served as what was known as the county's "poor farm."

In 1906, the county approved a bond issue for building a new

facility on the site. In 1907, construction began on the structure, which had seven acres of floor space and a capacity of 450.

The new county home was dedicated in 1908 and was called Patterson Hall. In 1911, the complex received the new name of Jackson County Home for the Aged and Infirm.

But by the 1920s, people still were referring to the facility as the "poor farm," and Truman wanted to upgrade the facility.

"The poor folks that were in the home out there didn't have a hospital," Rufus Burrus, lawyer and longtime Truman friend, said in 1985. "And he wanted $500,000 used to establish a hospital."

In 1928, Jackson County voters approved a bond issue, championed by Truman, that generated $6.5 million for building 224 miles of new roads, and additional funds with which to build a county hospital.

Construction was completed in 1930. "The hospital is up at less cost than any similar institution," Truman wrote at the time. "The per bed cost is one half the City's and St. Luke's and any others you want to name."

A cornerstone on the facility bears Truman's name.

The hospital was named for Truman shortly after he died in 1972.

The complex that is now Truman Medical Center Lakewood began when Jackson County voters approved a bond issue championed by Truman.
Photo by Ray Geselbracht.

Harry Truman speaking during his 1940 Senate campaign.

CHAPTER 6

SENATOR

Harry Truman spent more than nine years as a United States senator in Washington.

But he never allowed himself to forget where he came from, and sometimes he enjoyed putting a western Missouri spin on issues debated in the Senate chamber.

In a 1937 speech, while attempting to depict the scale of the chicanery he believed the nation's railroad financiers had been guilty of, he described a railroad robbery committed in 1873.

"The man who committed that robbery used a gun and a horse and got up early in the morning," Truman said. "He and his gang took a chance of being killed and eventually most were. That railroad robber's name was Jesse James. The same Jesse James held up the Missouri Pacific in 1876 and took the paltry sum of seventeen thousand dollars from the express car."

Decades later, Truman added, some "tin-plate millionaires" ruined the railroad "and got away with seventy million dollars or more. They did it by means of holding companies. Senators can see what 'pikers' Mr. James and his crowd were alongside of some real artists."

By invoking the outlaw from Clay County, just north of the Missouri River from his own Jackson County, Truman placed his regard for mid-twentieth-century railroad financing in accessible context. Throughout his Senate career Truman often brought a good measure of Missouri to his tasks. In

this he may have felt justified, as twice – in the Senate elections of 1934 and 1940 – Missouri voters elected him despite the conventional wisdom that held that Truman either was a weak candidate or a candidate with no chance at all.

When he took the oath of office on January 3, 1935, Truman was arriving at the Senate, in his own words, "under a cloud." He was derided as the "Senator from Pendergast," and there was no denying that machine votes, thousands of them suspect, had proved crucial to his surviving the Democratic primary against two opponents during the previous summer.

In the Senate chamber, he was assigned a desk in the last row of desks. These were new desks installed along the rear of the Democratic side of the aisle, as so many Democrats, like Truman, had ridden President Franklin Roosevelt's popularity to Washington.

Roosevelt, however, didn't agree to receive Truman until five months after he arrived. The scheduled fifteen-minute meeting at the White House lasted seven.

And yet, by 1944, Truman had risen to be regarded as one of the Senate's most respected members and a logical choice for Roosevelt's vice presidential running mate in that year's campaign. Democratic Party officials, looking for a reliable running

Sound car for the Truman campaign for senator in 1934. During one of the hottest summers in Missouri, Truman drove back and forth across the state.

mate for the ailing Roosevelt, felt comfortable with Truman's clear capacity for work. As Roosevelt adviser Harry Hopkins said, "Truman wasn't somebody pulled out of a hat."

Truman accomplished this transformation largely by sheer force of will. "It's been my policy to do every job assigned to me just a little better than anyone else has done it," he wrote to his daughter, Margaret. "It takes work to do anything well."

Yet his Senate career had not started well.

In 1934 Boss Tom Pendergast needed a candidate to run in that year's Democratic primary against Jacob L. "Tuck" Milligan and John J. Cochran, both with experience in the United States House of Representatives. Cochran represented the St. Louis Democratic Party organization, and Milligan was a patron of U.S. Senator Bennett Clark, Missouri's other senator, who wanted to challenge Pendergast's power in Missouri.

It's often said that Truman was selected when at least three other choices of Pendergast – U.S. Representative Joe Shannon; James P. Aylward, lawyer and head of the Missouri Democratic Committee;

and James A. Reed, former Kansas City mayor and U.S. senator – all begged off. But Truman scholar Robert Ferrell has written that Aylward also presented Pendergast with a list of ten more names.

Pendergast said he recognized none of them.

That's when Aylward brought up Truman. When Pendergast accepted the idea, Truman was tracked down at a Warsaw, Missouri, hotel, where he was in the middle of a speaking tour in support of a state bond issue to help with unemployment. Truman was instructed to drive to Sedalia, where he met with Aylward and Jim Pendergast, the boss's nephew and Truman's old friend.

Truman accepted the offer of Pendergast's endorsement as candidate for the Senate. The night before he began his campaign he stayed up late, writing his thoughts down in a room in Kansas City's Pickwick Hotel.

Several Missouri newspapers thought Truman an unimpressive candidate. Critics seized on what they considered Truman's chief vulnerability, which was his obvious connection with the Pendergast machine. Clark, campaigning for Milligan, derided "the judge's record of subservience in Jackson County."

Truman, however, was game. During one of the hottest summers in Missouri history, he drove across and back across the state. Over a six-week period Truman made it a goal to speak in every Missouri county. As a candidate he appealed to farmers, veterans, and Masons. Also, among the more than three hundred county judges across Missouri, Truman was a respected colleague. After completing his Jackson County road-building project, Truman had mailed each of them copies of *Jackson County - Results of County Planning*, a handsome volume detailing the new road system.

The judges who received these books now had bedtime reading that documented Truman's administrative abilities.

He prevailed in the primary by some 40,000 votes out of about 660,000 cast. While the Truman and Cochran votes in Kansas City and St. Louis, respectively, had largely canceled one another out, Truman had vindicated himself in the state's rural districts. When the St. Louis and Kansas City votes were taken out of the totals, Truman had won rural Missouri by more than 21,000 votes.

He defeated his Republican opponent that November.

A former labor supervisor on the Santa Fe rail line in eastern Jackson County in 1901, Truman enjoyed his work investigating railroad financing.

A former Kansas City bank clerk, Truman wasn't intimidated by higher finance and quickly mastered the concept of holding companies, a concept which he believed many of the nation's railroad financiers to have been abusing. Where other senators had proved reluctant to wade into the tedious work of unraveling the intricate financial structures and holding companies the railroads were suffering under, Truman volunteered.

Truman's emerging agenda on civil rights surfaced in the Senate. He supported legislation that would abolish the poll tax and prevent lynchings. In 1938, in a Senate battle over an anti-lynching bill, he voted to limit debate on the bill in an unsuccessful effort to break a filibuster against it.

As a senator he also passed out jobs to supporters of the Pendergast machine. Just as he had appointed his brother, Vivian, a Jackson County road overseer after he won the 1922 election to Jackson County eastern judge, Truman now appointed Vivian head of the Federal Housing Agency in Kansas City. He saw that his friend Edgar Hinde served as Independence postmaster.

In Washington, he missed his family. While Bess and Margaret Truman spent their springs in the capital, they often returned to Independence for the summer and fall.

He didn't try to deny his connection to the Pendergast machine. Truman placed a portrait of Pendergast in his Senate office. Pendergast, meanwhile, had never been more powerful in Missouri than during the mid-1930s. As Truman opponents had enjoyed saying during the 1934 primary election, Pendergast's Jackson Democratic Club at 1908 Main Street in Kansas City was the true capitol of Missouri.

The big white building with the large rotunda in Jefferson City, meanwhile, was merely known as Uncle Tom's Cabin.

When the Pendergast machine began to unravel with federal investigations of massive vote frauds in the 1936 elections, Truman, in a 1938 speech, attacked Maurice Milligan, younger brother of Jacob Milligan and U.S. attorney for Missouri's western district. "I say, Mr. President, that a Jackson County, Missouri, Democrat has as much chance of a fair trial in the Federal

District Court of Western Missouri as a Jew would have in a Hitler court or a Trotsky follower before Stalin."

Reaction to the speech was so negative that Truman thought his political career was

chance. That included several of Truman's close friends, who gathered at the Hotel Statler in St. Louis in January 1940 to discuss Truman's re-election prospects

Nevertheless Truman announced that he

Truman for Senator banner in Sedalia, Missouri, was part of Truman's 1940 campaign.

close to being over. So did many others, chief among them Missouri Governor Lloyd Stark who, though he initially had been elected with Pendergast support, now targeted the machine as well as Truman.

When Tom Pendergast pleaded guilty in the spring of 1939 to income tax evasion, Stark's momentum seemed clear. That September he announced that he was running for Truman's Senate seat.

As in 1934, few gave Truman much of a

was filing for re-election the next month. The campaign had trouble finding money to pay for stamps, and, on occasion, Truman slept in his car while campaigning. Stark, meanwhile, remained relentless in his attacks on Truman's connection to the now-disgraced Pendergast machine.

Worse, that July, the Jackson County court foreclosed on a court-held mortgage on the Truman farm in Grandview. Truman was convinced this had been done strictly to

VOTE FOR

DEMOCRATIC CANDIDATES

HARRY S. TRUMAN
United States Senator

LLOYD W. KING
State Superintendent of Schools

C. A. LEEDY, JR.
Judge Supreme Court
Division No. 2

JOHN T. FITZSIMMONS
Judge Supreme Court
Division No. 1

These Candidates Stand for Roosevelt and Recovery
GENERAL ELECTION, TUESDAY, NOVEMBER 6, 1934

Democratic candidate handbill

embarrass him during the campaign.

And yet Truman still won. He prevailed in the primary by about 8,000 votes out of about 665,000 cast. When he returned to the Senate chamber in Washington three days after the primary, his colleagues descended upon him, offering congratulations. Again, he defeated his Republican opponent that November.

In 1940, as he was running for re-election to the Senate, Truman also decided to leave the Senate for the U.S. Army. After the passage of the Draft Act in September 1940, Truman pulled out a uniform and presented himself to General George C.

Marshall, Army chief of staff. When Truman asked Marshall that he be assigned as a field artillery officer, Marshall told him he was too old.

Yet it was in a different military role that Truman would achieve what many consider his greatest distinction while serving in the Senate: the creation of the Truman Committee.

Pork didn't hold much interest for Senator Truman. In November 1940 the Army had shifted a large area training center from Iowa to Fort Leonard Wood in the Missouri Ozarks. For the site of a large ammunition plant, the federal government had chosen an area just east of Independence, where soon the Lake City ordnance plant would be in full production

Senator Truman visits his mother, Martha Ellen Truman, on August 12, 1934.

during World War II.

Missouri, Truman believed, had received more than half of all the defense expenditures between the Mississippi River and the Rocky Mountains.

But when his Senate office continued to receive complaints of massive waste and inefficiencies in the construction of Fort Leonard Wood, Truman visited several military camps then under construction near Washington. Alarmed by what he saw there, he took a road trip, driving as far south as Florida and then into the Midwest, and then into Michigan.

There, as at Fort Leonard Wood, Truman discovered waste on a vast scale. Sometimes it was equipment lying on the ground, exposed to the elements. Other

times it was employees drawing pay for doing nothing.

On February 10, 1941, Truman proposed in a Senate speech that a committee be established to look into the awarding of defense contracts and the efficiency with which those contracts were fulfilled. The Senate approved the committee the next month. Its official title was the Senate Special Committee to Investigate the National Defense Program.

Everyone called it the Truman Committee.

Its first task was the investigation of camp construction, and testimony before the committee confirmed the sheer size of the waste then going unchecked. Later estimates held that reforms in camp construction urged by the Truman Committee saved the federal government some $250 million.

The committee also investigated shortages of aluminum and magnesium, faulty aircraft engines, and the quality of steel plate used in the building of new ships. By 1943 the committee had produced twenty-one reports on a variety of topics, including gasoline rationing, lumber, and farm machinery. In its March 8, 1943, issue, *Time* magazine placed Truman on its cover and described the man it called "Investigator Truman" as a "scrupulously honest" politician.

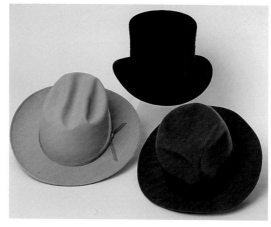

Truman's hats included this top hat worn at his inauguration in 1949, a well-worn fedora, and one of his trademark western-style hats. Although the western hat pictured here is a Resistol, Truman also wore similar hats made by Stetson, Portis, Calvert, and Dobbs. His hat size was 7 3/8.

It was in 1943 that Truman's name first began being mentioned in connection with the vice presidency.

Margaret, Bess, and Harry in the living room of the Truman Independence home, August 9, 1934.

Harry Truman, vice president-elect,
in a car between President Franklin D.
Roosevelt and Vice President Henry
Wallace, November 10, 1944, three
days after the presidential election.
National Park Service, Abbie Row

CHAPTER 7

VICE PRESIDENT

To his inauguration as vice president, Harry Truman wore a business suit.

In shunning formal attire, both Truman and President Franklin D. Roosevelt personified the government's policy of wartime austerity.

Not only was it the first inaugural during a war since Abraham Lincoln, but it also was the first ever at the executive mansion. The fifteen-minute ceremony in January 1945 proceeded on the White House south portico, overlooking a lawn dusted with snow.

Later, Truman left the post-inaugural reception and returned to his Senate office to answer mail and telephone his mother. When a reporter asked how he felt after taking the oath of office, Truman suggested that January 20, 1945, was just another day.

"I don't feel a bit different," he said.

In recent years, historians have wondered how the former farmer, artillery battery captain, and failed haberdasher really felt in the months surrounding his election to vice president. Before the nomination Truman, the senator from Missouri, had routinely professed reluctance to serve with Roosevelt, who had led the nation through the Depression and World War II, but who was now clearly not well.

Today much in the vast sea of correspondence, memoir, and oral history on file at the Harry S. Truman Presidential Museum & Library supports that position.

One example can be found in the recollections of Harry Easley, a Webb City,

Missouri, banker who one night soon after the November 1944 election sat up late with the new vice president at Kansas City's Muehlebach Hotel. In his 1992 biography of Truman, David McCullough cites Easley's account as solid evidence of a reluctant Truman.

"He knew that he would be president before the term was out," Easley said in a 1967 oral history filed at the Truman Museum. And that thought, Easley added, "scared the very devil out of him."

But different researchers have followed the same paper trail to different conclusions. Historian Robert Ferrell, focusing on still another page of the Easley oral history, found more to ponder for his 1994 book on the selection of Truman at the 1944 Democratic National Convention in Chicago. Ferrell noted that Easley, in the same recollection, went on to say that "I never did hear him say that he didn't want the nomination and I think he thoroughly enjoyed it after he got in there."

And, now and then, a new document will float to the surface. There is, for instance, the scrap of Senate stationery recently found by Truman Museum archivists amid car insurance invoices and thank-you notes in Truman's personal papers from January and February 1945. It is a list in Truman's hand of fourteen names, including those of American heroes Ulysses S. Grant and

Stonewall Jackson. Also named are Napoleon, Frederick the Great, and Richard the Lion-Hearted.

Behind each name is a number. Truman Museum archivists believe the numbers represent the ages of the historical figures.

Truman's taste for individual greatness went back to his tenth birthday, when he received a four-volume set of biographies entitled *Great Men and Famous Women.* The books gripped the boy's imagination; he later called their arrival a turning point in his life.

Any sense of self-satisfaction, however, might have been slow in arriving. The Truman family was upset when he accepted the vice presidential nomination on July 21, 1944, at the Chicago convention.

The Truman family fretted that election opponents would make much of Bess Truman's presence on the Senate office payroll. That happened. Truman's office staff, in turn, insisted that for her $4,500 annual salary, Bess Truman handled her husband's personal mail and edited Senate committee reports.

Edward D. McKim, Kansas City resident who served as a private in Battery D; longtime Truman friend and political aide. On how McKim tried to persuade Truman to accept the nomination as Franklin Roosevelt's vice presidential running mate during the 1944 Democratic National Convention in Chicago:

"Finally, I said, 'I think, Senator, that you're going to do it.' And he got a little belligerent with me and said, 'What makes you think that I'm going to do it?' I said, 'Because there's a little old ninety-year-old mother down in Grandview, Missouri, that would like to see her son president of the United States.' And with that the tears came in his eyes and he stomped out of the room; he wouldn't speak to me...I said 'president of the United States' because it was the consensus of opinion at the whole convention that whoever was nominated for the vice presidency would be the president of the United States."

Perhaps expecting greatness to drop upon him, maybe even dreading it, Truman appears to have spent at least one idle moment as president-in-waiting, trying greatness on for size.

If so, the numbers would have told Truman that greatness had been late in arriving. At sixty, he was eighteen years older than Grant at Appomattox.

Yet it seems a brief moment of reverie couldn't be resisted.

Truman also feared the press would exhume the 1903 suicide of his father-in-law. That didn't happen.

But perhaps even more serious, Truman had long told his wife that he wasn't interested in the job. In a 1943 letter to Bess, Truman described how a Senate colleague asked whether he wanted the nomination. "I told him in words of one syllable that I would not, that I had only recently become senator and that I wanted to work at it for

Mary Ethel Noland, first cousin to Harry Truman, on Harry Truman's apparent unwillingness to join the Democratic Party presidential ticket in 1944 before leaving Independence for the party's national convention in Chicago:

"Well, I don't remember having any doubts that he would, but when he was nominated for vice president, he didn't want to be vice president, and I remember he came here to see us before he went to the convention; and my mother was upstairs and he went to see her, and he said, 'Aunt Ella, I'm going to the convention to defeat myself; I don't want to be vice president.' "

about ten years," he wrote.

Margaret Truman has dated her parents' conversations on the subject to early 1944. That was when Truman nominated his St. Louis friend, Bob Hannegan, to head the Democratic National Committee.

"When Bob got the job," Margaret Truman wrote in her biography of her mother, "the *St. Louis Post-Dispatch* promptly declared that this appointment moved Truman into prime consideration for the vice presidency."

That spring at the Kansas City Club, another friend, Kansas City radio station executive Tom Evans, handed Truman a copy of the *Saturday Evening Post* that contained speculation about Truman and the vice presidency.

"He, of course, laughed it off," Evans said in his own Truman Museum oral history. "I mean, it was just a huge joke as far as Mr. Truman was concerned."

Relatives got the same impression that July.

"I remember he came here to see us before we went to the convention," Truman cousin Mary Ethel Noland said in her Truman Museum oral history. "My

mother was upstairs and he went to see her, and he said, 'Aunt Ella, I'm going to the convention to defeat myself; I don't want to be vice president.' "

Despite such stated misgivings, Truman, a longtime poker player, may have bluffed his way to power at the Chicago convention.

Historian Ferrell has wondered whether Truman's apparent hesitation was just part of his own calculated plan. As a candidate, Truman had several strengths. He was from Missouri, a border state with ties to both the North and South. He had won grudging admiration from the Roosevelt administration for his Senate committee's investigation of the national defense industry.

All Democratic Party insiders, meanwhile, knew that Roosevelt's health was failing. That made the choice of vice president crucial.

Before and during the convention, Democratic Party strategists conspired to influence Roosevelt to dump sitting Vice President Henry Wallace, whom they found remote or too disinterested in politics. Possible replacements included James Byrnes, a former South Carolina senator who now served as War Mobilization director and often received the title of Roosevelt's " assistant president." But he posed a liability with black voters, since in 1938 he was among Southern senators who had opposed a proposed federal anti-lynching law.

Adding to the confusion was the ever-opaque Roosevelt, who refused to clearly state his preference.

Roosevelt led both Wallace and Byrnes on with half-truths and guarded statements. Before the convention he told Wallace, "I hope it will be the same old team." But in an endorsement letter that Wallace requested, Roosevelt proved cagey. He wrote that if he were a convention delegate, he would vote for Wallace. With Byrnes, Roosevelt was ambiguous. In a telephone conversation, Roosevelt told Byrnes only that, of all the vice presidential candidates, Byrnes was his closest friend.

But from the rugby scrum that ensued in Chicago, Truman emerged holding the ball. At the convention, Truman won the nomination on the second ballot. And if some still believe him to have been a reluctant candidate, Ferrell has thought otherwise.

Ferrell's exhibit A: Truman's sudden, uncharacteristic silence on paper.

Throughout adulthood Truman believed in the recorded life. He wrote more than twelve hundred letters to his wife. Several of the letters detail political machinations in Jackson County and Washington. Further, Truman developed a habit of retiring to private rooms to literally write to himself. Truman's 1934 decision to run for the U.S. Senate apparently was so emotional that he fled to a room at Kansas City's old Pickwick Hotel, where he scribbled down his most intimate thoughts on the opportunity.

Yet when national party leaders began maneuvering in earnest ten years later to name Truman as Roosevelt's running mate, Truman's silence was thunderous, according

to Ferrell.

Still another historian believes Truman may have been unable to rein in his inner political savvy. Richard Lawrence Miller, author of *Truman: The Rise to Power,* finds it interesting that though Truman visited several assorted factions and delegations in Chicago, ostensibly to endorse Byrnes for vice president, many of these same delegations later found themselves favoring Truman.

Ultimately, Truman accepted the running-mate position in a Chicago hotel room, after Roosevelt, over the telephone, asked that Truman take the job.

The brief vice presidential interlude brought a degree of serenity for Truman, though he found himself underwhelmed with the ritual of the office.

"And then the Senate meets and it's my job to get 'em prayed for – and goodness knows they need it," Truman wrote in an April 11 letter to his sister and mother describing the ceremonial duties of his new job, which included presiding over the Senate and overseeing the occasional invocation.

He got the Senate's business going, he wrote, "by staying in the chair for an hour and then [seeing] more Senators and curiosity people who want to see what a V.P. looks like and if he walks and has teeth."

Truman's access to Roosevelt would be limited. The president kept Truman uninformed on several matters, chief among them the development of the atomic bomb. While Ferrell believes Truman had inklings of the project through his Senate committee's investigation of defense contracts, Roosevelt didn't deign to pass on any details.

The lack of communication between the two is suggested by Truman's April 5, 1945, handwritten note to the president. The note, today held by the Truman Museum, suggests Hannegan for postmaster general.

"Hate to bother you," Truman wrote, "but I have a suggestion to make."

Beyond the lack of access, Truman may have begun to sense the burden on his shoulders. Several friends later recalled a sudden loneliness in the new vice president.

Truman may have thought that he would serve as vice president for perhaps a year or two.

Instead, he served eighty-two days.

Another friend, Eddie McKim, heard Truman admit to anxiety following a White

Barkley told a story. It concerned a Kentucky Republican who had headed for Frankfort in 1895, looking for a job after the state elected a Republican governor. Six months later, the still-jobless Republican headed back home on his mule.

"All my life I've heard that the office should seek the man," the man told a friend on the road. "Well, I've been here six months and haven't seen an office seeking a man yet. If you happen to run across one after I've gone, will you please tell it

---

ORAL HISTORIES

Edward D. McKim, Kansas City resident who served as a private in Battery D; long-time Truman friend and political aide. After leaving a White House reception during Truman's brief vice presidency:

"When we left we walked down to the other gate and that's when I stopped Truman and told him to turn around and take a look at that place; that was where he was going to be living. And he said, 'I'm afraid you're right, Eddie.' And he said, 'And it scares the hell out of me.'"

House reception before Roosevelt's death.

"When we left we walked down to the other gate and that's when I stopped Truman and told him to turn around and take a look at that place; that was where he was going to be living," McKim said in his Truman Museum oral history.

"And he said, 'I'm afraid you're right, Eddie.' And he said, 'And it scares the hell out of me.'"

But others – especially fellow politicians – weren't buying the demure Truman. One was Alben Barkley, the Kentucky senator who later became Truman's own vice president. One night during their administration Truman and Barkley spoke at the same banquet.

that I'm a-ridin' out of Somerset Pike, and ridin' damn slow."

As late as the 1960s, Truman routinely insisted that he hadn't sought the office. "I never wanted to run for vice president and discouraged the talk about it," Truman said in an outtake from a television interview from the early 1960s and released by the Truman Museum in 2003. "But it didn't do any good.

"When I got to Chicago I went around to the various leaders of the organizations over the country, and I knew 'em all at the time. And not a single one of them would agree to support Byrnes. They said, 'If we can't have Henry Wallace, we want you.' Well, I said, 'I'm not a candidate, I don't want to be vice president.'"

Truman then described how Hannegan, Democratic party leader, convinced him to follow him to a hotel room filled with party elders. Soon President Roosevelt was on the telephone, and he asked Hannegan whether he had that "fellow" lined up. Hannegan replied that he had not, that Truman represented the "contrariest Missouri mule I ever came in contact with."

Roosevelt's response was emphatic, said Truman in the 1960s interview, his voice rising in an imitation of Roosevelt's patrician tones.

" 'Well,' the president said – when the president talked to you on the telephone, all he needed to do was raise the window; he didn't need a phone to talk to you, from one end of the country to the other – he said, 'You tell him, if he wants to break up the Democratic Pah-ty in the middle of a war, and maybe lose that war, that's his responsibility.'

"Well, I was floored. I was sunk."

AVOIDING SCANDAL

 ne day in the 1920's, while serving as Jackson County presiding judge, Truman knocked on a door inside a Kansas City hotel.

When a blonde woman wearing only a negligee opened the door, the future president turned and ran.

The story was told some forty years later by Edgar Hinde, longtime Truman friend and Independence postmaster, who witnessed the episode after being asked by Truman to accompany him to the hotel. Truman, who had been asked to report to the hotel room, apparently had smelled something and had brought along Hinde for protection.

It was typical of Harry Truman to have personal radar so sensitive to possible entrapment, Hinde said. "He had a phobia" about such situations, Hinde added. Truman's relentless decorum seemed strange even to Hinde, who also recalled how Truman

remained on alert for compromising situations while attending American Legion conventions.

"He had his room there, and naturally everybody would kind of gravitate to his room," Hinde said in 1962. "If some fellow brought a woman in there, or his wife, even, I've seen him [Truman] pick up his hat and coat and take off out of there, and that would be the last you'd see of him until those women left."

If Harry Truman was so averse to personal scandal in the 1920s, he may have been only more so in 1944, when he insisted to friends that he didn't want the vice presidential nomination at the 1944 Democratic National Convention.

He said as much to longtime friend Tom Evans, who couldn't understand why

Truman didn't want to be President Franklin Roosevelt's running mate. But Truman, Evans remembered in a 1963 oral history, said he didn't want to drag a lot of "skeletons out of the closet."

"And he said, 'Well, the worst thing is that I've had the boss,' meaning Mrs. Truman, 'on the payroll in my Senate office and I'm not going to have her name drug over the front pages of the paper and over the radio,' " Evans said.

Soon after Truman accepted the nomination and the campaign began, the news of Bess Truman's office salary hit the papers.

But Truman could only blame himself. He had appointed Bess to the payroll in 1941 at a $4,500 annual salary that was the highest among his office staff. In 1943, he added his sister, Mary Jane, to the payroll at $1,800 a year. It's possible the family simply needed the money. In the same 1944 conversation with Evans, Truman told him he was still in debt from his 1940 Senate campaign and couldn't afford any new campaign expenses while running for vice president.

But to Bess Truman, the true nightmare was not her presence on the payroll being made public, but her father's 1903 suicide. Having that discussed in the press would have been disaster inside 219 North Delaware. Even Margaret Truman did not know of the nature of her grandfather's death until an aunt casually mentioned it to her in 1944.

"I waited until Dad arrived later in the evening, and I asked him what he knew about it," Margaret later wrote.

"I have never seen him so angry and upset. He seized my arm in a grip that he must have learned when he was wrestling calves and hogs around the farm yard. 'Don't you ever mention that to your mother,' he said."

Clearly the suicide represented radioactive material, not only to Bess Truman, but to her mother, Madge Gates Wallace.

The suicide never surfaced, but Truman enemies made do with other perceived shortcomings. Truman's alleged membership in the Ku Klux Klan surfaced late in the 1944 campaign. In 1949, newspapers investigated the "five-percenters," or influence peddlers within the Truman administration who allegedly took 5 percent of the dollar value of all government contracts secured. One motivated Truman basher, William Bradford Huie, editor of the *American Mercury* magazine, traveled to Independence in the early 1950s to further research his topic.

One of his stops was to visit Sue Gentry, a longtime journalist with the *Examiner* of Independence and Truman family friend. "He came into the office and said, 'I know all this Pollyanna stuff about Harry Truman, but I am looking for some dirt, ' " Gentry said. "I said, 'Sir, if I knew any dirt about Harry Truman I would certainly never tell you.' "

Harry Truman would take a drink, and enjoyed small-stakes gambling around the poker table. But the overwhelming preponderance of evidence is that, when it came to sex, Truman was the same man who fled hotel rooms in the 1920s. In a 1988 interview, Secret Service officer Floyd Boring recalled an Army officer who, during the 1945 Potsdam conference near Berlin, noticed that President Truman was not traveling with his wife. He wondered whether, if the president wanted for anything, perhaps he could arrange it.

"And he [the president] said, 'Hold it, don't say anything more,'" Boring said. "He said, 'I love my wife, and my wife is my sweetheart.' He said, 'I don't want to do that kind of stuff.' And he said, 'I don't want you to ever say that again to me.' "

CHAPTER 8

THE PRESIDENTIAL YEARS

In 1900 William McKinley campaigned on the full dinner pail.

But in 1945 it was Harry Truman who received the full plate.

His first decision, made minutes after being sworn in to replace Franklin Roosevelt as president on April 12, was to confirm plans to proceed with the United Nations organizing conference, scheduled to begin in San Francisco later that month. He then scheduled a meeting with Secretary of War Henry Stimson, who wanted to talk to Truman about a secret weapon of terrible power.

On April 16, Truman addressed a joint session of Congress.

On April 23, Truman received V. M. Molotov, Soviet foreign minister, for the first time and told him that the United States wouldn't recognize any government in Poland that didn't allow free elections.

On April 25, Truman received his first full briefing on the Manhattan Project, about which, many historians believe, Truman had known next to nothing.

On May 8, Truman's sixty-first birthday, he announced the end of the war in Europe.

In the midst of this, Truman received a series of letters from his sister, Mary Jane Truman, who since April 12 had been dealing with interview requests for both her and

Jackson County courthouse in Independence, where Truman had presided over the county court only a few years earlier, formed a background for his return as president of the United States in June 1945. His daughter, Margaret, sat beside him, and brother, Vivian Truman, was the other occupant of the back seat.

her mother, Martha Ellen Young Truman, back in Grandview, Missouri. What about Mother's Day? she asked. Was Truman coming home to Missouri, or should they come to Washington? If so, their mother needed new clothes.

There was just too much for her to do, Mary Jane wrote, and she wasn't sure if she could get it all done.

The president, writing back, asked his sister to bear up.

For the next seven years and nine months, Truman had little choice but to bear up himself, as threats and crises both at home and abroad threatened to buffet him and the nation.

Some fifteen years before becoming president, as presiding judge of Jackson County, Missouri, Truman sometimes fled from the pressures of office, seeking sanctuary in Kansas City's Pickwick Hotel, or in retreats in Arkansas.

As president, there was no escaping for Truman. When he did leave the White House for Key West, Florida, as he often did, he was trailed by an entourage of advisers and correspondents. Yet while it is unrealistic for any president to try to disappear, neither did Truman seem inclined to. Years after Truman's presidency, his physician, Wallace Graham, recalled only that in moments of stress, Truman suffered a mild buildup of

President Truman entering the U.S. courthouse in Kansas City, June 1945. Fred Canfil, U.S. marshal, proudly held the umbrella for the president, who briefly visited his courthouse office.

fluid in his lungs.

Sometimes he strained his eyes, often reading official papers late into the night. But that appeared to be the only effects of the pressures of the White House upon Truman's physical health. In fact, Truman's principal dislike about the White House was merely that quite often wife Bess Truman or daughter Margaret Truman were not in residence there with him. Bess would desert Washington for Independence, often to be with her elderly mother, and Margaret would sometimes accompany her.

Alone, Truman would persevere.

Today it's appropriate that much of the American cultural shorthand used to invoke Harry Truman involves his refusal to retreat:If you can't stand the heat, get out of the kitchen. The buck stops here. Give 'em hell. All of these recall the resolve that President Truman brought to his task.

If reduced to telegraphic terms, the crises that Truman faced during his administration seem numbing. The war. The bomb. Steel strike. Railroad strike. The Cold War. Containing communism. Marshall Plan. Civil rights. Israel. The Berlin airlift. The "Gone Goose" (how one-time Republican congresswoman Clare Boothe Luce derided Truman during the 1948 Republican National Convention). Whistlestop. NATO. Korea. MacArthur.

The permanent exhibit devoted to Truman's presidential administration that the Truman Presidential Museum & Library in Independence unveiled in 2001 seeks to make coherent this dizzying succession of events. The exhibit's first artifact showcased is the small, standard-issue Gideon Bible found in the White House on April 12, 1945, and pressed into service to swear Truman in upon the death of

President Franklin Roosevelt.

"Boys, if you ever pray, pray for me now," Truman told reporters after encountering a crowd of them while visiting the Capitol the next day.

A quick left turn, and visitors to the Truman Museum exhibit find themselves fully immersed in the latter weeks of the Pacific War.

There, visitors confront four video monitors simultaneously detailing the race to produce the atomic bomb, the fire bombings of Japanese cities in 1945, the military campaigns that same year on the Pacific Islands of Iwo Jima and Okinawa, and the ongoing American propaganda offensive against the Japanese.

If visitors find the experience overwhelming, it's likely pretty close to what Harry Truman was feeling in the summer months of 1945.

In July, Truman learned of the successful test of an atomic bomb in New Mexico, and soon authorized its use against Japan.

The United States bombed Hiroshima on August 6, 1945, and Nagasaki on August 9.

The Japanese surrendered on August 14.

The entire country celebrated. Then the hangover arrived. For the next several months, the economy struggled to regain its footing. During the war the government had employed price and wage controls to restrain inflation. Washington removed those controls in 1946 and inflation soon followed. Further, by February 1946, more than two million workers had gone on strike in the country's steel, car, mining, and railroad industries. That November, during the 1946 elections, the Democratic Party lost both houses of Congress.

Meanwhile, Truman had to deal with a former ally, the Soviet Union, whose expansionist ambitions were becoming more and more clear. Then, in 1947, Great Britain announced that it could no longer afford to offer assistance to Greece and Turkey.

In response, Truman proposed a package of military and economic aid to the two nations in a March 1947 address to Congress. The speech outlined what came to be known as the Truman Doctrine. In his eighteen-minute talk, Truman warned of the dangers of inaction in Europe.

"I believe it must be the policy of the United States to support free peoples who are resisting attempted subjugation by armed minorities or by outside pressures," Truman said. Should America fail to act, he added, "the effect will be far reaching to the West as well as to the East."

In April 1947, Congress approved $400 million in aid to Greece and Turkey. The next month Truman signed the authorizing documents at Kansas City's Muehlebach Hotel.

Yet, in regard to Europe, Truman wasn't done. George Marshall, secretary of state under Truman, proposed a massive economic program for European recovery during a June 1947 speech at Harvard University. Truman had asked Marshall to affix his name to the plan, knowing the respect Marshall commanded among members of both parties. Congress approved the Marshall Plan in April 1948.

By the early 1950s, Europe would emerge from economic crisis.

The Cold War, characterized by diplomatic skirmishes between the United States and the Soviet Union since the end of World War II, took an ominous turn in

Bess and Margaret Truman, back home for a short stay in November 1944 after joining Harry Truman's campaign tour.

The Independence home of President Truman undergoing repairs in May 1945 in anticipation of its becoming the Summer White House.

food, coal, and other necessities. In the Truman Museum's presidential years exhibit, the hundreds of planes that landed every day are symbolized by 594 miniature airplanes suspended from above. Ultimately the Soviets would lift the blockade in May 1949.

In February 1948, Truman sent a special

June 1948. The Soviet Union, hoping to force the Allies to abandon Berlin, blocked all rail, highway, and water traffic in and out of the city, isolating the approximately 2.5 million people living in Berlin's Allied sectors.

Truman, knowing that forcing open a land route might prompt a shooting war, instead chose to approve an air-supply operation to aid West Berlin. Planes flew in

civil rights message to Congress. He was the first president to do so. The message, based on the findings of Truman's civil rights commission, called for a federal law against lynching, more effective protections of voting rights, and a possible integration of the country's armed forces.

In May 1948, Truman chose to extend de facto recognition of the new state of

Israel. The United States was the first country to do so. The decision was a great disappointment to George Marshall, the one man in Washington whom Truman may have admired above all others.

But Truman had been aware of Zionist dreams of a Jewish state in Palestine.

recognition to Israel on May 14.

Some wonder whether Truman's decision was influenced in part to win Jewish support in the upcoming 1948 presidential election. That spring, Truman's approval rating slumped to 36 percent. Many commentators speculated as to whether

President Truman greets representatives from *The Kansas City Star* outside his Independence home in June 1945.

Further, he received at the White House Jewish friends from Kansas City, chief among them his former haberdashery partner, Eddie Jacobson.

Jacobson lobbied Truman to allow Chaim Weizmann, a world Zionist leader, to visit him. Truman, at first angered that Jacobson would push him on the issue, ultimately agreed to meet Weizmann.

Ultimately, the United States extended

Truman should resign, allowing the Democratic Party to nominate a candidate with a better chance of winning.

Truman was presiding over a three-way split in the Democratic Party. Southern members, known as Dixiecrats, resenting the many civil rights initiatives of Truman, bolted the party. Led by South Carolina Governor Strom Thurmond, they formed the States Rights Democratic Party.

Meanwhile, former Vice President Henry Wallace, dumped in 1944 by party officials in favor of Truman, was leading the Progressive Party.

Few gave Truman any chance of winning. Republicans, confident of victory, voted to increase the $50,000 salary of the next president, who they were certain was

train, bringing what came to be called his "whistlestop" campaign to scores of small communities. Soon, supporters could be heard to yell, "Give 'em hell, Harry!" By election day on November 2, 1948, syndicated columnists already were speculating on the first initiatives launched by President Dewey. One newspaper, the

Mary Ethel Noland, first cousin to Harry Truman. On election night, November 2, 1948:

"Then the day came for election and the broadcasting company asked if they might set up a broadcasting station here – and they set it up in the front room. We thought, 'If it will help them any, yes, go ahead and set it up, but we're not interested at all.'

"Along in the evening the returns had begun to come in. We were sitting in the next room trying to read our paper or something because we hated to hear that everything was going against him. One of the men said, 'Don't you want to hear this? It's getting better, you'd better come in.'

"And so we went into the front room, and it did get better, and our friends began to drop in, and we had a roomful. We began to serve coffee; we began to hunt for cookies and doughnuts and something to eat; and we began to get pretty cheerful. And that went on all night long."

going to be New York Governor Thomas Dewey.

But Truman electrified the delegates attending the Democratic National Convention in Philadelphia. Arriving at the podium with vice presidential nominee Alben Barkley at about two A.M., Truman came out swinging. "Senator Barkley and I will win this election and make these Republicans like it – don't you forget that." The Democrats left their convention energized, as did Truman.

The president traveled the country by

Chicago Daily Tribune, had printed an early election edition declaring Dewey the winner.

It was a copy of this edition that someone handed Truman while the newly elected president had stopped in St. Louis en route back to Washington.

The subsequent inauguration the following January was held in dazzling winter sunshine.

But the fair weather didn't last. In the fall of 1949, the United States learned that the Soviet Union had tested an atomic bomb. With the tensions of the Cold War escalating, fear of Communist infiltration in the homeland led to a repressive climate today symbolized by the rise of Wisconsin senator Joseph McCarthy. In February 1950, McCarthy claimed to have a list of Communists employed by the State Department.

McCarthy's tactics angered Truman.

atomic bomb.

In June 1950, Truman was visiting his Independence home when he received a telephone call from Secretary of State Dean Acheson telling him that North Korea had invaded South Korea. Truman authorized sending American troops to South Korea and persuaded the United Nations to lend

But back in 1947, the president also had issued Executive Order 9835, establishing a federal employees loyalty and security program, a move never before made during peacetime. The program subjected federal employees to loyalty background checks. It also afforded political cover for Truman, who now could deny he was coddling Communists in the government.

In March 1950 Truman approved a project to build a hydrogen bomb, a weapon far more destructive than the original

support. But by 1951, Korea had become a stalemate, eroding much of Truman's popularity.

Meanwhile, General Douglas MacArthur, head of the United Nations force in Korea, was advocating bombing cities in China, which had since entered the conflict. Truman refused, feeling it could prompt a still wider war. Ultimately Truman fired the popular MacArthur to demonstrate that American military policy still was directed by civilians, not military officers.

In June 1945 Truman made his first visit back to Jackson County after becoming president. One stop was for dinner with Independence Mayor Roger T. Sermon, seen here to the right of the president. Also present were Charlie Ross, Truman's press secretary, to the right of Sermon, and at the far left, James Pendergast, Truman's political associate.

More than 36,000 Americans died in the Korean War. Truman's approval ratings sank. The heartbroken parents of some soldiers who had died in the war wrote the president, sometimes returning their sons' medals or decorations.

Truman kept one such Purple Heart close to him the rest of his life. He chose not to run for re-election and returned to Independence in January 1953, after the inauguration of President Dwight Eisenhower.

President Truman at an Army/Navy football game.

"Train pulled out amid cheers & tears," Truman wrote in his diary on January 20, 1953, describing his and Bess's departure from Washington's Union Station following Eisenhower's inauguration. "Crowd at Silver Spring, Md., some three or four hundred. Crowd at Harpers Ferry, Grafton, and it was reported to me at every stop all night long. Same way across Indiana and Illinois."

The legacy of the Truman presidential administration is testified to every spring by speakers invited to Independence and Kansas City to receive annual awards in Truman's name.

There are two awards: the Harry S. Truman Award for Public Service, given by the city of Independence, and the Harry S. Truman Good Neighbor Award, presented by a private foundation.

So numerous are the challenges faced by Truman during his presidency that speakers sometimes have trouble focusing on just one. Sam Nunn, former U.S. senator from Georgia and former head of the Senate Armed Service Committee, chose to wonder in 1997 what might have happened had not Truman resolved to fire the popular Douglas MacArthur in 1951.

"Would we still have civilian control of the military?" asked Nunn. But Nunn described other initially unpopular Truman decisions, such as the integration of the U.S. military and the Marshall Plan, which rebuilt much of Europe. Such decisions, despite being controversial, now are credited with preventing world history from unfolding in some unknown and probably unfortunate ways, Nunn said.

"We can all thank God that we have not had to face the consequences," he added.

Historian John Hope Franklin in 1999 cited Truman's establishment of a presidential civil rights commission whose subsequent report, "To Secure These Rights," released in 1947, influenced the ensuing fifty years of American race relations.

"He was the first president of the United States to appoint a commission to study the question and bring in recommendations," Franklin said of Truman. "There had been no president of the U.S. who had ever spoken out against segregation, in any way, until President Truman came around."

Truman's decision to use the atomic bomb near the end of World War II stands up despite recent criticism by some historians, said cartoonist Bill Mauldin in 1996.

"It always seemed to me that a lot of the flak about him, with the bombing of Hiroshima, showed a lack of knowledge of what the situation was in those days," Mauldin said. "I thought he did right."

Espionage thriller author Tom Clancy also saluted Truman for his courage in deploying the atomic weapons in 1945. "Of course he did the right thing," Clancy said in 1998. "Is there anybody here who doubts that?" Clancy also credited Truman with the establishment of the North Atlantic Treaty Organization, the integration of the U.S. military, and the ultimate containment of communism.

President Truman, while on his morning walk in Independence, stops to give his autograph to a young girl.

Bess and Harry Truman in the family quarters of the White House at Christmastime.

"All in all, not a bad legacy for a man who never wanted to be president but got stuck with the job," he said. Finally, there was Truman's personal character and integrity, Clancy added.

"What kind of man was Harry Truman?" Clancy asked. "Well, for one thing, you could trust your daughter around him."

In 1998 former Republican president Gerald Ford praised Truman's bipartisanship when he appointed Herbert Hoover, another former Republican president, to survey the world food crisis after World War II.

"In utilizing such expertise, Mr. Truman displayed a generosity and a bipartisan spirit that modern politicians in this era would do well to imitate," Ford said.

Former Missouri Senator John Danforth, another Republican, in 1994 commented upon Truman's wisdom in perceiving how the memories of voters sometimes soften over the years. "A statesman," Danforth said, quoting Truman, "is a politician who's been dead ten or fifteen years."

Finally, the long list of crises that Truman faced while president can be seen today as an example of the leadership that presidents, as well as all elected officials, can provide, Paul Simon, Democrat and former senator from Illinois, said in 2003.

"If Truman were alive today," Simon said, "he'd say, 'Face your problems, don't duck them.'"

President Truman is welcomed
home to Kansas City in 1947.

While delivering an address to Congress on March 1, 1945, Franklin Roosevelt's hands had trembled while turning the pages of his speech.

Among those who noticed was Vice President Harry Truman.

And yet, judging by Truman's diary excerpts written only several weeks later, Roosevelt's death on April 12, 1945, came as a surprise.

"I am not easily shocked but was certainly shocked when I was told of the President's death and the weight of the Government had fallen on my shoulders," Truman wrote in one diary excerpt. And yet in the very next paragraph, Truman struck a jaunty note. He recounted returning to his Connecticut Avenue apartment to find wife Bess, daughter Margaret, and mother-in-law Madge Gates Wallace eating turkey in a neighbor's flat. Truman had his own turkey sandwich, then went back across the hall.

"Went to bed, went to sleep and did not worry anymore," he wrote.

Before Roosevelt died of a cerebral hemorrhage in Warm Springs, Georgia, at 4:45 P.M. Washington time, Truman's day had been routine.

In his mail that morning, Truman had heard from Kansas City friend Jim Pendergast. The Pendergast Wholesale Liquor Company, Truman learned, was having trouble finding sufficient supplies of bottles and cartons needed to distribute eleven thousand barrels of whiskey stored in Kentucky.

"We will see what we can do right away," Truman dictated in a reply.

Truman spent the rest of the day presiding over the Senate. The main business concerned a water treaty with Mexico. During the deliberations, Truman scribbled one of his many letters to his mother Martha Ellen and sister Mary Jane back in Grandview, Missouri.

"I am trying to write you a letter today from the desk of the President of the Senate," Truman wrote, "while a windy Senator from Wisconsin is making a speech on a subject with which he is in no way familiar."

Truman's letter noted that it was raining that day.

The Senate recessed at four minutes until five P.M. Truman then reported to House Speaker Sam Rayburn's "hideaway" office at the Capitol. As he mixed a drink, he returned a call from Steve Early, Roosevelt's press secretary.

Truman's face then drained of color. He swore an oath invoking Jesus Christ, Andrew Jackson or both, according to various sources.

Truman, age sixty, took off at a sprint. He dashed the length of the Capitol to his office and grabbed his hat. He rode with his chauffeur to the White House.

"Mrs. Roosevelt and Steve Early were there," Truman wrote in the same diary excerpt. "Mrs. Roosevelt put her arm around my shoulder and said `The President is dead.' That was the first inkling I had of the seriousness of the situation."

This was at 5:25 P.M. For the next ninety minutes, official Washington scrambled. Cabinet members were summoned, as was U.S. Supreme Court Chief Justice Harlan Stone. Truman himself rang his Connecticut Avenue apartment.

In her memoir of her mother, Margaret Truman remembers that call coming at about six P.M., and that her father's voice had an "odd, tight" quality. He asked to speak to his wife.

At the White House, they needed a Bible. The only volume available was a standard-issue Gideon that had to be dusted off. With Bess and Margaret standing nearby, Truman took the oath of office at 7:09 P.M. *The New York Times* reporters present described Truman's face as "grave."

Truman's first decision was to give the official go-ahead for the San Francisco United Nations conference. He briefly addressed the Cabinet, asking for its support.

The thirty-third president then remembered to call Eddie McKim, his former artillery battery member, to cancel a planned poker game that night at a nearby hotel. Then he called Tom Evans, a longtime Kansas City confidant, then recuperating from a vocal cord ailment.

"Now I just want to tell you one thing," Truman told him. "You are not to come back to Washington until I give the orders. I want you to know that I've got plenty of power now and if you don't do as I tell you to do, you're going to be in all kinds of trouble."

The press, meanwhile, wondered what kind of trouble Truman might now be in. The first reporter to gain entry to the Oval Office was Roy Roberts of *The Kansas City Star*. In exchange for the access, Roberts damned with faint praise.

"What a story in democracy," Roberts wrote in a piece widely syndicated, "that a man approaching 40 and still looking at the rear of a horse as he plowed the corn rows, apparently not a success in life, just a little less than twenty years ago, should find himself today President of the greatest and most powerful nation on earth."

In their April 23 issue, the same *Time* magazine editors who had chosen Truman for

their magazine's cover just two years before now found themselves underwhelmed.

"With almost complete unanimity, Harry Truman's friends – in Washington and across the land – agreed last week that he 'would not be a great president,' " they announced.

No doubt the wire-rimmed Missourian suffered by comparison with the pince-nezed New

President Truman chats with Jim Pendergast while Bess talks to Independence Mayor Roger T. Sermon on a visit back to Independence.

Yorker who had led the country through the Great Depression and world war since 1933.

Much of the country was in shock. Many young adults, like Margaret Truman, could not recall anyone else occupying the White House. Radio didn't transmit an advertisement or soap opera for four days. Instead, broadcasters filled airtime with mournful eulogies and recordings of Roosevelt speeches.

"Coming from funeral train – old and young were crying in the streets," Truman recorded in his diary.

On April 16 Truman addressed a joint session of Congress. After twelve years of Roosevelt's elegant speaking voice, some Americans might have felt a symphony timpani had been replaced by an Ozark washboard. Where Roosevelt

had rendered "pah-ti" from *party* and "moth-uh" from *mother*. Truman's dialect rang with Southernisms, wrote one *New York Times* contributor. Truman sometimes broke up a vowel into a diphthong, transforming *fill* into "fih-uhl" and *soul* into "soh-uhl."

While Truman was no doubt

stunned by Roosevelt's death, historian Robert Ferrell has pointed out that Roosevelt had been pushing Truman around for about ten years.

When Truman first had arrived in Washington in 1935, the president ignored the new senator. By 1939, however, Roosevelt had developed an interest in Missouri politics. During a March meeting with Truman, he displayed detailed knowledge of Otto P. Higgins, the Pendergast police chief in Kansas City who wanted Washington intervention against Maurice Milligan, a federal attorney digging into Kansas City vote fraud.

For Truman, who had flourished under Boss Tom Pendergast's sponsorship, this could not have been comforting. The next month, a federal grand jury indicted Pendergast for tax evasion.

When Missouri Governor Lloyd Stark soon made a bid for Truman's Senate seat, it became clear that Roosevelt was scheming with Stark. In January 1940 a Roosevelt staff member called to offer Truman a lifetime appointment on the Interstate Commerce Commission, a job that paid better than that of senator. An angry Truman declined and went on to defeat Stark in the Democratic primary.

But Roosevelt wasn't through. He apparently downplayed Truman's new defense investigation committee. In 1941, South Carolina Senator James Byrnes, in charge of committee budgets, gave Truman's panel only $15,000. "I think Byrnes went to Roosevelt, who said `Starve him,' " Robert Ferrell said. Later, when the committee proved a success, Roosevelt claimed credit.

Despite all that, Truman wound up with the vice presidential nomination in 1944 when party insiders angled to remove Henry Wallace from the ticket. But Roosevelt remained aloof from his running mate, meeting only twice with him during Truman's eighty-two days as vice president.

Faced by the unknown, Truman turned to the familiar. His close friends, many of them with military backgrounds, began reporting for duty. The first visitor to Truman's office on April 13 was Eddie McKim, a former member of Truman's World War I artillery battery who arrived at 9 A.M. Truman made McKim an administrative assistant.

From a distance, another old friend urged him on. "Get in there and pitch," Jim Pendergast, Tom's nephew, said in a telegram.

"You can handle it."

Truman also received British Foreign Secretary Anthony Eden, who later cabled British Prime Minister Winston Churchill that the new president seemed "honest and friendly."

In his first week Truman signed the Mexican water treaty that had been debated by the Senate during Truman's last day presiding there as vice president – an eternity ago, it must have seemed like.

Truman's first full day in office had been Friday the 13th. But for his next few months, luck stayed with the thirty-third president. In May, Americans accorded him an 87 percent Gallup approval rating, higher than Roosevelt ever had enjoyed.

His popularity, however, had fallen in Grandview, home of Truman's mother, Martha Ellen, and sister, Mary Jane. Truman's new role as president had resulted in a plague of press, with reporters and photographers all wanting time with both women. "Why do such things have to happen when I have so much to do?" Mary Jane wrote her brother, the president, in late April.

"You both have done fine under this terrible blow," Truman replied.

President Truman smiles for the hundreds of
persons gathered to watch him leave the
U.S. courthouse in Kansas City, where he
had spent several hours working in his office
in June 1945.

TRUMAN AND POKER

It's April 12, 1945.

A telephone rings in a room at the Statler Hotel in Washington. There, Eddie McKim, a former private in Harry Truman's World War I artillery battery, has prepared the evening's poker game. A green felt table has been delivered by a hotel bellhop. McKim himself, upon Truman's instructions, has gone to the vice president's Capitol Hill office and taken several bottles of scotch and bourbon for the game.

At about five P.M., McKim received a message that the vice president would be on his way over as soon as he returned a telephone call from the White House. But Harry hasn't shown. Then McKim switches on the room's radio and hears that President Franklin Roosevelt has died that afternoon in Warm Springs, Georgia, and that Truman will be sworn in as the new president.

At some point the telephone rings again. McKim picks it up and a voice says, "Eddie?"

"Mr. President," McKim says.

"I guess the party's off," President Truman says.

So goes the story that McKim told a Truman Library researcher in 1964. The canceled poker party of April 12, 1945, is not mentioned in most Truman literature. But there's little doubt that Truman loved to play poker, and he respected the game's rituals and etiquette. From his perspective, Roosevelt's shocking death had not only elevated him to the presidency—it also had left several poker players without their host.

This was rare, as not even matters of the most profound importance could keep President Truman from his poker games. In a July 1945 letter to Bess from Berlin, where Truman was attending the Potsdam conference, the president defended his purchase of a luncheon set of Belgian lace, which had proved pricey. "But I came out a few dollars to the good in the game of chance on the boat, so it's invested in a luxury for you . . ."

The game figured in Truman's subsequent presidential administration in several ways.

In March 1946, when former British prime minister Winston Churchill rode the presidential train from Washington to central Missouri to deliver his "Iron Curtain" speech at Westminster College in Fulton, he played poker with Truman and several of the president's aides.

The game was one way Truman and Churchill, who met the year before in Potsdam, could take one another's measure. Upon Roosevelt's death the previous year Churchill had, from a distance, found Truman wanting. But the ensuing poker game proved the beginning of a genuine friendship, notwithstanding some delicate moments during the game itself.

In 1948, the game figured in the official recognition by the United States of the infant state of Israel.

Two prominent members of the Kansas City Jewish community – A. J. Granoff, a lawyer, and Eddie Jacobson, Truman's former Kansas City haberdashery partner – had played poker with Truman throughout the 1930s. In 1948, while President Truman grappled with the benefits and drawbacks of de facto recognition of Israel, both Granoff and Jacobson visited Truman in the White House.

Jacobson in particular asked Truman to receive the Jewish leaders who wished to plead their case in person. Truman ultimately agreed to meet the diplomats and later, on May 14, 1948, extended the official recognition that both Granoff and Jacobson wanted.

The game also contributed the principal icon of the Truman presidency, the brown wooden desk ornament bearing the legend THE BUCK STOPS HERE. The word *buck* derived from the buckhorn-handled knife that in frontier days sometimes was used as a marker in a poker game.

Those not wishing to deal the cards simply passed the marker, or buck, to the next player.

Some historians have noted how Truman's public affection for poker contributed to the image of the plain-speaking president with a common touch. Yet the same game proved one way for Truman to find his place within the membership of the exclusive Kansas City Club, which he joined in 1945. He was made a member of 822, the card club named for the room that members occupied in the high-rise club building in downtown Kansas City.

Ultimately the game serves as metaphor for the crafty Missouri politician who, some say, was a reluctant president, but nevertheless in 1944 allowed himself to be named Franklin Roosevelt's running mate at a time when

President Truman's poker chips with a wooden carrier and deck of cards. The leather card case was stamped "Senator H. S. Truman," but remained in use and was shipped back from the White House.

After the war Truman and his army buddies formed the Harpie Club, an Independence poker fellowship, which met on the second floor of this building. In 2003 the building was occupied by Keepsake Fudge and Finery, but a plaque reminds visitors of its earlier history. *Photos by Tammy Ljungblad*

insiders – Truman especially – knew that the president was in ill health.

Truman's long involvement with poker dates back at least to World War I. Edgar Hinde, a fellow officer with Truman in the 129th Field Artillery, recalls games occurring whenever the officers from Independence and Kansas City would gather in France. "Oh, we played every time we got together," said Hinde, adding, "It was just about the only recreation we had."

The players reconvened in peacetime, forming the Harpie Club, an Independence poker fellowship that met Monday nights. The club took its name from a harmonica-playing contest a member won in a local theater. Club members sometimes convened in private homes, but more often assembled in one of several buildings on Independence Square. Truman Museum archivists identify the principal Harpie Club site as 101 North Main Street.

Truman friend Edgar Hinde recalled Truman attending Harpie Club events perhaps twice while president. Hinde also recalled warning a *Look*

magazine photographer who had expressed interest in examining the club's interior that such an intrusion wouldn't be considered neighborly.

Besides, Hinde said, the place wasn't that interesting.

"All they had up there was a poker table and an ice box and a beer pump," he said years later. "That was about all that was there – and chairs, because that was all we did, play poker once a month." Added Hinde: "They never did get a picture of the inside of the club. Why, good gosh, that would have been pitiful."

As president, Truman used the game as a release. By then, Truman's poker retreat was a floating one, the presidential yacht *Williamsburg*.

"The President deals left-handed [and] loves to taunt anyone needing a particular card," columnist Drew Pearson once wrote. "When dealing, if he has dropped out of play, he will peek mischievously at the card before dealing, then slap it down and chuckle gleefully if it's the wrong card. Sometimes he takes a poll of what his guests want to play, then deals something else."

The Churchill-Truman poker encounter was not quite like that. Churchill had suggested playing the game while on the train heading for Fulton. Then he had excused himself.

According to a memoir written by former special counsel Clark Clifford, Truman turned to his aides and appealed to their patriotism. In what Clifford described as "total seriousness," Truman described the task ahead as worthy of their best efforts.

"This man has been playing poker for more than forty years," Truman said, adding that the "reputation of American poker is at stake and I expect every man to do his duty."

When the game began, however, Clifford wrote, "the truth emerged." Churchill was not very good.

After an hour Churchill excused himself yet again. Again, Truman turned to his aides, this time with an expression that Clifford described as "grave." Churchill was about three hundred dollars in the hole. This time Truman instructed his aides to ease up.

They did. Clifford watched as Charlie Ross, Truman's press secretary, folded while holding a winning hand worth a hundred dollars. The British-American alliance held.

Franklin Roosevelt's April 1945 death, by the way, did not cancel the Statler Hotel poker game. It only postponed it.

The following month, Truman and McKim organized the poker game again, this time held inside the White House. The game was interrupted by news, soon proved incorrect, that Germany had surrendered. Truman and his poker buddies left their cards to go down to the Oval Office to tell assembled reporters that there was no truth to the story.

The reporters left to file their stories. Then, according to McKim, the president paused.

"Well, I'm not making any money here," Truman said.

Everyone went back to their hands. McKim drew two sixes. Truman won with a pair of sevens.

The Harpie Club, according to Edgar Hinde, met regularly up until the late 1950s.

In 2002, new owners of the building at 101 North Main Street, on Independence Square, began renovating the building's upper floors to build loft apartments. The construction revealed traces of poker games decades past: a half-pint of gin, a can of Prince Albert tobacco, and two playing cards.

In 2003, the relics were on display inside Keepsake Fudge & Finery, the store that then occupied the site.

Sometime in the 1930s, Truman was invited to play poker by a member of the exclusive Kansas City Club. Later he was made a member of 822, the card club named for the room that members occupied in the high-rise Kansas City building.
Photo by Ray Geselbracht

The United Nations may not have worked without Harry Truman.

His first act as president, on April 12, 1945, was to reaffirm the United States' commitment to creating the world organization. Then, when Communist forces invaded South Korea in 1950, Truman turned to the United Nations, boosting its standing and credibility in the international community.

Yet the promises of the United Nations proved elusive. News articles about the United Nations' twenty-fifth anniversary in 1970 listed several perceived failures. And in recent years, others considered a more sinister meaning behind the talk of world unity.

After the Truman Museum began flying the United Nations flag in 1994, some angry callers demanded its removal. One night in January 1995, thieves stole the flag. That April, three hundred protesters at a "Patriot's Day rally" marched to the library and demanded the flag be taken down.

Truman, however, had always thought the organization deserved a chance.

Tentative plans for a postwar peace organization emerged in 1944 during the Dumbarton Oaks Conference in Washington. Then, in early 1945 at Yalta, Allied leaders scheduled a United Nations conference that April in San Francisco.

Until his death on April 12, 1945, President Franklin Roosevelt had championed the United Nations. Truman, who had been vice president for less than three months, had not been involved. But after taking the oath of office on April 12, the first question presented to Truman concerned the upcoming San Francisco organizing conference. Would it open in late April, as planned?

Yes, Truman said. In his first address to Congress as president on April 16, he described the necessity for a "strong and lasting" United Nations. On April 25, delegates from fifty nations gathered in San Francisco. On June 25, they unanimously adopted the organization's charter. On June 26 Truman flew to San Francisco to sign the charter at San Francisco's War Memorial Opera House.

In Independence on June 27, Truman told an audience of his high hopes for the United Nations. In Kansas City on June 28, Truman described the organization's role to a crowd in Municipal Auditorium. "Now, if Kansas and Colorado have a quarrel over a watershed, they don't call out the National Guard of each state and go to war over it. They bring suit in the Supreme Court and abide by its decision. There isn't a reason in the world why we can't do that diplomatically."

Truman was mindful of how Roosevelt had often, in the White House Cabinet Room, sat beneath a portrait of Woodrow Wilson, who had tried and failed to enlist the United States in the League of Nations after World War I. Wilson had blundered by not including any U.S. senators or influential Republicans among the peace delegation to Paris in 1919.

Republicans later balked at the peace treaty, including membership in the fledgling League of Nations. In desperation, Wilson launched a nationwide speaking campaign to rally support. He collapsed and then suffered a stroke.

The treaty failed in the Senate.

While waiting to ship home from France after World War I, Truman had glimpsed Wilson on his way to a Paris peace conference. At the same time,

President Truman told an audience at the RLDS Auditorium in Independence on June 27, 1945, that he had high hopes for the United Nations.

Truman seemed to have little use for any new world order.

"For my part . . . I don't give a whoop (to put it mildly) whether there's a League of Nations or whether Russia has a Red government or a purple one," he wrote in one letter home. But twenty-six years later, when he became president himself, he quickly affirmed the eight delegates Roosevelt had named to the United Nations conference. They included Republican senators Arthur Vandenberg and Harold Stassen.

The young organization still would be a long way from mediating international disputes.

When Great Britain notified the United States in February 1947 that it was backing out of Greece and Turkey, Truman filled the void. The next month he asked Congress for $400 million in economic and military aid for the two nations. Congress agreed and thereby established a policy, often called the Truman Doctrine, based on containing the threat posed by the Communist Soviet Union. That May, Truman authorized the Greece and Turkey aid package in a brief ceremony at Kansas City's Muehlebach Hotel.

Through the entire process, Truman never mentioned the United Nations.

He took a different tack in 1950, when Communist forces invaded South Korea. He could have ordered U.S. military action without going to the United Nations. But he asked the U.N. Security Council for backing.

Though Truman was a prolific letter writer, he left few personal thoughts on paper about the U.N.

In 1970, he did send a message on the organization's twenty-fifth anniversary.

"If in the intervening twenty-five years the United Nations has not always lived up to our fondest hopes," Truman wrote, "it has nevertheless managed to make substantial contributions to peacekeeping and is deserving of our continued support and cooperation."

No one protested in April 2003 when officials dedicated a new United Nations Peace Plaza located near the Community of Christ Auditorium, where Truman had appeared in June 1945.

THE ATOMIC BOMB

The devastation of the ruined German capital seemed familiar to the former artillery battery commander. He had seen what war was like in France in 1918. But the slump-shouldered refugees of Berlin in 1945 gnawed at him.

"We saw old men, old women, young women, children from tots to teens carrying packs, pushing carts, pulling carts," he wrote in a contemporary diary entry found in 1979, "evidently ejected by the conquerors and carrying what they could of their belongings to nowhere in particular."

The president kept writing, in something of a fury. He invoked Alexander the Great, Genghis Khan, and William Tecumseh Sherman.

Though Harry Truman could have added his own name to the list of conquerors, he didn't. As he was writing on July 16, 1945, he may not even have known that the world's first atomic bomb had been detonated that day at Alamogordo, New Mexico.

Secretary of War Henry Stimson, a member of the American delegation at the post-war conference of Allied powers at Potsdam, near Berlin, did not receive the telegram confirming the test's success until 7:30 P.M. About a week later, while still in Germany, Truman would resolve to use the terrible swift weapon to bring World War II to an end. In only a few days more, fireballs would appear over southern Japan, consuming between 80,000 and 140,000 people in Hiroshima and perhaps half that many in Nagasaki.

The exact figures remain in dispute, as does much of the history surrounding the decision to deploy the atomic bombs.

What is not contested is that Japan surrendered afterward.

The fiftieth anniversary of the Hiroshima and Nagasaki bombings in 1995 stirred long-simmering arguments regarding the wisdom or motives in using the Bomb. Some historians argued that Japan would have surrendered by the end of 1945 even without the use of atomic weapons. Others challenged that assumption, insisting that some Japanese leaders interviewed after the war's end conceded that the bombs had helped persuade them to stop fighting.

The issue was polarizing. The Smithsonian Institution scrapped plans for an exhibit on the bombings after some American veterans and members of Congress complained it would have presented Japan as a victim of the bombings without presenting an adequate picture of Japan's aggression.

Even with the exhibit's cancellation, several points remained in dispute. Among them:

- The casualties that might be expected from an invasion of Japan
- The intentions of the Japanese government, itself split between moderates wishing to surrender and militants insisting on fighting to the end
- The desire of the United States to intimidate and restrain the Kremlin after the war
- Whether early American assurances to Japan of retaining the emperor in a limited ceremonial role might have prompted a surrender without either the atomic bombings or the planned invasion

Largely lost in the argument was the make-up of the man who issued the final decision.

Today the enduring perception of the ultimate button-pusher is of the Missouri plain speaker who worked the math of human misery, made the call, and thought no more of it throughout the remaining twenty-seven years of

The original safety plug from ``Fat Man,'' the atomic bomb dropped on Nagasaki on August 9, 1945, appeared on exhibit at the Truman Museum in 2000.

his life.

Truman himself presented this version in later years when he made breezy statements of bravado, serenely suggesting that the decision was the emotional equivalent of a shrug of the shoulders.

"It was merely another powerful weapon in the arsenal of righteousness," he told students at Columbia University in 1959. "The dropping of the bombs stopped the war, saved millions of lives. It was just the same as artillery on our side. Napoleon said that victory is always on the side of the artillery." And later the same day: "That was not any decision that you had to worry about."

Still, the numbing catalog of bomb-related documents available today at the Truman Museum in Independence suggests that allegation to be baloney.

It shoves aside the president's own letters and diary entries, which detail his personal distress over the weapon. Unlike President Franklin Roosevelt, who authorized the Manhattan Project, Truman actually had led men in battle.

"We have discovered the most terrible bomb in the history of the world," Truman wrote in a July 25, 1945, diary entry at

Potsdam. "It may be the fire destruction prophesied in the Euphrates Valley Era, after Noah and his fabulous Ark."

Truman couldn't help thinking in Old Testament terms. Six years of global conflict had left millions dead, economies shattered, and misery on a biblical scale.

And it seemed far from over. More than two million Japanese troops and thirty million militia members were waiting for the fight on their home islands. What would it take to overcome them?

In 1995, George Elsey, a U.S. Navy intelligence officer who during World War II served in the White House map room, recalled the sight of Truman standing transfixed before the room's large map of Japan. "This weighed on him," Elsey said. "We had just been through the horrible experiences of Okinawa and Iwo Jima."

Seven thousand American soldiers and Marines had died, along with 5,000 sailors, in the three-month Okinawa campaign, which began a few days before Truman came to office on April 12. The number of wounded was 36,000. The total of 12,000 American battle deaths was the worst of any single battle in the Central Pacific campaign, easily surpassing the 6,800 U.S. dead at Iwo Jima. Japanese kamikaze pilots sank 34 American ships, and some 5,000 planes still were based in Japan.

"I have to decide Japanese strategy," Truman wrote the day before a June 18 White House meeting. "Shall we invade Japan proper or shall we bomb and blockade? That is my hardest decision to date. But I'll make it when I have all the facts."

At the meeting, General George C. Marshall, Army chief of staff, told Truman that landing on Kyushu, Japan's southernmost island, appeared to be the "least costly worthwhile operation following Okinawa."

Kyushu could serve as a staging area for the invasion of Honshu, Japan's main island. The assembled brass recommended a November 1, 1945, date for a Kyushu invasion and a March 1,

1946, date for Honshu.

Marshall began by estimating a Kyushu invasion force of 766,000 American troops, twice as many soldiers as had landed during the Normandy invasion the year before. Casualties over the first thirty days, he said, probably would not exceed those experienced in recapturing the Philippine island of Luzon – 31,000 men killed, wounded, or missing in action.

The Navy chief of staff, Admiral Ernest King, guessed at 41,000 casualties. King also passed along the estimate of Admiral Chester Nimitz, the Navy's Pacific commander, of 49,000 casualties.

would mean 40,000 dead, 150,000 wounded and 3,500 missing in action – a total of 193,500 U.S. casualties. Former President Herbert Hoover, meanwhile, estimated that between 500,000 and 1 million Americans would die in an invasion of Japan.

Those numbers would seem appalling enough. But in later years Truman administration policymakers would cite higher figures – suggesting to critics that Truman and his colleagues were struggling to justify their decision to use the atomic weapons.

Documents recently discovered at the Truman Museum, however, indicate that the

This duplicate bomb casing of the ``Fat Man'' atomic bomb used against Nagasaki appeared in a Truman Museum exhibit in 2000. An estimated twenty thousand people died instantly when the bomb fell, and thousands more died during the successive weeks from the effects of radiation.

Admiral William Leahy, the president's chief of staff, mentioned how American forces had suffered 35 percent casualties in taking Okinawa. Given Marshall's estimate of 766,000 troops, that meant total casualties of more than 268,000.

About the same time, military planners had prepared a report with their own numbers: Landings on Kyushu, followed by Honshu,

president found Hoover's memo to be significant and ordered that written appraisals of it be completed by several of his civilian advisers. None had a problem with the figures. "As it turns out," military historian D. M. Giangreco wrote in the spring of 2003, "Truman had a much higher opinion of Hoover than do today's historians."

During the June 18 meeting, no one knew

that the atomic bombs then under development would actually work. When Truman learned one month later that the device performed as advertised, the international equation changed.

In a July 18 letter from Potsdam to his wife Bess, Truman mentioned the pledge of Soviet premier Joseph Stalin to enter the war against the Japanese on August 15. "I'll say that we'll end the war a year sooner now, and think of the kids who won't be killed!" he wrote. "That is the important thing."

The same day in his diary, however, Truman indulged in a more confidential tone.

"Believe [the Japanese] will fold up before Russia comes in," he wrote. "I am sure they will when Manhattan appears over their homeland."

The success of the Manhattan Project rendered previous strategies irrelevant. Richard Rhodes, author of *The Making of the Atomic Bomb*, has maintained that before the successful bomb test in New Mexico, the main goal of the United States was to make sure the Soviet Union entered the war against Japan. U.S. planners were concerned about 1 million Japanese troops positioned in China and Manchuria.

But news of the successful July 16 test persuaded American officials that they didn't need the Soviets. A report on the bomb's successful test arrived at Potsdam on July 21. Where before Truman had been prudent in his dealings

with Stalin and British Prime Minister Winston Churchill, he now grew aggressive.

"Now I know what happened to Truman yesterday," Churchill told Stimson on July 22, after Stimson had shown him the report from New Mexico.

"I couldn't understand it.

In a July 18 letter from Potsdam to his wife Bess, Truman mentioned the pledge of Soviet premier Joseph Stalin to enter the war against the Japanese on August 15. "I'll say that we'll end the war a year sooner now, and think of the kids who won't be killed!" he wrote. "That is the important thing."

When he got to the meeting after having read this report he was a changed man. He told the Russians just where they got on and off and generally bossed the whole meeting."

A week later, Truman scribbled on the back of a cable asking for the bomb's authorization: "Suggestion approved. Release when ready but not sooner than August 2."

At Potsdam, the Allies released an ultimatum: unconditional surrender of all Japanese armed forces. The alternative, according to the July 26 document, was "prompt and utter destruction."

The document didn't refer specifically to Japan's earthly deity, Emperor Hirohito. It said only that occupation forces would be removed after a "peaceful and responsible" government was established according to the freely expressed will of the Japanese people.

Had Truman been more specific about letting Japan keep its revered emperor, some historians speculated, the fighting eventually could have ended without either of the atomic bombs or an invasion.

Others pointed out, however, that Truman inherited a war policy that had included since 1943 Japan's unconditional surrender and Hirohito's capitulation from power. Truman himself reiterated the requirement for unconditional surrender, to thunderous applause, in his first address to Congress on April 16, 1945.

Further, a July 1945 Gallup Poll suggested that Americans were not in a forgiving mood. One-third favored executing Hirohito as a war criminal, and 20 percent wanted him jailed. Only 7 percent said the emperor should stay on.

In that climate, any initial overture by Truman to the emperor may have been unrealistic. One Truman diary entry, however, suggested that the president may have been doubtful about any Japanese surrender. "The target will be a purely military one and we will issue a warning statement asking the Japanese to surrender and

157

save lives," he wrote on July 25. "I'm sure they will not do that, but we will have given them the chance."

On the same day Truman wrote that he had instructed Stimson that the bomb should be used for military objectives only and not to target women and children.

But that would not be possible. The war's civilian death toll had long been rising. The February 1945 raids on Dresden, Germany, by British and American bombers had killed an estimated 135,000 people with incendiary bombs. On March 9 and 10 more than 100,000 Tokyo residents had died in a firebombing. In Europe, American bombers often attempted precision daylight raids on military targets, but in Japan that was more difficult because defense installations often were scattered throughout civilian neighborhoods.

Besides the worry of civilian deaths, Truman also had to consider just which civilians would suffer the atomic bomb's effects and which would not.

"Even if [the Japanese] are savages, ruthless, merciless and fanatic, we as the leader of the world for the common welfare cannot drop this terrible bomb on the old capital or the new," Truman wrote on July 25.

Both Kyoto and Tokyo would, in fact, be spared. A separate target committee had grappled with selecting which cities would be attacked. Hiroshima was first on the list, along with Kyoto, Kokura, and Nigata. Kyoto, Japan's capital from 794 to 1868, was removed from the list at the specific request of Henry Stimson. But Hiroshima was the southern headquarters and depot for Japan's homeland army.

Some historians have won-

President Truman, British Prime Minister Winston Churchill, and Soviet Premier Joseph Stalin met at Potsdam, Germany, for a postwar conference in the summer of 1945. After Japanese leaders rejected the Potsdam Declaration, which called for their unconditional surrender, Truman authorized use of the atomic bomb.

dered whether the bomb could have been demonstrated in a remote area instead of used on a population center. A July 1945 poll of 150 Manhattan Project scientists showed that 124 favored some sort of demonstration.

But J. Robert Oppenheimer, director of the secret Los Alamos laboratory where the bomb was built, and General Leslie Groves, who supervised the Manhattan Project, favored the use of the device on an actual military target. Still others worried that the bomb wouldn't go off. The specific warning to the Japanese about atomic bombs that Truman mentioned in his diary was never given.

Hiroshima was bombed August 6, Nagasaki on August 9. Some advisers wanted a third bomb dropped on Tokyo. Truman declined.

The thought of wiping out another city was too horrible for Truman, Commerce Secretary Henry Wallace wrote in his diary, adding that the president made special men-

---

In 1959, Truman repeatedly shrugged off the bomb's emotional burden during his speech at Columbia University. He described himself as annoyed by "these wonderful Monday morning quarterbacks, the experts who are supposed to be right."

---

tion at an August 10 cabinet meeting of how he hated the idea of killing "all those kids."

The Japanese agreed to surrender on August 14.

In 1959, Truman repeatedly shrugged off the bomb's emotional burden during his speech at Columbia University. He described himself as annoyed by "these wonderful Monday morning quarterbacks, the experts who are supposed to be right.

"All this uproar about what we did and what could have been stopped . . ." he said. "They don't know what they are talking about. I was there. I did it. I would do it again."

Similar comments made on national television found their way to Hiroshima, where the city council responded by passing a resolution calling Truman's comments a "gross defilement committed on the people of Hiroshima and their fallen victims."

The city forwarded the resolution to Truman.

"The feeling of the people of your city is easily understood," Truman responded, "and I am not in any way offended by the resolution which their city council passed." However, the need for such a decision, he added, "never would have arisen, had

we not been shot in the back by Japan at Pearl Harbor in December 1941."

Back in 1945 at Potsdam Truman had proved more contemplative on the topic of atomic weapons. His July 16 diary entry included what now seems a prescient postscript to the nuclear standoff that followed the end of World War II.

"I hope for some sort of peace – but I fear that machines are ahead of morals by some centuries and when morals catch up perhaps there'll be no reason for any of it," he wrote.

Truman added that "we are only termites on a planet and maybe when we bore too deeply into the planet there'll [be] a reckoning – who knows?"

Since 1995, a group known as the Harry S. Truman Appreciation Society has organized ceremonies every summer at the Truman Museum in Independence. The ceremonies are meant to show gratitude for Truman's decision to deploy the atomic bombs against Japan, which society members say, saved the lives of thousands of young Americans who otherwise would have died in an invasion of Japan.

**F**or a moment in the mid-1940s, Bess Truman was the most famous bridge player in the country.

Not that Mrs. Truman ever had that in mind. But that's what happened after she invited ten members of the Tuesday Bridge Club of Independence to convene a meeting in the White House in January 1946.

After several months of receiving only a poker face from Mrs. Truman, the Washington press corps scrambled.

An additional twenty-five women reporters appeared at that week's Bess Truman press briefing. Mrs. Truman, as had been her habit, did not appear. In fact, from the time her husband became president in April 1945, Mrs. Truman had not seen much need to satisfy the curiosities of the Washington press corps.

Washington journalists had spent the previous twelve years covering Eleanor Roosevelt, who had embraced the high-profile role Bess Truman disdained.

In this context, the Independence bridge club was a revelation. "Mrs. Main Street, multiplied by ten, is hanging up her nylons in the Lincoln bedroom these nights," wrote syndicated columnist Doris Fleeson that April, after the ten Independence bridge players arrived at the White House. "It is Mrs. Truman's first assertion of her personality since she took over a year ago from

one of the most controversial women in the world. Washington, which was beginning to be rather wistful about her reticence, is delighted."

Subsequent bridge club coverage alternated between warm and condescending, sometimes in the same magazine.

In 1946, *Life* magazine described a photograph of Bess Truman during a visit to Chicago as "her last important appearance before receiving the bridge club." The same publication, after Harry Truman had been elected in 1948, dispatched a writer to Independence, where the details of the bridge club served as an open window into the unknown world of Mrs. Truman. The relentless reserve so familiar to many Washington journalists, *Life* readers learned, apparently was never on display among bridge club members. During one club meeting, scheduled shortly after Mrs. Truman once had arrived back in Independence from Washington, the members rose on a pre-arranged signal, bowed at the waist, and said, "Welcome home, Madam President."

Mrs. Truman, in reply, had said, "Oh, sit down. Sit down. You all make me so mad."

The young Bess Wallace had played cards in public as far back as 1903, according to social page notes of the Independence *Examiner*, which that year noted the occurrence of whist, a primitive form of bridge, at the Wallace home on North Delaware Street.

Eventually the club became to be known as the Tuesday Bridge Club of Independence. Members, upon receiving Mrs. Truman's 1946 invitation, estimated that Bess had been a member since at least the mid-1920s.

About fifteen reporters and photographers covered the bridge club members' arrival in Washington. The ladies attended a concert, went to the circus, and enjoyed a cruise down the Potomac on the *Williamsburg*, the presidential yacht. It was on the Potomac that the only bridge was played. First prize, a pair of nylon stockings, was won by Adelaide Twyman. The club declined challenge matches from nearby bridge clubs in Yorktown and Richmond, Virginia.

That the women enjoyed themselves is evident in the scrapbook kept by bridge club member Thelma Pallette Siebel, who recorded the White House sleeping arrangements. Leslie Shaw and Maggie Noel, she recorded, drew the Lincoln bedroom.

The club's visit, wrote Margaret Truman in her 1986 biography of her mother, "was one of the few positive stories the press wrote about the Trumans in 1946, although Bess did not have an iota of politics in mind when she issued the invitation."

In the 1990s, the Truman Presidential Museum & Library often climaxed a week's worth of events observing Bess Wallace Truman's February 13 birthday with an annual "Day of Bridge."

Bess Truman's Independence bridge club members leave Kansas City's Municipal Airport to visit Bess at the White House in April 1946.

CHRISTMAS 1945

Christmas 1945 was Harry Truman's first as president, and he made sure he was home in Independence before it was over.

But few places could be as cold as the summer White House in winter.

A photograph of Truman holding an armful of wrapped Christmas gifts suggests the president was brimming with holiday spirit that year. But the reality was far different.

First, the nation's newspapers were scolding the president for taking an airplane trip home in terrible weather.

Far worse, his wife was angry at him.

Her remark to him when he arrived at 219 North Delaware, as reconstructed by her daughter Margaret Truman in her 1986 biography of her mother, went something like this:

"So you've finally arrived. I guess you couldn't think of any more reasons to stay away. As far as I'm concerned, you might as well have stayed in Washington."

It's possible, then, that

when the commander-in-chief smiled for photographers holding his armful of packages, he was just waiting for any excuse to get out of the house. But it was no more inviting outside, because even though it was the first Christmas after the nation's victory in World War II, it wasn't just the president's wife who was grumpy.

Returned veterans were demonstrating in Denver over a housing shortage, carrying signs reading WE CAN'T LIVE IN FOXHOLES HERE. A series of industrial strikes was continuing in Flint, Michigan, with picketing autoworkers pushing back the cars of General Motors executives who were trying to

enter their offices.

Worst of all, Bess and their daughter, Margaret, had fled Washington for Independence a week before.

Truman decided to fly home on Christmas Day, so family members could celebrate the holiday together, as they had done since World War I.

Much of the nation was in the

Bess Truman was angry with Harry when he flew home in dangerous weather to be with his family on Christmas Day.

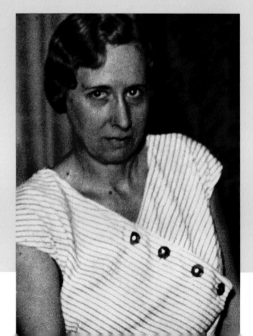

grip of a snow-and-ice storm. All commercial flights out of Washington's National Airport had been canceled.

Truman waited four hours, and then ordered his plane to take off.

Sacred Cow, the presidential aircraft, lifted off in a driving rain from a sleet-covered runway. Late in the afternoon, Truman arrived in Kansas City after a six-hour, white-knuckle ride.

Many were not impressed,

The *Kansas City Star* had an exclusive when Truman left his home on December 26 to deliver Christmas packages to family members.

chief among them eighteen White House correspondents who followed him to Missouri. The trip, said *The New York Times*, was "one of the most hazardous 'sentimental journeys' ever undertaken by an American chief of state."

Least impressed was Bess Truman. Maybe that's one reason the president, early on

December 26, undertook an unscheduled errand. Truman walked out the front door of his house holding several Christmas presents for his cousins, the Nolands, who lived across the street.

The sudden sight of the president startled two *Kansas City Star* staff members, apparently the only members of the press on duty, in the *Star's* temporary office in a home across North Delaware. A *Star* photographer got a shot of Truman, and then raced downtown to make the early edition of what then was an afternoon paper.

The picture appeared on the front page. Then there was heck to pay, James "Bud" Porter, the *Star's* one-person Independence bureau at the time, later related. "The [press] from Washington had kind of slept in," Porter said in a 1974 Truman Museum oral history. "So about two o'clock when the paper came out . . . here's Truman with all these gifts and they start getting stuff from Chicago,

'Where's our picture of Truman?' And Los Angeles, 'Where's our picture of Truman with the packages?' So it caused quite a furor and some of the guys got some real hard times over that."

Truman got word of it.

"So about three o'clock in the afternoon . . . here came old Truman out again with an armload of packages," Porter said. "Now I know dang well that Truman didn't have any idea of coming out in the afternoon with an another armload of packages, but he just did it so the guys could get a picture."

Truman flew back to Washington several days later, when he wrote a letter and sent it special delivery. Just what the letter said will never be known, because the next day Truman called his daughter, Margaret, with specific instructions. She was to go to the Independence post office and ask Edgar Hinde, longtime Truman friend and Independence postmaster, to hand her the letter.

That's what Margaret did. Then, still following her father's instructions, she burned it in the backyard incinerator.

Then Truman wrote a separate letter to Bess.

"You can never appreciate what it means to come home as I did the other evening after doing at least one hundred things I didn't want to do and have the only person in the world whose approval and good opinion I value look at me like I'm something the cat dragged in," Truman wrote.

His anger vented, Truman then appealed for help.

Truman wrote Bess that "you, Margie and everyone else who may have any influence on my actions must give me help and assistance; because no one ever needed help and assistance as I do now. If I can get the use of the best brains in the country and a little bit of help from those I have on a pedestal at home, the job will be done."

Some twenty-seven years later, when Truman died on December 26, 1972, the second letter was found in his desk at the Truman Museum. Apparently, it was never mailed.

Kansas City welcomed President Truman home with a gathering of nearly five thousand people at Union Station, on June 16, 1948.

1948

Harry Truman needed a diversion.

On November 2, 1948 – Election Day – the president waited in his Independence home while a motorcycle roared out of his driveway, heading west on Van Horn Road to Kansas City.

Reporters climbed into their own cars, gave chase – and got lost. The motorcyclist was Mike Westwood, an Independence police officer who later served as Truman's personal bodyguard.

"Mike wasn't going anywhere," Sue Gentry, longtime journalist with the *Examiner* in Independence, said in 1998. "Mike knew that part of town well, so he lost the reporters. While he was doing that, Mr. Truman slipped out the back door, crossed somebody's backyard, and got into a car parked on Maple Avenue."

Truman's car headed north to Excelsior Springs, site of the Elms resort, where Truman spent the night. Perhaps he wanted to face alone the humiliating defeat that everyone had been predicting for months. Yet by the next morning Truman had defeated Republican Party presidential nominee Thomas Dewey, and much of the nation's press was revealed to have been lost for months.

Today the upset endures in American political culture as a cautionary tale for overconfident candidates as well as an inspiration for any underdog. These days Truman is often considered one of America's greatest presidents, and Van Horn Road is now known as Truman Road.

But it all began badly.

In the spring of 1948, Truman's approval rating had slipped to 36 percent. TRUMAN SHOULD QUIT, read the cover headline on the *New Republic* of April 5. Even the president's nomination was in doubt.

Some Democratic Party strategists wanted Dwight Eisenhower to head their ticket. He declined. To help cinch his renomination, Truman scheduled a June "nonpolitical" train trip out west.

Bad idea.

In Omaha, the president spoke to a nearly empty auditorium. A photograph of the "acres of empty seats" appeared in *Life* magazine.

In Carey, Idaho, Truman helped dedicate an airfield that he believed had been named after a local war hero. In fact, it had been named for a local girl who had died in a civilian plane accident.

"The trip had not been well planned," George Elsey, then a Truman assistant, said.

"There were many gaffes and blunders."

One result was a new Truman research division. The low-profile team of writers was sequestered in spartan accommodations near Washington's DuPont Circle. "There was a row of beds in a big open space," Frank Kelly, a former *Kansas City Star* and *Times* reporter

After marking his ballot, President Truman folds it in preparation for casting his vote in the general election of November 2, 1948

President Truman casts his ballot on November 2, 1948, at his polling place in the Memorial Building in Independence.

who served four months with the group, said in 1998. "It was like a monastery."

In offices nearby, the researchers converted complex topics into handy briefs. These files came along on the "whistlestop" railroad campaign that Truman decided to undertake after he was safely nominated that summer.

The writers also compiled details on the many smaller cities that Truman would visit.

"Though the Truman campaign was an enormous national campaign, it was also extremely local," Kelly said. "Everywhere he went, audiences were surprised what the president knew about their town."

The familiar "Give 'em hell, Harry" comes from the 1948 campaign. As the president's train prepared to leave Washington's Union Station in September, his running mate, Alben Barkley, called to him, saying, "Mow 'em down, Harry."

"I'm going to give 'em hell," Truman replied.

Truman would address a particular campaign issue, but only one, at each stop. "He would never repeat himself in the course of a day," said Elsey.

"Reporters on the train – never knowing what Truman was going to be talking about but knowing it would be a red-hot issue – would scramble back to the press car after every speech. So, over the course of the day, flowing over the wires would be this series of stories on Truman for the afternoon and evening papers."

Dewey, as George Elsey recalled it, only addressed elevated themes.

"He spoke beautifully, but he would talk in platitudes," Elsey said. "Some reporters on the Dewey train later told me they would never leave the press car while Dewey spoke."

Truman discussed Dewey not at all. Instead, he ripped the Republican-controlled "do-nothing" Congress.

"He liked to call the GOP the party of `grand old platitudes,' " said Ken Hechler, a former Truman White House assistant who later served as West Virginia secretary of state. "Sometimes he would ratchet it up and talk about `gluttons of privilege.' "

Between hammering away at Republicans at every stop, Truman greeted local politicians.

Lewis Clymer, who later became the first African-American judge for the Jackson County, Missouri, Circuit Court, recalled being photographed on Truman's railroad car with other black Democratic Party officials. "He was very cordial to us," Clymer said in 1998.

Civil rights, Clymer knew, had become a defining issue after liberals forced a progressive plank onto the Democratic Party platform.

"This was to Truman's ultimate advantage," said Hechler. "It not only energized Democrats who had been tepid toward him, but it also ensured the loyalty of black voters, who saw that the party was not in the control of the segregationists."

Truman addressed other issues, such as agriculture. A former farmer, Truman needed little prompting. In Dexter, Iowa, that September, he told farmers that Republicans had "stuck a pitchfork in the farmer's back."

One especially vivid moment occurred when actress Tallulah Bankhead introduced Truman from her New York dressing room

Ballot box used in Jackson County, Missouri, circa 1940s.

Truman learns of his victory over Dewey in his penthouse suite at the Muehlebach Hotel on November 3, 1948.

before the president delivered a radio campaign address.

"She was the Marilyn Monroe of her day," recalled Frank Kelly. "And, with this really throaty voice, she said, 'I want you to vote for Harry Truman because he is a true man.'

"Truman smiled and kind of went pink in the face. He said, 'If that's what she thinks of me, what does she think of Dewey?'"

Truman had hit his stride. On October 30, when he delivered an especially emotional speech in St. Louis, he set his prepared text aside.

But it was too late, many correspondents believed.

"After 16 years of Democratic rule of the White House, the voters want a change," Duke Shoop, a

Kansas City Star and *Times* Washington correspondent, wrote on October 31.

Pollster Elmo Roper, meanwhile, had stopped taking surveys in September.

Even close Truman family members had no hope.

"I was confident of defeat," Truman's first cousin, Mary Ethel Noland, said in 1965. "Oh, it was terrible, and I just could not bear to think of how crushed he would be at that time. I was very miserable when I thought about it during that entire campaign. It was a campaign when bitter things were said. Everything disagreeable that could be said was said, and all I could hope for was 'This too will pass. It can't last forever.'"

At dawn on November 3, 1948, Truman arrived at the Hotel Muehlebach, his Kansas City campaign headquarters, confident that he would win.

His escape to the Elms, however mysterious, did have precedent. Many years earlier, disappointed that he had not been Boss Tom Pendergast's choice for governor, Truman also had booked a room at the resort.

First to shake his hand at the Muehlebach that morning was Kansas City lawyer Lyman Field. "He was utterly unchanged," Field said in 1998.

Truman's serenity in the face of apparent defeat had impressed many. Elsey's own

glimpse of it occurred in mid-October, as the Truman train crossed Minnesota. "The president asked me to write down a list of the states," Elsey said. "He knew the number of electoral votes that went with each, and he predicted how each state would go."

"When we were through he said, 'What's the total?'

"I said, 'You've got 340.' Actually he was overconfident, because he only got 303. But he was absolutely convinced he was going to win."

Buoyed by the civil rights issue, Truman carried all thirteen of the country's biggest cities. He also won five farm states that Franklin Roosevelt had lost in 1944.

Truman's upset was stunning in part because polls had convinced so many he had no chance. Newspapers like the *Chicago Daily Tribune*, which published an early edition bearing the headline DEWEY DEFEATS TRUMAN, depended on advance polls instead of the exit polls that are common today, said Frank Mitchell, a University of Southern California professor.

But another factor contributing to the public's wholesale amazement, Mitchell said, was a "campaign of deliberate

Truman holds aloft *Chicago Daily Tribune* headline "Dewey Defeats Truman." *From the collections of The St. Louis Mercantile Library at the University of Missouri - St. Louis.*

bias on the part of the news media."

Especially brazen, Mitchell said, was the Time-Life-Fortune empire of Henry Luce. The "acres of many seats" that *Life* had described in Omaha didn't explain how as many as 160,000 of the city's residents had seen Truman during a parade earlier in the day. And since *Time* magazine carried such clout with the Washington press corps, many correspondents discounted the large crowds that Truman continued to attract.

Kelly can vouch for that.

"One of them told me, 'They like him, but they are not going to vote for him,' Kelly said. "Just the blindness of the press was interesting. They didn't see what was going on right in front of them."

Truman was handed the DEWEY DEFEATS TRUMAN edition of the *Chicago Daily Tribune* during a train stop in St. Louis two days after the election. He held up the newspaper for photographers, and smiled.

The glory proved ephemeral.

The Korean War, plus Truman's break with General Douglas MacArthur, later diminished the president's status. Truman didn't run for re-election in 1952.

Still, Truman's 1948 campaign has left its own legacy. The term "whistlestop" now has entered the language as the definition of a hard-hitting grass-roots campaign.

Republican presidential nominee George Bush invoked Truman's 1948 upset in 1988 when he was seventeen points behind Democratic Party nominee Michael Dukakis. Bush won. Four years later, Bush recalled Truman again. But Democratic challenger Bill Clinton also praised him.

And Bush, it soon was learned, had not voted for Truman in 1948.

"And what's so screwy," political comedian Mark Russell later sang, "he voted for Dewey."

The 1948 election ultimately emphasized the difference that individual votes can make. Days after the election, Frank Kelly spoke at Boston University, where he had taken a job as a journalism professor.

"Many people came up to me and said, 'I voted for Truman but I didn't think anybody else did,' " Kelly said. Kelly, as it happened, was substituting that day for pollster Elmo Roper, who had been scheduled to deliver a speech entitled "Why Dewey Won."

"Apparently, he had gotten ill," Kelly said.

President Truman flanked by his family as he leaves for Washington, December 29, 1948. From left, brother Vivian, President Truman, Bess Truman, sister Mary Jane, and daughter Margaret.

On May 8, 2003, the 360 guests attending the annual Harry S. Truman Good Neighbor Award banquet lifted small glasses of sherry and toasted the thirty-third president, born 119 years before.

The luncheon was held in the Muehlebach Tower of the Kansas City Marriott Downtown. The building is the latest incarnation of the Muehlebach Hotel, quite likely Kansas City's most famous hotel and – during the late 1940s and 1950s, when President Harry Truman was a frequent guest – one of the most familiar hotels in the country.

On April 12, 1947, Truman broadcast from his Muehlebach suite a radio salute to former President Franklin Roosevelt, who had died two years before. On May 22 of that year, at the Muehlebach, Truman signed documents authorizing millions of dollars in aid for Greece and Turkey. Again that same year he stayed several days in the hotel, commuting back and forth between the Muehlebach and the Grandview, Missouri, home of his mother, who had suffered a stroke.

The hotel's most storied association with Truman, however, occurred in November 1948. On November 3, Truman arrived at the hotel at dawn. Several hours later New York Governor Thomas Dewey conceded the previous day's presidential election, prompting a celebration in the hotel's eleventh-floor suite occupied by the presidential party.

Truman's relationship with the hotel, at the southwest corner of 12th Street and Baltimore Avenue, may have begun in 1919, when he and business partner Eddie Jacobson opened their haberdashery on West 12th Street, just north of the hotel.

When Truman's World War I artillery battery held one of their first reunions in 1920, the Muehlebach hosted it. Decades later, in the 1960s and 1970s, surviving Battery D alumni chose to hold their reunions in the Muehlebach,

in honor of Truman, their former captain. Other admirers of the thirty-third president often organized Muehlebach birthday celebrations for Truman following his return from the White House in 1953.

But the hotel was celebrated well before Truman.

It opened in 1915 and soon became Kansas City's unofficial center of gravity. Not long after the hotel opened, the operator of Kansas City's Strauss-Peyton photography studio opened a Muehlebach Hotel office. Today the glass plate portraits of Fred Astaire, Jean Harlow, and the Marx Brothers taken by Strauss-Peyton photographers testify to the kind of traffic that came through the Muehlebach.

For decades, the hotel served as Kansas City's home to the stars, with Mary Pickford, Debbie Reynolds, and Jimmy Durante among those checking in. Upon the arrival of major league baseball in Kansas City in 1955, visiting teams stayed at the Muehlebach.

In 1956, a 350-room hotel addition, called the Muehlebach Towers, made the now 950-room Muehlebach the largest hotel between Chicago and the West Coast. When the Beatles played Kansas City's Municipal Stadium in 1964, they stayed in an eighteenth-floor suite at the Muehlebach Towers, and even hosted a Muehlebach press conference.

Kansas City Star photographers, so used to photographing entertainers as well as prominent business leaders at the hotel, began calling their Muehlebach Hotel portraits "Muehl-mugs."

But much of the Muehlebach's cachet was generated by the politicians who chose to stay or gather there.

Hotel management claimed that the many

The Muehlebach Hotel presidential suite on the eleventh floor served as Truman's headquarters in Kansas City from the time of his vice presidential campaign in 1944 until he left the presidency in 1953. *Photos by Ray Geselbracht*

sitting, former, and future presidents who stayed there began with Theodore Roosevelt. Clearly Truman felt comfortable there. On election day in November 1944, when voters elected him vice president, Truman played piano and rested on the hotel's eleventh floor. In August 1960, during that year's presidential campaign, Truman hosted a luncheon for Democratic presidential candidate John Kennedy.

It wasn't long, however, before the Muehlebach, along with the rest of downtown Kansas City, went into a decline.

President Richard Nixon, visiting Kansas City in 1971, chose to check into a Holiday Inn a few blocks away from the Muehlebach. During the 1976 Republican National Convention, President Gerald Ford established his headquarters at the new Crown Center Hotel, while challenger Ronald Reagan checked into the Alameda Plaza, recently built across Brush Creek in the Country Club Plaza.

Television news correspondent Charles Kuralt, meanwhile, found a bug in his bed at the Muehlebach, and said so on national television.

In 1996, the old Muehlebach Towers was imploded, and soon a new facility rose in its place. Today the building is known as the Muehlebach Tower of the Kansas City Marriott Downtown. The Harry S. Truman Library Institute, the Truman Museum's nonprofit support group, often holds its annual "Wild About Harry" programs in the hotel.

In 2003, the hotel's older portion, which includes the original Truman presidential suite, was not accessible to visitors. However, the new Muehlebach Tower includes a Truman Suite.

In May 2003, C-Span cable television network founder Brian Lamb stayed in the suite when accepting that year's Harry Truman Good Neighbor Award.

Bess Wallace Truman died in 1982.

Not long after, Margaret Truman donated her mother's vast archive of letters written to her by husband Harry Truman to the American people. After historians studied and published the letters, they noted their sheer number (more than twelve hundred, starting in 1910 and running through the 1950s), their candor, and their warmth.

They also noted the letters' occasional racial slurs.

Young Harry Truman's attitude toward African Americans was, some historians maintained, a product of his time and place. Both his paternal and maternal grandparents—all of whom were born in Kentucky—had owned slaves.

Missouri, where his grandparents soon would migrate, was a border state during the Civil War. Jackson County, where all four grandparents settled, shared Missouri's western boundary with Kansas. It was called home by both Unionists and Confederate sympathizers,

and thus emerged from the war a smoking ruin. Some sixty years later, while deluging Bess Wallace of Independence with letters, young Harry Truman had found it appropriate to make the occasional unfortunate remark.

In 1922, during his race for Jackson County eastern judge, Truman apparently briefly considered joining the Ku Klux Klan, which held many rallies throughout the county in the 1920s.

It all makes Truman's civil rights record as president only more remarkable.

During a November 1950 visit back home, Truman met with three Kansas City African-American leaders: left to right, J. A. Bradford, Byrdie D. Jackson, and Girard T. Bryant.

In December 1946, Truman appointed the President's Committee on Civil Rights.

In June 1947, Truman became the first president to address the National Association for the Advancement of Colored People.

That October, the president's civil rights committee released its report, which included almost three dozen recommendations, including the approval of an anti-lynching law and the end of discrimination in the United States' armed forces.

In February 1948, Truman sent a special civil rights message to Congress, endorsing many of his committee's recommendations. No president had ever sent Congress such a document.

That July, Truman issued Executive Order 9981, initiating the integration of the United States armed forces. The same day he also issued Executive Order 9980, which created a fair employment board to eliminate racial discrimination in federal employment.

That October, during the 1948 presidential campaign, Truman became the first president to campaign in Harlem. In other actions he bolstered the Justice Department's civil rights division, and appointed the first black judge to the federal bench.

Several historians since have marveled at the president's "conversion" on civil rights, suggesting that the transformation had occurred sometime after Truman's arrival in the White House. Some accounts argue that stories of outrages against returning black World War II veterans finally convinced Truman to act.

It's true that Truman had established the presidential commission in 1946 some two months after a delegation described for Truman a former World War II sergeant who, hours after receiving his separation papers from the Army, had been blinded by two police officers in South Carolina.

"My God," historians quote Truman as saying, "I had no idea it was as terrible as that. We've got to do something."

But Truman's evolution on civil rights didn't occur in the White House. His earlier attitudes toward ethnicity and religion had been challenged by his war experiences. His artillery battery during the war was largely Catholic; his business partner after the war was Jewish.

As a candidate supported by the Pendergast political machine, Truman came to appreciate the importance of the minority vote. Prior to the turn of the century, Kansas City housing codes often restricted blacks to the city's North End and West Bottoms, areas often controlled by James Pendergast, alderman and Pendergast machine patriarch.

But beyond political motivation, Truman seemed genuinely concerned for the African Americans of Jackson County and Missouri.

As presiding judge, Truman supported and maintained budgets for county homes for elderly blacks as well as young African-American men. Truman often visited the facilities. Truman also remained alert to minority patronage: 330 African Americans held jobs in Truman's Jackson County administration in 1928.

Truman's actions in Jackson County impressed one hard-to-impress observer: C. A. Franklin, editor of the *Call* of Kansas City, a black weekly newspaper.

Franklin was an ardent Republican who endorsed Thomas Dewey over Truman for president in 1948 and sent a staff member, Lucile Bluford, to New York to chronicle Dewey's many civil rights initiatives in his home state.

But Truman's efforts on behalf of Jackson County's black residents had moved Franklin to endorse Truman in elections in 1930, 1934, and 1940.

In 1930, when Truman ran for re-election as Jackson County presiding judge, he was one of the few Democrats endorsed by the *Call*. Four years later, when Truman ran for the U.S. Senate, Franklin endorsed him again. In the August 1934 primary, Truman carried every black precinct in Kansas City.

Truman's race for re-election in 1940 proved especially difficult, with the candidate struggling to survive following the spectacular fall of his political patron, Tom Pendergast. In 1939 the Boss had pleaded guilty to income tax evasion and had been sent to federal prison in

Leavenworth, Kansas.

Truman opened his 1940 re-election campaign with a June 15 speech in Sedalia, Missouri—and made special mention of his civil rights agenda.

"And when we speak of man and his labor," Truman said, "at least in this country and more particularly in this locality, we must consider the problem of our Negro population and bend our every effort that, at least under the law, they may claim their heritage in our Bill of Rights to life, liberty, and the pursuit of happiness.

"Their social life," Truman added, "will naturally remain their own, but as free men they must have their equality before the law."

Truman prevailed by a slim margin in the Democratic primary. In November 1940, Truman was the only Democrat receiving the *Call's* endorsement.

Back in Washington, Truman heeded Franklin's calls to see black workers hired during an expansion of Fort Riley, Kansas, as well as in the new North American Aviation aircraft plant in Kansas City, Kansas.

But Truman's landmark civil rights initiative may well be Executive Order 9981. Issued by Truman on July 26, 1948, it called for the initiation of the integration of the country's military.

The idea didn't originate with Truman. Black labor leader A. Philip Randolph, along with the Urban League and NAACP, had campaigned for such a measure for years. In June 1948 Randolph informed Truman that unless the president issued an executive order ending segregation in the armed forces, African-American youth would not obey the country's draft laws.

A Gallup poll that same month found that 63 percent of Americans opposed an integrated military.

Still, Truman issued the executive order in July, and many saw the move as pure politics. "His object was obviously to stack up political hay before Congress even had a chance to tackle the civil rights issue," a *Kansas City Star* editorial read.

Politics were a factor. One month after the

president's civil rights committee had issued its report in 1947, Truman advisers had presented to Truman a lengthy memo detailing the importance of the black vote in the coming presidential race.

Still, just within his own party, the fallout from Truman's civil rights activism was bitter. Many southern politicians originally had taken Truman for one of their own when he joined the party's presidential ticket in 1944. After Truman's February 1948 message to Congress, some southern senators visited the president to ask whether he could modify his stance.

"But my very stomach turned over when I learned that Negro soldiers, just back from overseas, were being dumped out of army trucks in Mississippi and beaten," Truman later wrote to the senators. "Whatever my inclinations as a native of Missouri might have been, as President I know this is bad. I shall fight to end evils like this."

As his intentions became more clear with his July integration order, the same politicians ultimately turned away. South Carolina Governor Strom Thurmond became the presidential nominee of the States Rights Democratic Party, or "Dixiecrats."

Truman, himself an Army veteran, had no illusions about its overnight integration. Truman's order mandated a vast social change in a rigid hierarchy, and the president found it necessary to appoint the Fahy Committee in January 1949 to supervise the order's enforcement.

For the next eighteen months, the committee and the Army squared off in bureaucratic stalemate. Sometimes Army officials fed committee members false information regarding military facilities available to blacks. To obtain reliable reports, the committee secretary would leave his Pentagon office unlocked so informants could leave details there.

Then, in June 1950, the Korean War began.

Under fire, Army priorities changed. After years of postwar demobilization, the force was not at battle strength. Combat units were being decimated, and field commanders looking for replacements often plugged in black troops to make up the difference.

One historian, Steven Schlossman, believes

momentum for Army integration originated in the field, from the bottom up. But in a commencement speech at Washington's Howard University in 1952, Truman complimented Matthew Ridgway, head of the United Nations command in Korea who, he said, "ordered the progressive integration of all the troops in his command, and you have seen the results in the wonderful performance of our troops in Korea."

In April 1951, Ridgway requested that the Army allow him to integrate all African Americans within his command.

In his 1952 speech, Truman tried to establish solidarity with the Howard students. "I know what it means not to have opportunity," he told them. "I wasn't able to go to college at all."

Yet the modern civil rights movements that emerged in the late 1950s and early 1960s didn't impress Truman. He opposed sit-ins, and said so to reporters. In a 1960 letter, Dean Acheson, former secretary of state, respectfully asked the former president to keep his opinions regarding contemporary civil rights protests to himself, all to better the chances of Democratic Party success in that year's presidential election.

Yet, in recent years, Truman's civil rights legacy has been clear to many. Colin Powell, for one, needed no convincing in 1998. That year Powell, then a retired Army general and former head of the Joint Chiefs of Staff, visited Independence on the fiftieth anniversary of Executive Order 9981. In signing the order, Powell said, Truman helped to dismantle "a system of apartheid almost as evil as slavery and far more duplicitous."

The Harlem-born son of Jamaican immigrants, Powell described his military career as

an example of what Truman helped make possible. In a forty-minute address, Powell conceded that Truman was guilty of unfortunate racial attitudes before his term as president. "He was from a border state," Powell said, "and his biographers will tell you that on occasions he used words that we would not use today."

But Powell, who joined the Army in 1958, said the desegregated American military offered him opportunity.

"It was the only place when I was coming out of college, the only institution in all of America—because of Harry Truman—where a young black kid could now dream," he said.

It was the one place, he added, "where . . . the color of your guts and the color of your blood was more important than the color of your skin."

In 1998 Colin Powell, then a retired Army general and former head of the Joint Chiefs of Staff, praised Truman's civil rights legacy in a speech at the RLDS Auditorium.

At the birth of the North Atlantic Treaty Organization in 1949, something else died: the 150-year tradition of isolationist influence in America.

As president, Harry Truman presided at the NATO treaty-signing ceremonies in April 1949. As an artillery battery captain during World War I, Truman, in letters home, sometimes had shrugged off the complexities of international politics in his eagerness to return to Jackson County. But Truman also personally witnessed the role the United States played in the global conflict and from then on operated from that perspective.

As president thirty years after World War I, Truman was interested in containing communism. The end of World War II had brought a precarious peace. By 1947 Hungary, Bulgaria, Romania, and Poland had fallen to Communists. In May of that year, the United States had provided $400 million in aid to Greece and Turkey, in part to inhibit the spread of Soviet influence. The next month, Secretary of State George Marshall had proposed what came to be called the Marshall Plan, an aid package to rebuild Western Europe after World War II.

In February 1948, the Soviet Union had seized power in Czechoslovakia. The next month, Great Britain, France, Belgium, the Netherlands, and Luxembourg signed a fifty-year collective defense treaty.

But what the leaders of those nations really wanted was American involvement. The salvation of the West, they believed, depended on the formation of a union backed by the United States.

the Truman administration, received a visit from John Hickerson, the department's director for European affairs.

"I don't care whether entangling alliances have been considered worse than original sin," Hickerson said. "We've got to negotiate a military alliance."

Secret negotiations began,

"What we are about to do here is a neighborly act," Truman said at the NATO treaty signing on April 4, 1949. *"We are like a group of householders, living in the same locality, who decide to express their community of interest by entering into a formal association for their mutual self-protection."*

America was slow to come around to the idea.

Ever since George Washington warned against entangling European alliances in his 1796 farewell address, the United States had avoided permanent alliances outside the Western hemisphere. In 1919 and 1920, the U.S. Senate had declined to approve the League of Nations covenant. The first president's caution still lingered on December 31, 1947, when Theodore Achilles, a State Department official in

as Achilles described later in a Truman Museum oral history. The resulting NATO treaty bound the United States as never before to go to the defense of its allies.

An attack on one nation would be considered an attack on all.

Some worried that any NATO treaty might undermine the charter of the new United Nations. Still others wondered whether a NATO treaty ignored the congressional prerogative of declaring war. But the State

Department included select senators in the treaty negotiations, chief among them Arthur Vandenberg of Michigan, head of the Senate Foreign Relations Committee who once, before Pearl Harbor, had argued against the loan of war materi-

ed in 1914 and 1939, Truman said, "I believe it would have prevented the acts of aggression which led to two world wars."

NATO never went to war with the Soviet Union, which broke apart in 1991.

NATO. For the event, museum curators brought out the small table on which Truman, at Kansas City's Hotel Muehlebach, had signed documents authorizing the $400 million in aid to Greece and Turkey in 1947.

als to Great Britain. Ultimately the Senate approved the treaty by an 82-13 vote.

"What we are about to do here is a neighborly act," Truman said at the NATO treaty signing on April 4, 1949. "We are like a group of householders, living in the same locality, who decide to express their community of interest by entering into a formal association for their mutual self-protection."

If such an alliance had exist-

The alliance's first attack on a sovereign nation did not occur until 1999, when it initiated air strikes in Yugoslavia.

In March 1999, Hungary, Poland, and the Czech Republic joined NATO in ceremonies at the Truman Museum in Independence. The Truman Museum was enlisted to host the event, said Secretary of State Madeleine Albright, in recognition of the thirty-third president's role in establishing

During a 1999 Truman Museum ceremony, Secretary of State Madeleine Albright signs documents admitting Hungary, Poland, and the Czech Republic into NATO. Looking on are, from left, Jan Kavan of the Czech Republic, Janos Martonyi of Hungary, and Bronislaw Geremak of Poland.

The foreign ministers of the three new NATO members used the table to sign papers documenting their entry into the alliance.

Harry Truman and Eddie Jacobson were poker buddies from way back. But Truman wasn't prepared for the card Jacobson played during a March 1948 White House social call. The indirect result was that some two months later, on May 14, 1948, the United States extended de facto recognition to the infant state of Israel.

It represented one of the turning points in world politics in the twentieth century. Not that Jacobson, who died in 1955, would have told it that way.

"My father always said that he was *beshert*, which is a Yiddish word meaning that it was just his fate to be at the right place at the right time," Gloria Schusterman, a daughter of Jacobson, once said.

"My father was a very modest man and when he said he was *beshert*, he was saying that he really didn't do anything special."

Still, following the end of World War II, two members of the Kansas City Jewish community exerted a profound influence on White House foreign policy in the Middle East.

One was Jacobson, who since 1945 had been the owner of a Kansas City clothing store. The other was A .J. Granoff, Jacobson's friend and Kansas City lawyer.

In the late 1940s the two made several self-financed trips to Washington, where they conducted off-the-record meetings with Truman to discuss the future of Palestine. Their only portfolio as self-appointed diplomats was their long friendship with Truman, which often revolved around

Kansas City card games dating back to the 1930s. Yet together Jacobson and Granoff influenced Truman's decisions regarding what would become Israel.

Most important was a March 1948 meeting during which Jacobson extracted from Truman a promise to receive Zionist leader Chaim Weizmann in the Oval Office. Truman received Weizmann days later, without the knowledge of the State Department.

During the meeting Weizmann received assurances from Truman that he would work toward the establishment and recognition of a Jewish state. All this would be to the frustration of State Department specialists who were struggling to steer the president through the minefield of Middle East policy.

"Eddie and my dad both knew something about Truman that the more jaundiced politicians didn't appreciate," Loeb Granoff, Kansas City lawyer and son of A. J. Granoff, once said. "And that was if Truman knew the facts, whatever they were, they could always depend on this guy to do the right thing, even if it wasn't politically expedient.

"That's the thing that made

him Harry Truman."

But it was complicated. The Joint Chiefs of Staff felt that a new Jewish state would represent a potential outpost for Soviet communism. The State Department believed the Arab nations surrounding any new state of Israel would push the outnumbered Jews into the Mediterranean.

But Jacobson and Granoff had their own agenda.

Jacobson, of course, was a former business partner of Truman's. Before leaving for Europe during World War I, the two had operated a successful canteen at their training base in Oklahoma. After the war through 1922 they had operated the haberdashery bearing their names on Kansas City's 12th Street. Even though their store failed in 1922, their friendship survived.

Granoff, who died in 1970, came to know Jacobson in the 1930s. Soon he would be playing cards at games that included Truman. Decades later, some wondered whether those games may have included solemn discussions about the future of a Jewish homeland.

"Never," said Granoff in a 1969 interview. "Never."

In fact, Jacobson was uncertain about Zionism, the movement whose followers often advocated the establishment of a Jewish state in Palestine.

"Neither Eddie Jacobson nor my father were card-carrying Zionists," said Loeb Granoff. "But they both believed very passionately in the importance of a Jewish state.

"Back then, with new nations emerging to statehood everyday, it was unthinkable that in the hour of their greatest need the Jewish

year-old dream of a Jewish state that Zionist leaders had been articulating since the late nineteenth century. After World War II the concept gained urgency as the extent of the Holocaust became known.

But Secretary of State George Marshall did not want to see a two-state solution in Palestine. He was convinced that American support of a Jewish state in Palestine would endanger long-range interests of the United States.

That was up to Harry Truman.

One problem: Truman had wearied of the whole business. A few Zionist leaders had insulted the president, one of them banging on the Oval Office desk. Further, Truman was said to be under the spell of Marshall, perhaps the military leader that Truman admired most of all – except for Andrew Jackson.

In the early 1930s Truman had seen to it that a sculpture of the seventh president was placed in

people would not have their own homeland."

Yet nothing was guaranteed after World War II.

In November 1947, the United Nations had voted to partition Palestine, then a British protectorate, into separate Arab and Jewish states. The vote gave clear momentum to a two-thousand-

The British mandate was to expire at six P.M., Eastern time, May 14, 1948. Zionist leaders, who had already begun organizing a government and military, promised to proclaim a Jewish state at that moment and proceed to defend it. Crucial to Israel's future would be official recognition from the United States.

President Truman visits former partner Eddie Jacobson at his Kansas City menswear store in 1945. Jacobson was influential in Truman's considering the recognition of Israel.

front of the new Jackson County Courthouse in downtown Kansas City.

Eddie Jacobson remembered that.

On Saturday, March 13, 1948, Jacobson walked into the White House without an appointment.

Although Jacobson had declined to abuse his friendship with Truman since 1945, others couldn't resist appealing to Jacobson. But in response to such entreaties from Zionist leaders, Jacobson already had made several such trips to the White House. Then, in February 1948, Jacobson received a call telling him that Truman was refusing to see Chaim Weizmann, a leading world Zionist leader who would become Israel's first president.

Jacobson soon left for Washington for another off-the-record White House meeting.

"I . . . brought up the Palestine subject," Jacobson later wrote. "He [Truman] immediately became tense in appearance, abrupt in speech, and very bitter in the words he was throwing my way."

Then Jacobson spied a small statue on Truman's desk: a miniature of the Andrew Jackson figure that stood outside the Jackson County courthouse.

"I too have a hero," Jacobson then told Truman. "A man I never met, but who is, I think, the greatest Jew who ever lived . . . I am talking about Chaim Weizmann; he is a very sick man, almost broken in health, but he traveled thousands and thousands of miles just to see you and plead the cause of my people. Now you refuse to see him just because you were insulted by some of our American Jewish leaders, even though you know that Weizmann had absolutely nothing to do with these insults and would be the last man to be party to them. It doesn't sound like you, Harry, because I thought you could take this stuff they have been handing out to you."

Jacobson later described to his daughter what happened next.

"He said Harry swiveled around in his chair and looked out at the window to the Rose Garden," Schusterman said. "And when he started strumming his fingers on the desk, my father knew Harry was changing his mind. He knew Harry so well."

Truman turned around and said, "You win . . . I will see him."

Jacobson left. Once clear of the White House, he did something he had never done before: He stopped at a hotel bar and threw down two double bourbons.

Today an auditorium named for Jacobson stands in a Tel Aviv B'nai B'rith building.

The mystery still remains, though, of just how much Jacobson really knew and admired Chaim Weizmann. A.J. Granoff, for one, had his doubts.

"I used to poke fun at him for that," A. J. Granoff said in 1969. "He had that story. That's Eddie's own story and I sort of let him know that I took it with a grain of salt."

Granoff's son Loeb believes that Jacobson saw an opening and seized it.

"It was a tribute to Jacobson's quick thinking," he said.

Photo by Ray Geselbracht

THE ELMS

On the afternoon of November 2, 1948, election day, the president of the United States managed to slip away from his home in Independence even though it was staked out by reporters.

Harry Truman's destination: the Elms Hotel in Excelsior Springs, Missouri, some thirty miles to the north.

Truman had been to the Elms before. Many years before he had retreated to the hotel after learning that Democratic machine boss Tom Pendergast would not support him in a run for Missouri governor. Perhaps Truman was preparing for disappointment again; all the journalists surrounding his Independence home were expecting Truman to be defeated by New York Governor Thomas Dewey.

Truman arrived at the hotel at 3:45 P.M., in the first of two limousines. The party was met at the front of the hotel by the hotel manager, who had been sworn to secrecy. The manager led Truman through the hotel's rear entrance and escorted him to Room 300 at the end of a hallway.

The origins of the Elms Hotel, as well as Excelsior Springs, dates to the late nineteenth century, when residents began to believe that the spring water found in the area had healing properties. Truman received a mineral bath and massage. At 6:30 P.M., he was in his room, eating a sandwich and listening to election returns by radio.

At nine P.M., he told his Secret Service detail that he was going to sleep, adding that the agents should wake him if anything important happened.

Truman awakened at midnight and turned on the radio to hear radio news commentator H. V. Kaltenborn announce that the president was ahead by 1.2 million votes. He went back to sleep. A Secret Service agent then woke Truman at around four A.M. The president now was leading Dewey by some 2 million votes.

Truman dressed and directed that his agents drive him to the Muehlebach Hotel, his downtown Kansas City headquarters. While Truman was there, Dewey conceded the election.

That afternoon, Truman returned to the Elms for another mineral bath.

In 2003, guests in Room 300 at the Elms Resort & Spa would find a small plaque near the door, identifying the room as the Truman Suite.

THE 1949 INAUGURATION

Harry Truman defeated Republican presidential nominee Thomas Dewey on November 2, 1948. At some point, the thought process in Kansas City and across Jackson County might have gone something like this:

Harry's been elected president. Presidents are inaugurated.

Hey, we know Harry.

Road trip.

Truman was the first native-born Missourian elected president, and upon Washington, Missouri descended.

Hundreds of Kansas City area residents rode special trains to Washington. Eddie Jacobson, Truman's former haberdashery partner, arrived at the inaugural with friends and family in his own railroad car.

Many Missouri residents, faced with full hotels, slept in their Pullman cars. Bess Truman, wrote her daughter, Margaret, played hostess to ``droves of Wallace and Truman relatives and every real and imaginary VIP in Missouri.'' *The Kansas City Star* published entire columns of print consisting of nothing but the names of those attending.

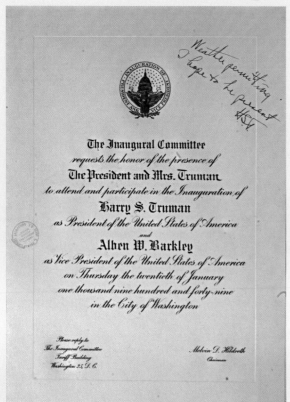

The Inaugural Committee
requests the honor of the presence of
The President and Mrs. Truman
to attend and participate in the Inauguration of
Harry S. Truman
as President of the United States of America
and
Alben W. Barkley
as Vice President of the United States of America
on Thursday the twentieth of January
one thousand nine hundred and forty-nine
in the City of Washington

Please reply to
The Inaugural Committee
Tariff Building
Washington 25 D.C.

Melvin D. Hildreth
Chairman

President Truman's humor comes through on this annotated invitation to his own inauguration. "Weather permitting, I hope to be present. H.S.T."

All a visitor needed at the Washington inaugural, wrote one *Star* reporter, was a Missouri badge pinned to your lapel and a ``a plunging fullback's physique'' to burst through the gridlock.

The theme of Truman inaugural week was sudden intimacy with your fellow Missourians, especially at the inaugural ball on Thursday night.

"It was crowded," Gloria Schusterman, daughter of Eddie Jacobson, said in 1989. In January 1949 Schusterman was an eighteen-year-old University of Oklahoma student who had been excused from final exams to attend the inauguration. "It took a lot of maneuvering to get out on the dance floor and then get back to where you started," she said.

It had been the same at the reception given by Missouri Governor Forrest Smith at Washington's Shoreham Hotel. Lyman Field, a Kansas City lawyer, found himself in a taxi that had been stalled in traffic outside the Shoreham. "Colonel Field," said the cab's ranking occupant, James Blair, recently elected Missouri lieutenant governor, "get out there and get our cab into the Shoreham."

During World War II, Field had achieved the rank of captain in the U.S. Marine Corps. But at this moment he was a member of the Missouri Colonels, a now-defunct ceremonial guard. Field left the cab and began directing traffic. Drivers, seeing Field's Missouri Colonels uniform, obeyed.

"It was a gorgeous black uniform, modeled

after the uniform of an Army artillery officer," Field said in 1989.

The inaugural typewritten schedule for the Truman family filled two pages, coordinated down to the minute and annotated with reminders of dress codes. "He will leave the Blair House at 12:50 P.M., arriving at the Hotel at 12:57 P.M. (Business Suit)," read the first entry for Wednesday, January 19, directing the president to a luncheon given by the Democratic National Committee at the Mayflower Hotel.

That was followed by the Missouri governor's reception given at the Shoreham; the Electors Dinner back at the Mayflower Hotel, to which Truman was to arrive at 6:55 P.M., and then that night's inaugural gala concert at Washington's Armory at nine P.M. Entertainers ranged from bandleader Lionel Hampton to film stars Gene Kelly and Jane Powell to singers Jane Froman, Lena Horne, and Dick Haymes to a comedy team called Lum and Abner, portraying Ozark old-timers.

For the crowd, Lum defined the word inauguration: "Every four years a Democrat is sworn in in Washington."

For Truman, inaugural day, Thursday, January 20, 1949, began before dawn.

One reporter noted the moon in the predawn Washington sky as Truman appeared

Battery D veterans leave for Truman's inauguration festivities in Washington.

outside of Blair House to leave for his 7 A.M. breakfast with his World War I artillery battery at the Mayflower Hotel.

A prayer service at St. John's Church in Lafayette Square began at ten A.M.

The inauguration itself began at the Capitol at noon.

At 12:50, after having been sworn in and delivering his inauguration speech, Truman left a Capitol luncheon to ride in an open limousine down Pennsylvania Avenue to a reviewing stand outside the White House.

The inaugural parade lasted several hours. An inaugural reception followed at the National Gallery of Art, itself followed by the inaugural

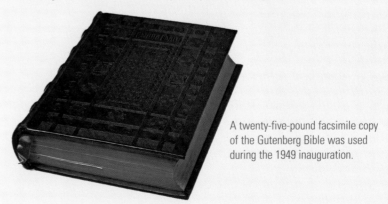

A twenty-five-pound facsimile copy of the Gutenberg Bible was used during the 1949 inauguration.

ball, back at the armory.

Richard Bolling, the former U.S. representative who had in November 1948 just been elected to represent the Kansas City area, fought off voters demanding tickets to all events. "I learned right away how much pressure you can get from constituents," Bolling said in 1989.

Jacobson had it worse.

"He was besieged by friends at the hotel," said Gloria Schusterman. "People were asking him to get them into this ball or that party," she said. "So it was exciting for him."

It was so exciting that on the morning of the inauguration Jacobson, who suffered from hypertension, woke up with high blood pressure and missed the ceremony.

For Truman's inauguration, Washington threw off the wartime austerity present during final swearing in of Franklin Roosevelt in 1944. The Republican Congress, confident of a Dewey victory, had appropriated $80,000 for Dewey's assumed inaugural. The Democrats, with Truman's blessing, decided to spend it all and more besides. Washington taverns applied for the right to stay open until four A.M. instead of two A.M.

Most Missouri residents, however, found one another in Washington hotels. One day Rufus Burrus Jr., son of the Independence lawyer and friend of Truman, accompanied his father

Women related to Battery D veterans look down the escalator at Kansas City's Union Station as they prepare to travel by train to Truman's inauguration festivities.

to the coffee shop in the Mayflower Hotel. There the younger Burrus met a boy two years his senior.

More than twenty-five years later, the younger Burrus would rise at an Independence restaurant and introduce, as a candidate for the U.S. House of Representatives, the boy he met that morning: Ike Skelton.

Skelton, who since 1977 has represented Missouri's fourth congressional district, remembers the 1949 inauguration for that chance encounter as well as another. At a reception for Missouri residents at Washington's Shoreham Hotel, Skelton, then seventeen years old and interested in running track, met a St. Louis lawyer who had run track at Cornell University.

"Instead of talking to other people, he talked to me," Skelton said. "Later in the evening he agreed to mail me information on training."

Skelton went on to run track for Wentworth Military Academy in Lexington, Missouri, and, only seven years later, ran for prosecuting attorney of Lafayette County, Missouri, just to the east of Jackson County. In both endeavors he received advice from his friend from the inauguration, Thomas Hennings who was elected to the U.S. Senate in 1950 and served until his death in 1960.

Skelton also recalled that in 1949 he stood across from the presidential reviewing stand on Pennsylvania Avenue and saw the car carrying South Carolina Governor Strom Thurmond approach the reviewing stand which held Truman. Thurmond had run for president as the candidate of the States Rights Democratic Party and had carried four states.

Passing the president's stand, Thurmond waved.

Some published accounts have Truman returning only a stony glare. Skelton, however, recalls that when Thurmond waved, Truman happened to be talking to someone else on the stand and simply didn't see Thurmond.

Whether Truman's snub was real or accidental, the story's conclusion didn't arrive until thirty-five years later in 1984. That's when Skelton was serving as chairman of a centennial anniversary joint session of Congress honoring Truman.

"Would you like to know who was president pro tem of the U.S. Senate and who sat on the dais?" Skelton said in 1989, referring to the centennial joint session. "Strom Thurmond. So I saw both ends of that piece of history."

Representing Missouri in the inaugural parade was a Missouri float pulled by six huge Percheron horses, a Jackson County "posse" of lawmen on horses, and a Lamar, Missouri, float pulled by four mules. Of the ninety-seven members of Battery D who marched beside the president's limousine, only two failed to complete the walk down Pennsylvania Avenue. Battery members wearing their identifying armbands also discovered that police and security guards often gave way before them.

"They pass through police and Secret Service lines with the same honors as a general," *The Star* reported.

Rejecting inaugural tradition, the committee organizing the inaugural ball decided to assign seat boxes by random drawing. Another decision, designed to maintain decorum, was to ban alcohol from official inaugural events like the ball.

"Nothing will be served in bottles," the inaugural committee had announced. This prompted mixed reviews, as some observers wondered if Democrats were displaying too much decorum. "You can tell the registered Democrats by their Lord Fauntleroy look and their Chesterfieldian airs," wrote syndicated columnist Inez Robb. "However, some Democrats are muttering, 'Just how significant can you get, question mark.' "

Thanks to the primitive television coverage of the time, more persons watched Truman's inaugural than had ever before seen a single event. "You could see Mr. Truman fiddling with his gloves when he first arrived," one Associated Press reporter wrote, watching in New York. An estimated ten million people watched as images of the inauguration came in sharp and clear in St. Louis, near the western end of the nation's existing television network. The Associated Press found it appropriate to report that a druggist in Sedalia, Missouri, some 150 miles west of St. Louis, reported good reception.

For several days, Harry Truman had ruled Washington. Some attending the inaugural ball wore Harry Truman masks. At the Missouri reception at the Shoreham Hotel, photographs of Truman were enclosed in frames of spun sugar.

Even the weather cooperated for the thirty-third president. The day before the inaugural was cold and cloudy. Then inauguration day dawned cold but bright. The next day a sleet storm arrived and one Washington newspaper announced that the president had given the weather back to the weather bureau.

At some point, during the pre-inaugural confusion, an official inaugural invitation had been sent to Harry Truman.

"Weather permitting," the president had written in the invitation's right-hand corner, "I hope to be present."

"**D**on't make this alarmist," Harry Truman said, reassuring reporters gathered at the Kansas City airport on the afternoon of Sunday, June 25, 1950. North Korean troops had crossed into South Korea, and while the outlook appeared ominous, Truman told the correspondents he remained hopeful.

But that's not what he told John Snyder, his treasury secretary, who climbed aboard Truman's airplane a short time later in St. Louis.

"We're in trouble, I think," Truman said.

When Truman's plane had touched down in Kansas City some twenty-four hours before, the agenda had been different.

His thirty-first wedding anniversary was the next Wednesday. He wanted, he had written Stanley Woodward, the ambassador to Canada, to do "some fence building – not political – order a new roof on the farmhouse and tell some politicians to go to hell. A grand visit – I hope?"

What happened over the next day was a juxtaposition of the momentous with the mundane.

On Saturday night Truman gathered with his family for dinner at 219 North Delaware. The clan later reassembled on the home's new screened-in back porch. Not long after dusk, the telephone rang for the president.

Truman took the call and came back to face the family, Margaret Truman later wrote.

"That was Dean Acheson," her father said, referring to his secretary of state. "The Communists have invaded South Korea. I'm going to stay here tonight. It may not be as serious as it sounds. Tomorrow I want everyone to pretend it's business as usual."

On Sunday morning *The Kansas City Star* greeted readers with a headline announcing the crisis. But on North Delaware, Margaret wrote, "We were all good soldiers. We went to Trinity Church and chatted with neighbors as if it was just another sleepy summer Sunday in Independence." Truman himself visited the family farm in Grandview, as well as his sister's house.

Meanwhile, the United Nations Security Council was preparing to consider a resolution, drafted overnight, calling for the immediate withdrawal of North Korean forces.

Truman returned to Independence before noon. As if on cue, the telephone rang with Acheson on the line. After the secretary confirmed the scale of the invasion, Truman made a quick decision to return to Washington.

His plane was in the air less than two hours later.

Until the invasion of Korea, Truman had been on a remarkable roll.

The spring of 1950 had marked the five-year anniversary of Truman's ascent to power, and reporters had observed the occasion with stories that conceded his strengths, chief among them the meeting and greeting of voters. He had spent much of the spring touring the Great Plains by rail and charming voters who responded to his common touch. An article in the *Washington Post* traced Truman's appeal back to his days working the counter in his Kansas City haberdashery.

"In this way he is making himself probably the most available president in the history of the nation," read the June 25 article.

But it's tempting to regard the invasion of Korea as a personal divide for Truman, after which his presidency appeared to go into a decline.

"So much for Mother's hope for a quiet anniversary," Margaret wrote. "It was gone – and so were the sunny political skies of 1949. So was the president's peace of mind."

Following the invasion of Korea, Truman did not make any more extended campaign trips in 1950. In midterm elections that November, Democrats lost twenty-eight House seats and five in the Senate. The 1950 elections served as a preview of the 1952 general election, when Republicans capitalized on the issues of "Korea, corruption, and communism."

There was some good news in December. Truman, back in his Independence home for the Christmas holiday, took another telephone call, this time from General Omar Bradley, chairman of the Joint Chiefs of Staff. Bradley told Truman that the evacuation of 105,000 United States and South Korean troops – the final act in a precarious retreat in the face of an overwhelming wave of 300,000 Chinese forces that had counterattacked in North Korea in late November – had been completed from the North Korean port of Hungnam.

"I thank God for the success of the Hungnam operation," Truman said in a statement released on Christmas Eve. "It is the best Christmas present I could have."

On Christmas morning, Truman took an eighteen-block walk through his Independence neighborhood. He flew out of Kansas City's downtown airport the next day for Washington. As the war continued, Truman's popularity plummeted. By March 1951 his public approval rating stood at 26 percent, then a record low.

When he fired General Douglas MacArthur the next month, Republican lawmakers discussed impeachment. By November 1951, Truman's approval rating bottomed out at 23 percent. Richard Nixon's approval rating, when he resigned in August 1974, had stood at 24 percent.

A grave President Truman speaks to reporters at the Municipal Airport before taking off for an unexpected return to Washington because of the Korean crisis, June 25, 1950.

In March 1952, Truman announced he would not run for re-election.

President Truman, here accompanied by a Secret Service agent, was often followed by neighbors and children as he took his morning walk when he was back in Independence. After the presidency, he became the most public private citizen in Independence, and neighbors continued to accompany him on his walks. When Truman left the presidency, the government did not provide him with Secret Service protection, but the Independence mayor assigned police officer Mike Westwood to serve as Truman's official guard and companion.

CHAPTER 9

BACK HOME IN INDEPENDENCE

Harry Truman's office telephone number in the Kansas City Federal Reserve Bank building was Baltimore 6150.

His home address in Independence was 219 North Delaware Street. His usually awoke at about 5:30 A.M., with his daily walk around his Independence neighborhood beginning about forty-five minutes later.

His route often was south on North Delaware and then left, on Maple Avenue, heading uptown to Independence Square. After his walk, it would be time for breakfast, and then time for the drive west – on Truman Road – to downtown Kansas City.

After returning to Jackson County from the White House in January 1953, Harry Truman resolved to resume life as a private citizen. "It's a pleasure indeed to be going home as a private citizen once more," he had said during his train trip back from Washington. "I look forward to a grand time doing what I please and going where I please."

While Truman did go and do as he pleased, he was never just another private citizen back home in Independence and Kansas City. For almost twenty years, from his January 1953 return to his December 1972 death, Harry Truman remained Jackson County's most public private citizen, and he and his wife spent their final years alternately embracing and avoiding the local spotlight.

In Independence and Kansas City, Truman wrote his memoirs, built his presidential library, gave away his daughter in marriage, campaigned in presidential and congressional elections, and received the several presidents or presidential candidates who came seeking his support.

So high was his local profile that the details of his everyday life – his routine, his home address, even his office telephone number – were reprinted in the newspapers. It would be a decade after the Trumans returned to Independence before former presidents received Secret Service protection.

Sometimes Harry and Bess Truman had to hold the world at arm's length, as common sense dictated. One of the first things

Tourists pose for pictures in front of the Truman home, 1960.

Truman in front of the
Independence Depot.

1976. "He was totally without protection and this was a gross injustice by the federal government."

Weatherford asked that Independence police officer Mike Westwood serve as Truman's official guard and companion.

Together the two would follow a familiar path through the Independence residential streets not long after dawn. Hazel Graham, an Independence neighbor, recalled that in the day before widespread residential air conditioning, she would hear through an open window the sound of Truman's cane tapping on the sidewalk in the morning.

Not everyone recognized the former president at first, as when Truman, while walking not long after returning from the White House, visited a construction site near his home.

"A shovel [automatic] and a drag line were working, as well as some laboring men digging in the old-fashioned way," Truman

that Bess Truman wanted to do upon returning home to Independence, Margaret Truman later wrote, was to remove the fence surrounding the Truman home, installed in 1947 as a security measure.

But the Trumans soon changed their mind once they saw the hundreds of people walking or driving past their home every week.

Hazel Graham, 1989, first executive director, Jackson County Historical Society; neighbor of Harry and Bess Truman. On why the Trumans eventually agreed to put up a fence around their home at 219 North Delaware in the late 1940s:

"I remember when the crowds got so thick sometimes and they would go up and try to take splinters off of the house. We were all incensed in the neighborhood that people were so rude."

The same thought occurred to Independence Mayor Robert Weatherford, as he saw hundreds of Independence residents lining the streets while accompanying the Trumans on their first drive home to 219 North Delaware from the Independence train station after their January 1953 arrival.

"The federal government did not at that time furnish any kind of protection whatsoever to a former president," Weatherford said in

later wrote. "The boss or the contractor was looking on and I asked him if he didn't need a good strawboss. He took a look at me and then watched the work a while and then took another look and broke out in a broad smile and said, 'Oh yes! You are out of a job, aren't you?' "

Soon various Independence residents became sufficiently emboldened to approach the former president. One elderly couple one day saw him on the sidewalk and, instead of

President Truman received dozens of handmade gifts including this cane bearing his name in raised letters.

crossing the street to talk to him, asked him to cross the street to talk to them.

Truman did, and accordingly signed the autograph book of a granddaughter.

"The granddaughter lived in Detroit," Truman later wrote in a May 1953 diary entry, "and was very sure that anybody in Independence [could] get me to do whatever was wanted. I'd never seen the old people before but I signed the granddaughter's autograph book."

On another occasion, a group of young people approached Truman.

"A day or so before that I was walking up the hill at Union and Maple and was stopped by a bunch of boys and girls for the purpose of having a picture made with a young man named Adams who was running for president of the Student Council," Truman wrote. "I wonder how he came out. That stunt may have beaten him."

Eventually Independence residents began to anticipate Truman's morning ritual, often greeting the former president when he emerged in the morning. He routinely dressed in office clothes, such as a coat and tie, with snappy Panama hat and cane.

"I feel a lot more comfortable," he once explained. "I never know who I'm likely to meet, so I try to be prepared."

As one of the state's principal tourist attractions, Truman felt he had a responsibility to take his walks.

"Sometimes whole delegations stand outside, looking in over the fence – school children, Girl Scouts, all kinds of people," he once wrote. " I realize they've come to see the striped mule of Missouri, and I don't want them to be disappointed."

Harry Truman's early morning walks provided inspiration for this whimsical organization made up of reporters, photographers, and Secret Service men. "Chief Follower" Tony Vaccaro was a White House correspondent for the Associated Press and a personal friend of President Truman.

ORAL HISTORIES

Hazel Graham, 1989, neighbor of Harry and Bess Truman.
On Harry Truman's walks around his North Delaware neighborhood:

"Well, Mr. Truman was always very anxious to speak to everybody in the neighborhood as he walked around, and if you didn't get out where he could talk to you, he often waved to you. Before he had to use the cane to lean on, he always had the cane and he waved with the cane. It was a normal thing to see Mr. Truman waving to somebody with his cane.

"In those days we didn't have as much air-conditioning as we have today; so I have been awakened any number of mornings by hearing this `tap, tap, tap' (through the open window) because he swung his cane as he walked, and it would go 'tap tap tap.' "

The doorway of the 822 Club in the prestigious Kansas City Club, which Truman joined to partake in fellowship and poker. *Photo by Ray Geselbracht*

Most of Jackson County resolved to respect the Truman family's privacy – to the point where the Trumans perhaps thought everyone respected it a little too much.

Artist Thomas Hart Benton, who came to know Truman while preparing the mural in the lobby of the former president's library, wrote that he thought the Trumans were waiting to be invited out. Randall Jessee, a prominent Kansas City's television news correspondent in the 1950s, thought the same.

"Then, along about in 1953 or '54, it might have been, one time I told my wife, 'I think that Mr. Truman and Mrs. Truman are lonely,' " Jessee said in 1964. "They don't get invited out as much as they should. I think people are just afraid to invite them out. They just think that 'Oh, they wouldn't want to come to our house.' "

Jessee asked, and the Trumans accepted.

Truman also was pleased when a longtime Kansas City friend Tom Evans cajoled him into joining the 822 Club, so named for the room in the exclusive Kansas City Club in which members convened for poker and fellowship.

Harry Truman had always been at home among people. After his 1972 death, Truman Library archivists made an inventory of the contents of his wallet, which bulged with membership cards. He had carried, for instance, a metal card crediting him as being an honorary precinct captain of the Cook County Illinois Democratic Party. No great lover of spectactor sports like baseball, he had nevertheless carried a 1968 stadium pass from the St. Louis Cardinals.

For those opening stores or championing nonprofit causes, the former president often was available. He helped open a grocery store, cutting the ribbon with a hacksaw wrapped in aluminum foil. He worked telephones to help raise money for the 1859 Jail, Marshal's Home and Museum in Independence.

ORAL HISTORIES

*Hazel Graham, 1989, neighbor of Harry and Bess Truman.
Of Bess Truman's favorite reading spot at 219 North Delaware:*

"Another time I came to bring something and she said, 'I was just sitting there on the stairway reading.' I guess she thought I looked a little bit surprised about why she was sitting on the stairs reading. She said, 'That was my favorite place from the time I was a child, because then of course we didn't have any air-conditioning and there was always a nice breeze, a cool breeze blowing up the stairway. That's where I read all my books.' She said, 'I still read some books sitting there on the stairway going up the stairs.'"

In formal wear, he conducted the Kansas City Philharmonic. When the Kansas City Athletics, the first major league baseball team to call Kansas City home, opened its first season in 1955, Truman threw out the first pitch.

He had decided to build his presidential library in Independence, and sometimes it was a good idea to be more public than private. Margaret Truman was amazed in May 1955, on Truman's seventy-first birthday, when Bess Truman invited some 150 guests to 219 North Delaware. But that was when Truman was looking for assistance in building his library. When the Independence Chamber of Commerce presented a check, the presentation took place on the back porch of the Truman home.

Truman seemed to resign himself eventually to being a curiosity, both in and outside of Jackson County. "I've had the usual reception here," Truman wrote in a diary while visiting New York in January 1954. "Wish my 'glamour' would come off so I can be a 'regular citizen' again. Looks now as if it never will."

The street on the north side of the Truman home – once named Van Horn Road – was now Truman Road, so renamed after his election in 1948. Truman had no problem with it, as long as everyone knew he had not instigated the idea. When Independence erected a sign identifying the city as the home of the thirty-third president, Truman's only complaint was that Grover Cleveland had served two separate terms, making Truman the thirty-second president.

In April 1956, when Margaret Truman married Clifton Daniel at Trinity Episcopal Church in Independence, the reception was

The last billfold carried by Harry S. Truman contained a few dollar bills, his driver's license, several credit cards, and almost fifty passes and membership cards.

Harry, Bess, and Margaret Truman are feted at a dinner in their honor in Independence, February 6, 1953.

a private affair at the Truman home. Yet just outside the home, bumper-to-bumper traffic crawled by – on Truman Road.

Following the 1963 assassination of President John Kennedy, Congress approved a bill authorizing Secret Service protection for former presidents. Bess Truman recoiled at the thought, and Harry Truman reacted negatively when one Secret Service agent told him that he no longer needed Mike Westwood. Only through the intervention of President Lyndon Johnson, who telephoned Bess Truman, did the Trumans ultimately accept the protection.

Even when the Trumans traveled, they could not escape their celebrity. In the summer of 1953, Harry and Bess Truman drove to Washington. They were thrilled with their status of private citizens, which lasted as

long as it took to drive to Hannibal, Missouri, where they were recognized at a restaurant. In Decatur, Illinois, they checked into a motel and soon discovered six police officers monitoring their room. On the way back from Washington, a police officer pulled the Trumans over on the Pennsylvania Turnpike. Truman said the officer merely wanted to shake his hand; the officer said Truman had cut off two motorists trying to pass.

It was the Trumans' last long car trip.

The Trumans boarded a cruise ship bound for Hawaii in 1953. In 1956 the

Left In formal wear Truman conducts the Kansas City Philharmonic, March 22, 1958.

Right Truman cuts the ribbon opening a local grocery store, using a hacksaw covered with aluminum foil.

Trumans traveled to France, Italy, and England. When they left from the Independence depot on May 8 of that year, the former president's seventy-second birthday, friends came to the small Independence train depot to see them off and cut a birthday cake. Upon the June 1957 birth of Clifton Truman Daniel, their first grandchild, Harry and Bess Truman the next day climbed on the first train east that went through the Independence station.

In 1958, Truman went to Yale, and then back to Europe. In November 1961, the Trumans traveled back to Washington, where they were special guests at a White House dinner given in their honor by John and Jacqueline Kennedy.

If Truman was retired from the White House, he never considered himself retired from politics. In 1956 Truman, appearing on local television, introduced James Pendergast, nephew of former Boss Tom Pendergast, and the leader of a Kansas City Democratic Party faction which was supporting various candidates in an upcoming primary.

During the 1958 congressional campaign, Truman gave thirty-five speeches in twenty states. He still fancied himself a player. In July 1960, he held a press conference at the Truman Library supporting Missouri Senator Stuart Symington for the Democratic Party nomination for president. Ultimately, however, he threw his support behind John Kennedy once Kennedy secured the nomination.

Former President Truman throws the first ball in a game played on April 12, 1955, by the Kansas City Athletics, Kansas City's first major league baseball team.

In 1960 Truman received Robert Kennedy at the Truman Library before a Democratic rally in Sugar Creek, the Standard Oil refinery town adjacent to Independence

Hazel Graham, 1989, neighbor of Harry and Bess Truman. On the apologies Harry and Bess Truman offered after a surprise visit from President Lyndon Johnson:

"I was supposed to take something that Mrs. Truman had ordered by the house as I went home to lunch. I went by and didn't stop because there was such a huge crowd of reporters and photographers all around. When I went back to the museum after lunch, they were still there, so I didn't stop then, either.

"In the early afternoon, Mrs. Truman called me and said, 'I am so sorry. We had no idea that the president was going to stop by here and I know that you couldn't have even gotten in, but we really do want to apologize.' I said, 'Well, no problem at all. I'll stop by as I go home.'

"I did stop by with the package as I was on my way home that evening, and Mrs. Truman was apologizing again. I didn't go into the house. I just handed it to her at the front door. She was apologizing again and Mr. Truman came in from the back hall and he was apologizing; he kept saying, 'I'm so sorry about that.' And he said, 'I thought he was never going to leave.' "

That year Truman hosted a luncheon for Kennedy at Kansas City's Muehlebach Hotel. He also received Robert Kennedy at the Truman Library before a Democratic rally in Sugar Creek, the Standard Oil refinery town adjacent to Independence.

In 1960, he delivered thirteen speeches in nine states in support of Kennedy.

After that, Truman's political appearances were more ceremonial. In July 1965, when President Lyndon Johnson signed the new Medicare bill, he did so at the auditorium of the Truman Museum. In March 1969 Truman welcomed President Richard Nixon, with wife Pat, to his home at 219 North

Former President and Mrs. Truman on the porch of their Independence home, August 5, 1969.

Delaware, and to the library as well.

From 1957, when the library was dedicated, through 1964, Truman came to his library office almost every day. After that his visits were less frequent. Truman stopped coming regularly in 1967.

When the members of Truman's World War I artillery battery gathered in Kansas City for a fiftieth anniversary celebration in 1968, the highlight was a reception at 219 North Delaware. The next year, on June 28, 1969, the Trumans celebrated their fiftieth wedding anniversary by receiving a few friends.

The world available to them was shrinking by then, and had begun to years before. In 1965, when Mary Paxton Keeley wrote Bess Truman, inviting them to visit her in Columbia, Missouri, some two hours east of Independence, Bess wrote back, saying they couldn't drive that far anymore.

Truman usually rose at 5:30 a.m. and took his daily walk around his Independence home about forty-five minutes later. Here he is walking circa 1960.

COMING HOME

On the train heading home to Independence from Washington in January 1953, Harry Truman couldn't stay in his private car. Instead, he kept coming forward, walking through diners and coaches. When passengers recognized him and stood, he told them to sit down. "Don't get up," he said. "I'm no longer president."

The day before, when he had slipped away from the Capitol after the inauguration of Dwight Eisenhower, Truman's limousine had stopped at a red light. Truman biographers consider this the first time since 1945 that a car in which Truman was riding had done that. Later that day, when the Trumans boarded a train at Washington's Union Station, no Secret Service agents accompanied them.

These may have been the first signs of Truman's encroaching private citizenship and in that context, Truman's forays into the coach cars represented the former president trying on his old Jackson County self and seeing if it still fit.

It's not clear what Harry and Bess Truman were expecting when their train stopped outside the small Independence station just after nine p.m. on January 21, 1953. But the crowd of 8,500 people that cheered the Trumans' arrival touched and amazed them.

"Thank you very much," Truman said after being led to a microphone. "I can't tell you how much we appreciate this reception. It's magnificent – much

more than we anticipated. It's a good feeling to be back home."

Bess Truman stepped to the microphone – an event in itself. "I'm just delighted to be home," she said. "This certainly is a wonderful welcome."

Accompanied by Independence Mayor Robert Weatherford and his wife, the Trumans were driven to their home at 219 North Delaware. There, another fifteen hundred spectators cheered when the Trumans stepped out of the car and climbed the steps to their front door serenaded by the William Chrisman High School band.

"I never saw anything like this in my life," Truman told the crowd. "If I had been elected to something, I could understand something like this, but this is hard to understand."

The Trumans entered their home, but a crowd of about two hundred lingered. Some forty-five minutes later, the Trumans reappeared. "A welcome like this is just out of this world," the former president said. "I never had a welcome equal to this anywhere in the world."

The crowd gave the Trumans

one final cheer, and then everyone went home.

The morning after, a reporter asked the former president what was the first thing he planned to do. In a remark that would become recognized as vintage Truman, he said he planned to "carry the grips up to the attic."

Harry Truman's homecoming in Independence on January 21, 1953. The crowd of 8,500 people that cheered their arrival amazed the Trumans.

TRUMAN AND THOMAS HART BENTON

They liked each other.

Both were born in southwest Missouri. Both knew politics; the great uncle of one was an early Missouri senator. Both drank bourbon.

They didn't like each other.

One of them, Harry Truman, called a painting rendered by the other, Thomas Hart Benton, a "monstrosity." Truman also once referred to the Benton mural in the capitol building in Jefferson City, Missouri, as the "horror" that spoiled the statehouse.

Benton, for his part, once wrote that he was "appalled" by Truman's notions of art.

None of this stopped Truman one day in 1960 from climbing a scaffolding and, with Benton beside him, applying his own brush strokes to the mural that is

today known as "Independence and the Opening of the West" at the Harry S. Truman Presidential Museum & Library.

Benton and Truman were two independent thinkers who rose above misunderstanding to become friends so thick that

Artist Thomas Hart Benton works on a sketch of former President Truman at his Independence home while Truman reads a book

Truman later called Benton "the best muralist in the country" and Benton considered Truman a model patron.

The story begins in the 1950s when, according to Benton's version of events, he had seen busier days. "The 1950s had been a bad time for my art," Benton wrote in a memoir *The Intimate Story, the President and Me.* "Although I still had a good deal of journalistic support, the art galleries and museums had little interest in my paintings."

Fortunately, he added, "my reputation as a muralist had survived."

So he saw as fortuitous the visit to his Kansas City studio by Wayne Grover, archivist of the United States, and David Lloyd, executive director of the corporation that built the Truman Museum in the 1950s. Both were considering a mural as a finishing touch to the building, which had been dedicated in 1957.

A wild card figured to be Truman, who had his own opinions of the art world. "I know nothing about Art with a capital A, particularly the frustrated brand known as modern," Truman wrote Benton's agent in 1955.

Whether Truman considered Benton's work to be modern was unclear. Benton, born some five years after Truman in 1889, had studied at the Chicago Art Institute and the Academie Julien in Paris. By the 1930s he had established his style, which many

"The Old President" by Thomas Hart Benton, 1971, 37 x 21 oil painting, owned by UMB Bank n.a. Trustee of the Rita and Thomas Hart Benton Testamentary Trusts. ©T.H. Benton and Rita P. Benton Testamentary Trusts/Licensed by VAGA, New York, NY

described as American Regionalist and which was thought to be shared by other artists like John Steuart Curry and Grant Wood.

The Truman Museum mural happened anyway, despite the following dust-ups:

• *Truman's opinion of Benton.*
In 1955, Benton's agent had invited Truman to the artist's Belleview Avenue studio in Kansas City so he could be pho-

tographed with Benton and a new painting entitled "The Kentuckian." The agent included a reproduction of the picture which Truman didn't like.

"Both of my grandfathers

Truman views the Benton mural in the Truman Museum.

were from Kentucky as were both of my grandmothers," Truman wrote. "All of the four had brothers and sisters most of whom I knew when I was a child. They did not look like that long-necked monstrosity of Mr. Thomas Hart Benton's." Truman closed by adding that he wouldn't encourage Benton to commit any more "horrors like those in Missouri's beautiful capitol."

• *Benton's Jefferson City mural.*

Benton's statehouse mural, depicting the social history of Missouri, was controversial as soon as Benton completed it in 1936. The mural included recog-

nizable Kansas City figures – chief among them was Boss Tom Pendergast, Truman's political sponsor. Truman apparently thought Benton included Pendergast without Pendergast's knowledge or permission. On the contrary, Pendergast posed for the picture, according to Benton.

Benton conspired with friend Randall Jessee, a Kansas City television news personality and friend of the Trumans. Both hosted parties to which the Trumans were invited. While Truman was leaving one of the parties, Benton slipped Truman an original Pendergast sketch. "By the way he accepted it, with a good

hearty grip of the hand, I knew that at least one difference between us had been done away with for good," Benton wrote.

• *Bourbon.*

According to Benton, Truman once told him, "I hear you like this," while pulling a bottle out of his desk. When the artist asked for water and two ice cubes for his drink, he said Truman told him, "Well, you don't drown it."

Benton wrote: "This performance on the part of a president of the United States embarrassed me. There is no good reason why it should have, because it was a common act of human hospitality, but there was still about Harry Truman an aura of power . . ."

When the bourbon ritual became more familiar, Benton perceived it in another way. Whenever Benton would ask for a second glass, Truman would say, "Tom, you're driving a car. You can't have another because you've got some work to do around here and I'm not going to take risks with you."

Benton wrote: "I was now, in effect, his man and he was going to protect me. And he did."

• *The mural's subject matter.*

By 1957, the president had accepted the idea of a mural and the idea of Benton rendering it. But just what Benton would paint had to be decided before a contract could be signed.

In early discussions, Truman kept telling Benton of his admiration for Thomas Jefferson and his foresight in the negotiations that led to the Louisiana Purchase. The mural, Truman thought, should incorporate that.

Benton, he wrote, was "appalled." He kept trying to rein in Truman's ambitions for the mural. He wrote that the president's thinking was verbal, not visual. Finally, Benton said, "Mr. President, there's no way I can paint President Jefferson's foresight and I can't paint negotiations, either."

Truman, Benton wrote, then said, "Well, what the . . . is it you can paint?"

Seeing the opening, Benton presented an outline of a mural that would emphasize Independence and its role in the opening of the West. "I said I would get it up with enough historic detail for him

to understand what I was trying to put over, and finally I said, 'And it'll be something I can paint.' He told me to 'Go ahead.' "

By comparison, other details, such as Benton's price for the mural, $60,000, sparked little debate. The principals signed the contract in June 1958. The ensuing project took more than two years. Benton first produced sketches, and then sculpted a three-dimensional clay model depicting the figures that would appear in the finished painting. He first began to paint in December 1959.

Truman never bothered him, Benton said. Once, he allowed Truman to climb the scaffolding and apply paint to a corner of the mural.

The completed painting, covering 495 square feet in the Truman Museum's main lobby, was completed in March 1961. Upon its dedication the next month, Truman called Benton "the best muralist in the country."

Later, Benton worked with Truman again, this time for a portrait.

Benton first had attempted to render a likeness of Truman not long after he finished the library mural, and began visiting the former president in his library office. But, Benton complained, library staff members volunteered their opinions on how the former president should be depicted, and the artist soon abandoned the project.

Then, several years later, both Truman and Benton agreed to try again. Benton made four trips to the Truman home for sketches, and then completed the painting in his Kansas City garage studio.

Soon it was on display in the lobby of the Truman Museum, and some employees were not pleased. As described at the time by Harry F. Rosenthal, Associated Press correspondent, the painting "shows a white-haired old man engrossed in a book held in gnarled, arthritic fingers. The shirt collar and suit are loose. About all that's familiar is the hawk nose, made more prominent by the lines in Truman's face. Like all Benton paintings, it's scrupulously detailed."

Benton, meanwhile, couldn't understand the disappointment of some.

"The old man looks better as an old man than he did as a young man," he told Rosenthal. "You get that fat off of him and you see that chicken-hawk face and also his sensitivity." He added: "You can see the man without the jowls and the fat. He has no need now to put on an act, any kind of public act. So he relaxes now. He's a very interesting old man."

Thomas Hart Benton gives Truman a check for the Harry S. Truman Scholarship Fund, May 7, 1960.

Benton, by the way, had received the endorsement of perhaps the most important critic of all.

"Mrs. Truman saw it," the artist told Rosenthal, "and said, 'That's him.' "

VIETTA GARR

At the Independence home of Harry and Bess Truman, Vietta Garr prepared dinner and served it.

But over decades of such service at the Truman home and the White House, she would do much more.

She would help rear Margaret, the Trumans' daughter. She also would serve as companion to Madge Gates Wallace, the president's mother-in-law. That was important because Wallace in the 1940s agreed to move to the White House if Garr went, too.

That meant Bess Truman, instead of having to remain in Independence and tend to her mother, also could stay in the White House. And, no longer distracted by domestic matters, Harry Truman then could run the country.

An exhibit at the Harry S Truman National Historic Site in Independence shed light on Garr's dual role in the Truman family. One display, featuring a flour sifter and a potato masher borrowed from the Truman home's kitchen, invoked her official role as cook.

But other artifacts, such as a photograph of Garr attending Margaret Truman's 1956 wedding, suggested her role as member of the extended Truman family.

Ione Vietta Garr was born in Independence in 1896 and she began working for the Truman-Wallace family in 1928. In 1945, when Franklin Roosevelt's death

made Harry Truman president, the Trumans sent for Garr, who instructed White House cooks in what the Trumans enjoyed. Later, when Margaret Truman toured the country in pursuit of a singing career, Garr accompanied her. No better evidence of Harry Truman's trust in Garr can be imagined.

Garr ultimately worked thirty-six years for the Truman-Wallace family. When Margaret Truman served as host of a segment of Edward R. Murrow's 1950s *Person to Person* television show from the Truman home in Independence, Garr was included, along with Margaret's parents.

Soon a new generation

came to appreciate Garr.

Clifton Truman Daniel, eldest son of Margaret Truman Daniel, still has specific memories of Garr's cooking, remembered from his many visits to the Truman home at 219 North Delaware Street.

"Before our visits, she'd make a batch of brownies and layer them in a tin, separated by wax paper," Daniel said. "The minute I hit the house, I headed straight for the pantry to make sure the tin was there, with the corner of the wax paper sticking out from under the lid.

"I didn't even say hi to Grandpa until I had seen that tin."

The Trumans' regard for Garr was such that they helped finance a small home in Independence for her. Margaret Truman Daniel helped Garr select the design for the house, which still stands in the 100 block of East Farmer Street, just northeast of Independence Square.

"Mother always complained that I chose the most expensive one," Margaret Truman Daniel said through Clifton in 2002. "And I did. I wanted Vietta to be comfortable."

While white Independence knew Garr as a cook, the African-American community of Independence recognized her as one of its leading citizens. On one occasion, when she left Independence to join the Truman family at the White House, many of her friends organized a small parade to the train station, with some carrying a banner which read "Our First Lady." Garr also was affiliated with the Knights and Daughters of Tabor (International Order of Twelve),

a now-defunct fraternal organization. The group offered its members not only community but also medical and burial insurance unavailable through some white-owned companies.

Garr died in 1973. It's unclear how much, if at all, Garr's constant presence through the decades may have influenced Harry Truman's attitudes on racial relations. Although his courtship letters to Bess Wallace as a young man contained the occasional racial slur, Truman's initiatives on civil rights as president often were without precedent.

The former president's grandson, however, has little doubt as to Garr's influence.

"Looking back," said Clifton Truman Daniel, "I can't help but think that if my brothers and I are free of racial prejudice, and I think we are, it's not only because our parents and grand-parents raised us that way, but also because Vietta was so much a part of the family."

Vietta Garr was the Trumans' cook and helper, but she was also a member of the extended Truman family.

TRUMAN AND CARS

Harry Truman, some historians say, was America's last nineteenth-century president. But Harry Truman learned what a lot of twentieth-century men have learned: that when it came to getting a date, a car makes all the difference.

In 1917 Truman had his Stafford remodeled into a hot sports roadster and took it to Camp Doniphan.

His first car was not just any car but a hand-built, five-passenger, right-hand-drive 1911 Stafford with a brass-framed windshield. He bought it used in 1914, and it made all the difference in courting Bess Wallace of Independence.

The distance from the Truman farm in Grandview to North Delaware Street in Independence was about sixteen miles. In horse-and-buggy time, that was several hours. Or, Truman could take a train to Kansas City, and then transfer to Independence.

But in a car, Harry could arrive in good time and in a style to which, he hoped, Bess Wallace could one day become accustomed. Photographs survive of Truman, Bess, and assorted friends and cousins in the car. Photographs don't exist of the occasional mishaps Truman had with the same car, bending an axle and crashing into a ditch during one memorable outing taken with his mother and an uncle.

"When you have an auto, there is nothing else to cuss about," Harry wrote once to Bess. One of the first letters that

Truman responded to after returning to Independence from the White House in 1953 was from an automotive writer who was researching Truman's old Stafford. "I had it remodeled into a hot sport roadster and took it to Camp Doniphan with me in 1917," Truman wrote. Truman ultimately sold the car for $200 before leaving for Europe.

After the Stafford, Truman drove Dodges, Plymouths, and Chryslers. Some cars Truman bought from Independence dealer J. E. "Honey" Latimer. In 1955, Truman lent his signature to an "owner endorsement," a document used by the Latimer dealership in which former owners vouched for their trade-ins.

"I have driven Dodges since 1919," Truman wrote on the sheet touting his 1953 Dodge four-door.

He was particular about his cars. "The car was washed every few days," Margaret Truman once recalled. "And the upholstery was vacuumed and cleaned and people did not throw gum wrappers around – they were put in the ashtray – and he did not like people to smoke because he had

Bess Wallace, Harry Truman, Nellie Noland, and Mary Jane Truman riding in the Stafford, circa 1915.

never smoked and the smoke would get into the upholstery . . . "

Cars figured in Truman's private and public lives. In 1922 he campaigned for eastern Jackson County judge by driving the length and width of the county. "I had an old Dodge roadster which was a very rough rider," Truman said in one memoir. "I kept two bags of cement in the back of it so it would not throw me through the windshield while driving on our terrible county roads."

When Truman was defeated for re-election in 1924, he made a living by selling memberships in the Kansas City Automobile Club.

As Jackson County presiding judge in the 1930s, Truman sold voters on a bond issue for new roads by explaining that every farm in Jackson County could be within a short distance of a good county road. As someone who had served as a Jackson County road overseer in 1914, Truman had a knowledge of roads.

When considering a new county courthouse for downtown Kansas City, Truman took a driving tour of the South and Midwest, looking at possible designs and finally finding one he liked in Louisiana.

In 1934, and again in 1940, he drove much of the state campaigning for the U.S. Senate. "Fact is, I like roads," he once said.

In November, 1940, Truman won re-election to the Senate in an election that even President Franklin Roosevelt had doubted

Truman driving, 1946.

he could win. Four days later, Truman decided to observe the occasion by buying two new 1941 Chryslers in the same transaction. Truman even sprang for options - radios and heaters being options at the time.

The Trumans drove back to Washington from Independence after the 1940 election, and soon Truman was off on another road trip, this time through the South and back up through Arkansas and Oklahoma. On this trip Truman made several inspections at the sites of military camps and other defense installations then under construction.

These visits and the information Truman gathered there led to the formation of the Senate Special Committee to Investigate the National Defense Program, better known as the "Truman Committee." The committee saved taxpayers millions while exposing waste in the nation's defense buildup. It also made Truman's name far more familiar to Americans, as he later noted in a White House interview with writer John Hersey after he had become president.

"If I hadn't taken that drive I'd still be just Senator Truman instead of being in all this fix," Truman told Hersey.

In the summer of 1944, Harry,

Bess, and Margaret drove to Chicago to attend that year's Democratic National Convention, during which Truman received the nomination as Franklin Roosevelt's running mate. This impressed Bess not at all. On the drive back to Independence, well before the advent of air conditioning, Margaret described the climate inside the car as "arctic."

With all the mileage that Truman logged behind the wheel, it's almost unfair to dwell on his occasional mishaps. But he was in two known accidents.

In 1934, while campaigning for the U.S. Senate and driving between appearances in Rolla and Jefferson City, he struck a car that had turned in front of him on the highway. Truman suffered two broken ribs and a welt on his head. Truman's car, a used Plymouth bought specifically for the campaign, was no longer usable, and Truman used his wife's car for the balance of the campaign.

In 1938, while driving between Washington and Independence Truman's car collided with another car after Truman didn't notice a stop sign that was partially hidden by a parked car. Truman received a cut on his forehead, Bess a strained neck. Margaret was pulled out unhurt through a car window.

Between 1945 and 1953, as president, Truman didn't drive nearly as often as he was driven. After his return from Washington to Independence in January 1953, Harry bought Bess a new black Chrysler. Later that spring, he bought another car, a two-tone green Dodge coupe, to drive to his office in downtown Kansas City.

Throughout the 1950s, 1960s, and 1970s, the Trumans owned a variety of Dodge or Chrysler models. Some area residents later spoke of seeing the former president filling his tank at the gas station at 800 West Maple Avenue, just southwest of his home at 219 North Delaware Street.

Today the "Truman gas station" still stands, renovated and restored. There was some derision directed at the building's restoration. In 1993, the Independence City Council approved demolition of the then-vacant structure. Though attempts to restore Truman's neighborhood and significant landmarks were no doubt appropriate, some wondered if such efforts should be extended to his former gas station.

But after several preservationists pleaded their case, the city council reversed its decision. Today the structure serves as headquarters for the neighborhood redevelopment company which helps property owners in the Independence "Truman district" receive tax abatements for restoring their properties.

Filmmaker Robert Altman featured the gas station in his 1996 film *Kansas City*, which depicted the Kansas City's Jazz Age, much of which Harry Truman helped preside over as Jackson County presiding judge or U.S. senator.

One Independence preservationist couldn't resist making the point that to find authentic Kansas City buildings Altman had to travel to Independence and the "Truman gas station."

As the Trumans aged in the 1960s, their world shrank. While Harry Truman no longer drove,

This gas station used by Truman, restored in the 1990s, was used as headquarters for the neighborhood development company working to restore the Truman district in Independence.
Photo by Tammy Ljungblad

he and Bess allowed Independence police officer Mike Westwood, who served as the family bodyguard, to drive them to places such as the Independence library.

In 1968, then eighty-four, Truman was among the first to line up to have his car inspected when the law requiring state inspection went into effect that December 1. The mechanic who looked for forty-five minutes found nothing wrong with his car. After receiving the inspection certificate, Truman climbed in and was driven back home by Westwood.

Truman's last car was a 1972 Chrysler Newport Royal four-door sedan, Missouri license plate 5745. The numbers translate to May 7, 1945, when Truman learned that the war in Europe had ended.

Scholars believe that Truman, who died in December 1972, never drove the car. It was still in the Truman home garage when Bess Truman died in 1982. The park service staff that today maintains

the home considers the Chrysler the site's largest museum object. Staff members believe the Secret Service agents protecting Mrs. Truman used the car for errands.

In 2003 the car was on blocks, with its fluids drained out and its odometer reading approximately eighteen thousand miles.

Among the first in Missouri to comply with the state's new vehicle inspection law was former President Harry S. Truman in December 1968.

Just before Christmas in 1971, Harry Truman was at home at 219 North Delaware in Independence when he saw two unfamiliar teenagers slip by the door of his study. He got up and found his daughter, Margaret, who had just arrived with her family from New York.

"Who are those two young men with the long hair?" he asked her.

"Those are your two oldest grandsons," she said.

One thing the elderly Harry Truman did not appreciate, in the early 1970s, was the fashion of long hair on men.

One thing that Clifton Truman Daniel and his younger brother, William Wallace Daniel, had in abundance when they visited the Truman home in Independence in 1971 was long hair.

The former president let it slide. His grandsons had been welcome at 219 North Delaware since Clifton Truman Daniel, the eldest, was first brought to Independence in the late 1950s.

Back then Daniel was still a toddler, and one photograph depicts the former president holding the wide-eyed two-year-old in his arms at the Independence train station. Photographs of other homecomings depict the two older Daniel boys grabbing and hanging from their grandfather's arms and legs. But by the late 1960s and early 1970s, the former president was not up for such roughhousing, and by 1971 Daniel felt a subtle reserve that he attributed mostly

to the vast distance between their respective generations.

Daniel described greeting his grandfather that year in the Truman home in Independence in a 1995 book, *Growing Up with My Grandfather: Memories of Harry S. Truman*. Just after the family arrived for the 1971 Christmas visit, his mother had come to the foot of the stairs and called up to where Clifton and his brother Will had been rummaging through the toys their grandparents stored for the family's visits.

"So, worried about being summoned to the inner sanctum, I followed Will downstairs, through the dining room, and to the study door where Grandpa was still standing, one hand on his cane, the other on the doorway," Daniel wrote. "His dark gray suit seemed too big, his tie and collar loose around his neck. His face was gaunt, and his eyes looked huge behind his thick glasses. But there was something about him that made him seem anything but frail. As we approached, he didn't say anything, just looked us up and down, his mouth set.

" 'Hello, Grandpa,' I said.

" 'What was that?' he asked, cupping his left ear and leaning

forward a little.

" 'We just came to say hello,' I said, louder.

"He straightened up again and nodded once sharply.

" 'Well, do it, then.' "

Daniel brought a specific perspective to the story of Harry and Bess Truman living out their later years. While it was the viewpoint of a Truman family insider, it was also that of a family member who had grown up in New York City, well outside Jackson County, Missouri. Then there was the gulf in years between the two. Harry S. Truman was born in 1884, during the Gilded Age; his grandson, born in 1957, grew up with television and rock 'n' roll.

To Daniel, the Truman home at 219 North Delaware – today a national historic site operated by the National Park Service – endures in his memory as a vast vacation home featuring small mysterious rooms, heating ducts resonant enough to carry conversations between floors, an attic ladder to the roof, and drawers full of trinkets presented to the Trumans by distant Democratic committees.

There was the kitchen pantry. On every visit Daniel went to see that a red-and-white cookie tin had been filled with homemade brownies by Vietta Garr, the Trumans' longtime cook.

There was the study, which the Daniel brothers knew to be careful around, as it was the room in which their grandfather spent the bulk of his time.

"Books were crammed into every square inch of shelf space," Daniel wrote. "Table-size picture books, well-thumbed old history books, thick biographies, faded magazines all bulged from the floor-to-ceiling shelves. If you tried to slip even a pamphlet into the pile, it would all come crashing down."

There was the attic. "There were stacks and stacks of dusty hatboxes," Daniel wrote, "and a dozen or so plain, round-handled canes, as if my grandparents planned to open a Harry S. Truman spare parts store."

To young boys it was a house made for adventures, and the Daniel brothers had several.

Perhaps the most dramatic occurred one Christmas when the two eldest Daniel brothers received toy guns from their grandmother.

"She loved spoiling us and often gave us toys that my parents wouldn't have dreamed of buying," Daniel wrote. Only a few minutes' worth of playing with the guns outside 219 North Delaware prompted the Secret Service into rapid response mode, with two agents rushing from their station across North Delaware into the Truman home yard.

Equally hair-raising, however, was the response of their grandfather when the Daniel brothers decided to fire the guns inside 219 North Delaware. The toy

Grandfather Harry S. Truman proudly carries his grandson, Clifton Daniel, age two, after meeting the train of his mother, Margaret Truman Daniel, in December 1959.

guns fired red plastic bullets, and the brothers transformed the living room into a pistol range, popping shots off at a soft drink can positioned on a coffee table.

All was well, Daniel wrote, until he felt the gun yanked out of his hands by his grandfather, who, if he needed a cane to steady his walk, still owned an iron grip.

But he said nothing. His grandfather, Daniel wrote, "who

spent his life giving speeches and press conferences, turned stone-cold silent when someone close to him disappointed him. It was an effective tactic. He hadn't uttered a word, but I knew I was never again going to fire another

toy gun in the house."

The two older Daniel brothers also distinguished themselves with their grandmother when they decided, during another visit, to climb the attic ladder to the roof. Again the Secret Service deployed, this time alerting Bess Wallace, who responded by locking the door to the attic and then hiding the key. Years later, after Bess Truman's 1982 death, National Park Service rangers found the key tucked in the back of a file cabinet drawer on the home's second floor.

For the record, the two older Daniel brothers were joined on the roof by their mother, Margaret. According to Daniel, when his mother saw the head of the Trumans' Secret Service detail racing into the Truman home she said something close to "Uh-oh."

One of Daniel's earliest recollections of his grandparents is when they served as babysitters at his parents' New York home.

"I was about three years old and I was riding one of those hobbyhorses mounted on springs," Daniel said in a 1994 interview. "This is a memory that has been honed and refined over the

Truman grandsons William Wallace Daniel and Clifton Truman Daniel throw a football back and forth at the Truman home after Truman's funeral in December 1972.

years." When the horse tipped over, Daniel recalled, he began to cry. As his grandmother got up to assist him, his grandfather told her not to.

"He told me, 'You are not hurt," Daniel said. " 'Get up, put the horse back up, and start riding again.' Apparently, I shut up and and got up."

Another Daniel family story detailed how Clifton and his

brother Will were discovered by their mother one morning in their grandfather's lap. The preschoolers were spellbound by the Greek philosophy that their grandfather was reading aloud.

"Apparently we were giving him our undivided attention," Daniel said. "But my grandfather had a way of doing that. He never yelled and never raised his voice. Still, I had the sense that this was somebody whom you listened to."

More wheels began to turn inside Daniel's head in 1965 when he saw Lyndon Johnson, the new president of the United States, in his pajamas.

The Daniel family had attended the Johnson inauguration as representatives of Harry and Bess Truman. The next morning the family dropped by the White House, where Lyndon and Lady Bird Johnson greeted them in their bathrobes.

"Mr. Johnson kept hopping up and getting us souvenirs," said Daniel, who then was seven. "He finally went too far when he gave me and my brother each a book of White House matches."

When Daniel's father, Clifton Daniel, mentioned that they were late for their train, Johnson said, "Don't worry, the train will wait."

"Well, we finally sprinted out of there," Daniel said. "We got to the station and we were all running to the train when we saw the conductor. He said, 'Don't worry folks, the president called.'

"That's when I began to get the indication that my grandfather was somebody special. Because I could see the president in his pajamas, and that our train would wait for us."

Harry Truman died in 1972, when Daniel was fifteen. "My grandfather and I had very few meaningful discussions," Daniel said. "He died before I was mature enough to realize that I should have been sitting down with him."

Daniel returned to Independence with his family to attend his grandfather's funeral.

When Daniel was seventeen, the rock group Chicago released the song "Harry Truman," which saluted the former president's integrity and direct style of speech during the height of the Watergate era. The idea that his grandfather was the subject of a rock song by a popular band of the 1970s got Daniel's attention in a way that other things could not.

"That was one of the little turning points in my life," Daniel said. Soon, Daniel found friends and acquaintances approaching him with questions and recollections about his grandfather.

"Nobody ever came up and wanted to talk about the complicated issues of those days," Daniel said. "They just wanted to talk to me about my grandfather's honesty, his hard work, his straightforward no-double-talk approach."

Daniel continued to visit his grandmother in Independence during the 1970s. By then, the house at 219 North Delaware possessed a palpable sense of place. The room that seized his imagination was his grandfather's small dressing room, which contained a single bed, two dressers, a rocking chair, and a wooden rack on which a suit often hung.

"I don't remember the year,"

Daniel wrote, describing another Christmas visit. "But I do remember, clearly, standing in the doorway, watching snow drift past the windows. The room was silent. The rocking chair was empty, and there was a gray suit on the rack. That memory is very comforting to me, the thought of the silence and the cold outside. I loved being in that big, warm house, watching the snow blanket the small town outside and feeling alone, like I was the only one in the house, maybe the only person in the whole town."

Daniel returned to Independence for his grandmother's funeral in 1982. He didn't visit Independence again until 1994, when he delivered the keynote address during an Independence Day celebration at the Harry S. Truman Presidential Museum & Library.

In 2003, Daniel, a member of the board of the Harry S. Truman Library Institute, was director of public relations for Harry S. Truman College in Chicago, Illinois.

Clifton Truman Daniel in 2003.

The Harry S. Truman Presidential Museum & Library today. *Photo by Tammy Ljungblad*

CHAPTER 10

THE TRUMAN PRESIDENTIAL LIBRARY

One morning in the early 1950s, former president Harry Truman left his home earlier than usual, driving several blocks west to Independence City Hall and arriving at six A.M. There he met Independence Mayor Robert Weatherford.

The two drove north several blocks, finally slowing to a stop in Slover Park, a city facility on the town's near north side. The park occupied a spot from which Truman and Weatherford could see much of the town, including the steeples of several churches and the Jackson County Courthouse on Independence Square.

"Mr. President," Weatherford said, "we can give you thirteen and a half acres here, and this is the best I can come up with."

Truman was pleased. "This is the place," he said, according to Weatherford, who thought he heard the thud of history being made at that moment. "I recalled the words of Brigham Young as he entered Salt Lake Valley," Weatherford added in a 1976 oral history.

With those words, Truman and Weatherford had agreed upon the site of what is now the Harry S. Truman Presidential Museum & Library. The surreptitious meeting, occurring at such an early hour, was necessary, as there had been curiosity as to just where Truman would try to acquire land to build his library.

But now the site had been found and Weatherford's relief was palpable. He said he hardly noticed that, upon leaving Slover Park, Truman accidentally slammed the car door on one of Weatherford's fingers.

"I never even felt pain," he said. "I was so relieved from the decision having been made."

Since it opened in 1957, the Truman Museum has served as a principal cultural center for the Kansas City area.

As one of the earliest presidential libraries, it has received several presidents and former presidents. For decades scholars have arrived to study the millions of government documents generated during the Truman Administration to gain a better comprehension of the principal events of American history from 1945 through 1953.

Just as important, as Truman imagined it, the museum has served young people as a portal to a better understanding of the democratic system of government, the role of presidents, and the history of their own country. In recent years, the Truman Museum staff has re-imagined the institution, overhauling its exhibits and aiming to capture the imagination of today's young people – a priority of the former president.

And yet the realization of Truman's dream was never inevitable.

Though Independence seemed the obvious place to build a Truman library, it only ended up there through a series of events, of which the six A.M. meeting of Truman and

The Benton mural today.
Photo by Tammy Ljungblad

Weatherford was only one.

Truman had decided to build the library in 1950. He was following the example of Franklin D. Roosevelt, who years earlier had donated his personal and presidential papers to the federal government. Roosevelt had pledged part of his estate at Hyde Park to the government, and the president's friends had formed a nonprofit corporation for the construction of the facility.

Truman followed a similar formula. Aside from writing his memoirs, the Truman library was Truman's principal interest after returning to Independence from the White House in 1953.

To raise funds, he gave speeches. At a 1954 auction in Independence, Truman watched as bidders bid on, among other items, a sterling silver letter opener that once belonged to Daniel Webster, a registered four-month-old Boxer pup, a pair of bowling shoes, and a load of crushed rock. At a 1955 donkey basketball game fundraiser in

Independence, he threw out the first ball. He began thinking as a steward of the nation's history, and testified before Congress on the need to microfilm all presidential records. When, in 1956, he visited the Pope Pius XII in Rome, Truman brought up the importance of microfilming historic documents.

In about eighteen months Truman raised more than $1 million.

Still, the decision as to just where to build the library was perhaps more complicated than Truman had anticipated. Even among his friends there were arguments. Some thought Truman wanted it built in Grandview. Two days after arriving back in Independence from the White House in January 1953, the former president went to the Truman property in Grandview to look over potential sites.

He also had dispatched aide George Elsey to Grandview where he had been shown about the Truman farm by Truman's younger brother, Vivian. As Elsey told it, Vivian led him to a dismal corner of low-lying land next to a railroad track. When Elsey and others pointed to a nearby high spot, Vivian replied that that was valuable land that deserved a better fate than any "dang library."

Ultimately even Truman seemed to realize that the Grandview option presented problems. He told Independence Mayor Weatherford that utility installations on the property would be expensive. But another problem – perhaps explaining Vivian's lack of excitement – was that turning over a prime piece of Grandview real estate to the library project would diminish the Truman family's financial legacy.

Another option was the campus of the University of Missouri in Columbia, but Truman told Weatherford that was too far away. Some residents of Kansas City, meanwhile, were requesting that Truman build it there, but Truman didn't like that idea.

"The people in Kansas City want it over there, but there's so many of them that have fought me over the years that I don't want it there," he told Weatherford.

Ultimately, Truman agreed on the Independence Slover Park site, and on May 8, 1955, his seventy-first birthday, he turned the first shovelful of dirt.

Truman liked the Slover Park location in part because of the magnitude of the gift from the city of Independence. The park acreage stood adjacent to a small strip of homes. The city purchased the homes, demolished many of them, joined that land to the park, and presented the entire package to the Truman library corporation. Weatherford estimated the nearby highway work to be worth half a million dollars.

But Truman also liked the site, he told Weatherford, because the library's relatively high elevation allowed him to "look down into Kansas City."

Truman led the building's July 6, 1957, dedication. Among those attending were Eleanor Roosevelt, former president Herbert Hoover, Sam Rayburn, speaker of the U.S. House of Representatives, and Dean Acheson, former secretary of state under

Masonic officers in full regalia parade with Chief Justice Earl Warren to lay a Masonic cornerstone at the library, July 6, 1957.

The Harry S. Truman Library, 1959.

Truman. Among the several thousand others were members of Battery D, Truman's World War I artillery unit, and Independence Mayor Weatherford, who remembered the occasion as "the hottest day I ever lived through."

Truman originally had imagined the museum looking like his grandfather Solomon Young's original farmhouse in Grandview. He contacted architect Edward Neild, who some twenty years before had restored the Independence county courthouse in a style that recalled Philadelphia's Independence Hall.

But for the Truman Library, Neild, along with local architect Alonzo Gentry, submitted a long, low modern design, dressed in white Indiana limestone. When a *New York Times* reporter, visiting just before the museum's dedication, remarked that the building recalled elements of architect Frank Lloyd Wright, Truman wasn't pleased.

"It's got too much of that fellow in it to suit me," he said.

After building the library, Truman donated it to the federal government, which took on the facility's operation. Truman came to his library office virtually every day from 1957 through 1964. "I wish people would stop calling it the Truman Memorial Library," Truman once told *Life* magazine. "I'm not dead and I feel fine."

He considered his library a novel classroom in which young people could study the inner workings of democracy. "I want this to be a place where young people can come and learn what the office of the president is, what a great office it is no matter who happens to be in it at the time," he once said.

Of the 101,530 persons who visited during the library's first year, 15,145 were school children, and Truman met a number of them personally. Often he met with young people in the museum's auditorium, answering a wide range of questions.

Visitors to Truman Library, on its dedication on July 6, 1957.

The children of the 1950s had an idea of who Truman was.

Children of the 1990s may not have been so sure. That's a principal reason why, in the early 1990s, Truman Museum leadership began the exploring the idea of a museum makeover. For decades the library had depended upon visitors who lived through Truman era themselves and were familiar with its principal players. By the mid-1990s, however, more than 80 percent of the library's clientele were senior citizens. In response, Truman library leadership embarked on a capital campaign to raise the funds for a $22.5 million library renovation.

In early discussions, library leaders imagined the renovated Truman Library as a blinking video-monitor mothership, top-heavy with computers and other interactive hardware, all the better to entertain the young people who arrived.

But in 2001, when the museum opened its twelve-thousand-square-foot permanent exhibit devoted to Truman's presidential

Waiting for his desk, Truman prepares to move into his new office at the Truman Library, July 3, 1957.

Truman is surrounded by excited schoolchildren from Wyandotte County, Kansas, at the Truman Library in 1964.

Truman addresses an audience in the library auditorium.

administration, it became clear that library exhibit designers had treated the concept of "interactive" in a more meaningful way. Putting a premium on engaging the visitors personally, exhibit designers had included "decision theaters." In these alcoves, visitors could ponder the 1948 decisions by Truman to recognize Israel, or order the desegregation of the United States armed forces, and also consider the delicate balance between the need for national security and the civil liberties that Americans have come to enjoy.

The exhibit also addressed the decision of Harry Truman to deploy atomic bombs against Japan in 1945. A similar exhibit mounted by the Smithsonian Institution years before had been scuttled because of controversy over the exhibit's text.

The Truman exhibit showcased a diversity of viewpoints and perspectives on the issue. Visitors to the exhibit confronted four video monitors simultaneously detailing the race to produce the bomb, the firebombing of Japanese cities in 1945, the military campaigns that same year on the Pacific islands

of Iwo Jima and Okinawa, and the ongoing American propaganda offensive against the Japanese.

A nearby display, entitled "The Debate Continues," presented contrasting opinions on the wisdom of dropping atomic weapons upon Hiroshima and Nagasaki. Represented were the views of Secretary of War Henry Stimson, who in 1947 agreed with Truman's decision. But the perspective of former president Dwight Eisenhower, who in 1963 said that the bomb's use might not have been necessary to end the war, also was represented. Visitors also heard audio from historians as well as Pacific War veterans and women on the home front, all discussing what Truman's decision meant to them.

It all was evidence of the brief disclaimer placed near the exhibit's start. "History," it read, "never speaks with one voice."

The White House Decision Center opened that same year. The experiential curriculum allowed area students to engage in role-playing, wrestling with some of the same issues that Truman addressed during his administration.

In early 2004 the Truman Museum planned to open a second permanent exhibit, this one devoted to the former president's personal life. Here, alongside the traditional exhibit cases, young people will be invited to assume the roles of Harry, Bess, or Margaret Truman by pulling on period clothing. Because Harry Truman served a short stint as postmaster of Grandview, visiting children will be able to sort mail.

There even will be an interactive game in which children can race one another electronically from Grandview to Independence, the route that the young Truman often took while courting Bess Wallace. One player will take the trains and trolleys available in pre-World War I Jackson County. Another player will take Truman's 1911 Stafford automobile.

It's hard to imagine the former president, who had memorized the routes between his family's Grandview farm and the Wallace home in Independence, being anything other than pleased.

"There are younger people who haven't always taken much history in school, and I'm talking as the parent of five kids," Truman Museum director Michael Devine said in 2001. "These are people who know that Truman was president some time way back there, a long time ago, maybe with Jefferson and Lincoln and those guys."

Then again, young people can surprise.

Not long ago, Billy Everett, a first-grader at James Walker Elementary School in Blue Springs, Missouri, stopped at a display case in the Truman Museum basement.

"Awwwwesommmmme," he said.

What Billy beheld was not a pair of in-line skates, or a Michael Jordan rookie card, or any Nintendo product.

It was White House china and flatware from the Truman Administration.

Former president Dwight D. Eisenhower is guided through the Truman Library by Harry Truman in November 1961.

The White House press corps was waiting.

But seven Harry Trumans were still meeting in their Cabinet room. Their course of action was clear but there was one final detail: Which Truman would meet the press?

"Anybody object to me being president?" asked one of the Trumans.

"Yeah, me," answered another.

Finally, the seven chief executives filed into the press room. Six sat in a front row of chairs while the seventh, selected by his peers, stood at the lectern and announced that the White House had called for negotiations after the June 1950 invasion of South Korea by North Korean troops.

"Why don't you use the atomic bomb?" one reporter asked.

"We don't want to start another world war," today's Harry Truman replied.

Crisis averted. Now: lunch.

So went a day at the White House Decision Center, a role-playing curriculum at the Truman Presidential Museum & Library in Independence.

The center, located in the basement of the Truman Museum, opened in October 2001. As developed by the Harry S. Truman Library Institute, the facility's nonprofit support arm, the center is a realization of the vision the thirty-third president often had articulated for his

library. Not only would the library serve as a research center for scholars, but it also would engage young people and demonstrate the challenges and responsibilities that come with being an American citizen. The center offers an experiential curriculum in which students assume the roles of President Harry Truman and members of his cabinet to deal with actual Truman-era events. In its first year, the decision center hosted 2,320 students from around fifty public and private schools in the Kansas City area.

A portion of the Truman Museum basement has been out-fitted in period detail to suggest the White House West Wing of the late 1940s and early 1950s. Students can retire to several mini-cabinet rooms, sit behind nameplates that read SECRETARY OF STATE or PRESS SECRETARY, and occasionally encounter archaic artifacts such as dial telephones.

Students and teachers visiting the center can choose one of three scenarios to investigate and re-enact: the 1950 invasion of South Korea by North Korea, the 1948 Soviet blockade of Berlin, and the integration of the United States armed forces that same year.

Once a scenario is chosen, students and teachers study lesson plans for several days before their visit to the decision center. Each student also receives an individual packet that contains copies of authentic documents from the Truman Museum that pertain to the scenario. Still another classroom session follows the decision center visit.

By the spring of 2003, the center had completed its second year, with some 4,800 students having arrived from around the Kansas City area, and from as far as Topeka and Lawrence in Kansas and St. Louis and Columbia in Missouri.

As of 2003, decision center staff members were developing a version of the program for adults.

Students follow a role-playing curriculum at the White House Decision Center. Opened in 2001, it is located in the basement of the Truman Museum.

In November 1961, former president Dwight Eisenhower visited the Truman Museum in Independence, Missouri. The dedication date of Eisenhower's presidential library in Abilene, Kansas, was approaching and Eisenhower wanted to see how Harry Truman's library, dedicated four years before, operated.

The visit also ended what *The New York Times* once described as "one of the most notable political feuds of recent years." For about eight years, from 1953 through 1961, Truman and Eisenhower had rarely met, written, or communicated.

So often these two had sweated the small stuff.

For his January 1953 inauguration Eisenhower had decided to depart from tradition and wear a homburg instead of a silk top hat. Truman agreed to forgo the top hat, only to be insulted when Eisenhower declined to come into the White House for a brief luncheon when his limousine stopped there before the inaugural.

Upon moving into the White House as president, Eisenhower had ordered Truman's portrait removed from public view. He also had decommissioned the *Williamsburg*, the presidential yacht so enjoyed by Truman. In October 1953, Eisenhower visited Kansas City. Truman was the only notable area government representative not invited to a reception at Kansas City's Muehlebach Hotel. When Truman tried to call the Muehlebach himself to schedule a time to pay his respects, he was told – according

to Truman – that Eisenhower's schedule was full.

Truman also was capable of petty moments. In 1956 Truman declined an invitation to attend that year's Gridiron Dinner, organized by Washington correspondents. Truman wrote to journalist Edward T. Folliard that he didn't want to be near Vice President Richard Nixon. "I just cannot sit with that fellow, or his boss, either," Truman wrote. Three times during the late 1950s, Eisenhower invited Truman to various receptions or events. Each time Truman sent his regrets, claiming scheduling conflicts.

Each believed that he had suffered more significant slights from the other.

For Truman's part, the thirty-third president was outraged that Eisenhower, during a 1952 presidential campaign speech in Milwaukee, deleted a statement of support for General George C. Marshall from his prepared text. Eisenhower apparently didn't want to offend Wisconsin Senator Joseph McCarthy, who had recently suggested that Marshall had behaved as a traitor.

In 1953, Herbert Brownell – attorney general under

Eisenhower – accused Truman of promoting a Soviet agent within the Treasury Department. The speech led to a subpoena directing Truman to appear before the House Un-American Activities Committee. Truman declined to appear.

For Eisenhower's part, the 1952 Republican presidential nominee resented the criticism Truman rained down upon him following the Marshall episode. "A man who betrays his friends in such a fashion is not to be trusted with the great office of president of the United States," Truman said in one speech.

Maybe one problem was that the two men were so alike. The last two presidents born in the nineteenth century grew up about 150 miles from one another in the Midwest; one in Independence, Missouri, the other in Abilene, Kansas.

Both knew disappointment. While each aimed to attend military academies, it was Eisenhower who graduated from West Point. Truman, hoping to attend the same school, found that his vision was too poor to qualify. But during World War I it was Truman who distinguished himself in combat. Eisenhower, who ached to serve in France, instead was ordered to train tank units in the United States. He proved such an effective training officer that his superiors didn't see fit to assign him to Europe until the war almost was over.

Historian Steve Neal, in his 2001 book, *Harry & Ike: The Partnership That Remade the Postwar World*, noted that President Franklin Roosevelt transformed the lives of both men. In December 1943 Roosevelt chose Eisenhower over

campaign.

They had gotten along well at first.

In a June 1945 ceremony at the White House, President Truman had pinned a decoration on Eisenhower. In a letter to his wife, Bess, back in Independence, Truman described Eisenhower as a "nice fellow and a good man." He added: "They are running him for president, which is o.k. with me. I'd turn it over to him now if I could."

pledged to support Eisenhower as the Democratic presidential nominee in 1948, and that Truman also offered to run as his vice presidential running mate.

Together in the years after World War II, Truman and Eisenhower shared the same agenda. In his book, Neal maintained that the two worked together to redefine America's role in the world in the face of an ever more assertive Soviet Union. From 1945 to 1960, the two

Former president Dwight D. Eisenhower is guided through the Truman Library by Harry Truman in November 1961.

George Marshall as supreme commander of Allied forces in Europe during World War II. Several months later, Roosevelt selected Truman as his vice presidential running mate in the 1944

In 2003, a Truman Library staff member discovered a diary that Truman had maintained in 1947. One entry in the journal confirmed what many historians long had believed: that Truman

Midwestern presidents also served as special White House representatives of the Kansas City region, and today several monuments to this influence stand.

One example is Kansas City

area flood control. After the July 1951 flood that devastated the Kansas River valley and Kansas City, President Truman flew in to inspect the damage. Truman's head of the U.S. Corps of Engineers, Major General Lewis Pick, also was co-author of the Pick-Sloan plan, which in part called for a network of dams and reservoirs to be built in the Kansas River valley.

Yet it was Eisenhower, the Kansan, who as president resisted the protests of some Kansas residents and ultimately approved the reservoirs that now help control run-off in the Kansas River valley.

Despite standing firm against expanding Soviet influence after World War II and helping transform the Missouri-Kansas region, Eisenhower and Truman seem more remembered for their feud.

The first move toward reconciliation came from neither Truman nor Eisenhower but from Joyce Hall, founder of Hallmark Cards Inc. of Kansas City and an organizer of the November 1961 rededication of the Liberty

Former president Dwight D. Eisenhower is shown around the Truman Library by Harry Truman in November 1961. At far right is Joyce Hall, founder of Hallmark Cards, who brought them together.

Memorial, a Kansas City World War I monument.

That month Hall informed Truman that Eisenhower wished to see the Truman Museum.

Truman agreed to receive Eisenhower. Eisenhower arrived in Kansas City by air on November 10, and headed for the Truman Museum in Hall's limousine.

Even during the official reconciliation of the two former presidents at the Truman Museum, aides to both former presidents skirmished over protocol. Eisenhower had been accompanied to the Truman Museum by Roy Roberts, president and editor of *The Kansas City Star* and adviser to Eisenhower. When Eisenhower's car arrived at the museum, Roberts told Rufus Burrus, Independence lawyer and Truman friend, that Truman was expected to come out and greet Eisenhower.

It didn't happen. Burrus informed Roberts that Eisenhower was calling on Truman, and that the thirty-fourth president would have to present himself to the thirty-third. He had been acting on specific instructions from Truman, Burrus said in a 1985 Truman Museum oral history: "He said, `They want me, I expect, to come out to the car and meet him and I'm not coming to the car and [meeting] him. I want you to tell them that.' "

Burrus, so ordered, went out to greet Eisenhower as he emerged from his limousine and then led him inside, where Truman was waiting. "Come in, come in," Truman said. "It's good to see you again."

The two shook hands and met privately for perhaps fifteen minutes. Then Truman led Eisenhower on a brief tour of the Truman Museum. Asked if Eisenhower should sign the guest book, Truman said, "Definitely," adding

that if anything turned up missing, "we'll know who to blame."

Truman wasn't above a few other digs. In examining the museum's Oval Office replica, Eisenhower noticed his own portrait hung prominently nearby. "Truman said, `Yes sir, General, and I had it put there,' " Burrus said in 1985. "Well, the general got red in the face when Mr. Truman told him that." It was, Burrus said, Truman's way of reminding Eisenhower how he had removed Truman's portrait from public view at the White House after Eisenhower's 1953 inauguration. "That was what Truman was demonstrating to him, sort of rubbing his nose into it," Burrus said.

One week after Eisenhower's visit, both he and Truman met again at the Bonham, Texas, funeral of Sam Rayburn, longtime speaker of the U.S. House of Representatives. In 1962, Eisenhower stood next to Harry and Bess Truman during the Hyde Park, New York, funeral of Eleanor Roosevelt.

In November 1963, the assassination of President John Kennedy prompted still another reunion. Before the funeral, Eisenhower asked Truman and his daughter, Margaret, if they would care to ride to the Kennedy services in his car. The Trumans accepted, and sat in the same cathedral pew with Dwight and Mamie Eisenhower. Following the funeral, Margaret Truman invited the Eisenhowers back to Blair

House, where the Trumans were staying.

Tom Gavin, a friend who had accompanied Harry Truman to the funeral, described the scene that followed as Truman and Eisenhower shared sandwiches and small talk. At one point, Eisenhower stood up and moved his chair to be closer to Truman. "It was just two old soldiers recalling the times and the people they had known," Gavin said in 1963. "Maybe you can say the funeral and all the things that had happened that weekend brought them together. But it was more than that. It was two men who had lived in the same time remembering things they cared about."

When the Eisenhowers rose to leave, the two former presidents shared a long handshake. Then Truman followed them out to the sidewalk.

"When the general left, President Truman didn't say anything," Gavin said. "But he has this gesture - putting both arms out like he's carrying a light package at waist level - and he made that gesture and just smiled. It was wonderful to see."

Truman and Eisenhower met for the last time less than three years later, during a June 1966 luncheon promoting the United Nations. The site: Kansas City's Muehlebach Hotel, where almost thirteen years earlier, Truman's name had not been on Eisenhower's guest list.

Harry Truman died at 7:50 A.M. Tuesday, December 26, 1972. Within hours, Independence police officers placed barricades on North Delaware Street outside the Truman residence. The news apparently compelled many residents to leave their homes and drive by the familiar white Victorian home that, since 1953, had housed the Kansas City area's most prominent resident.

But Truman's death had not been a shock, as he had been in precarious health for weeks. He had left his home for the last time on December 5 suffering from lung congestion, and had been taken to Research Hospital and Medical Center in Kansas City. Wallace Graham, Truman's longtime physician, prescribed antibiotics to fight the infection and described the former president's condition as "fair."

Doctors revised that to "critical" the next night. The former president's blood pressure dropped, his temperature fluctu-ated to a peak of almost 103 degrees, his heart rate raced to 120 beats a minute or more, and his respiration began to fail. Doctors placed an oxygen mask over his face. They administered antibi-otics by intravenous injection.

Treatment continued for almost three weeks. Doctors issued eighty medical bulletins to the press corps maintaining a vigil at the hospital. "He's getting kind of contrary," Margaret Truman Daniel said during one press con-ference in early December. "Is that a sign of progress? It's a very good indication."

Newspapers tracking Truman's condition published articles detailing his stamina while he had served as president in his early to middle sixties. During his term Truman had entered a hospital only once, in 1952, when he spent three days recovering from a virus infection.

He maintained his health after leaving the White House, making such a tradition of his morning walks – either while at home in Independence and while visiting in Washington or New York – that a puffing herd of jour-nalists routinely trailed the former president on the sidewalks.

In 1954 while attending Kansas City's Starlight Theater, Truman suffered a gallbladder attack that confined him to a hospital bed for two weeks.

As he grew older, the sug-gestion of death didn't seem to unnerve him. When Alden Whitman, chief obituary writer for *The New York Times*, visited Truman in his library in the early

Former President Truman entered his car when he was released from Research Medical Center after a gastrointestinal disorder, July 17, 1972. The woman at left is Bess Truman.

1960s, Truman noted the occasion by opening a bottle of bourbon and saying, "Let's start the morning right," according to Whitman. "I know why you're here," Truman added, "and I want to help you all I can."

In 1963 doctors repaired a hernia, and Truman remained in a hospital bed for twelve days.

In 1964 Truman slipped and fell in a second-floor bathroom at 219 North Delaware, breaking two ribs and suffering a gash over his right eye that took eleven stitches to close. Years later relatives would wonder whether Truman's decline began after that. In the late 1960s Truman's sister, Mary Jane, would note how drawn and gaunt the former president had become.

Between 1966 and 1969, Truman visited a local chiropractor more than 250 times seeking relief from an arthritic hip. In 1969 the flu prompted another hospital stay. By the late 1960s Truman was not up to visiting his library office more than occasionally. Episodes of vertigo in the late

1960s and early 1970s helped end his morning walks.

Truman was hospitalized for intestinal inflammation in January 1971 and again in July 1972. "Harry is not well at all," Bess Truman wrote her friend Mary Paxton Keeley that November.

The bulk of December 1972 Truman spent inside Research Hospital. Throughout his stay he suffered from bronchitis, heart irregularity, kidney blockage, and a failing digestive system. On December 18 Truman told doctors he felt "all right." Two days later he was able to follow movement with his eyes and make small gestures with his hand in response to questions.

On December 23 Truman slipped into a coma. Doctors told reporters that the former president was unresponsive and in critical condition. On Christmas Eve doctors described Truman as weakening, suffering from an abnormal heart rate and fluctuating blood pressure. A bulletin issued at seven P.M. on Christmas day noted that fluid was increasing in Truman's lungs and that his kidney activity was diminishing.

Throughout the three-week ordeal Bess Truman spent her days as well as many nights at her husband's bedside. Keeley, slipping past the Secret Service, found Bess there one day.

Margaret, who spent the month shuttling back and forth from her New York home, arrived at Kansas

Independence merchants wish Truman well, December 8, 1972.

City International Airport just after eight P.M. on Christmas day. Entering the hospital at nine P.M., she grew alarmed at her mother's fatigued state and after twenty minutes convinced Bess to return with her to 219 North Delaware.

Her father, she later wrote, was in a coma. There was nothing they could do.

The next morning they received Wallace Graham's telephone call informing them of Harry Truman's death. To the press, physicians attributed the former president's passing to a "complexity of organic failures causing collapse of the cardiovascular system." He was eighty-eight years old.

Accompanied by his long-time companion and guard, Lieutenant Mike Westwood of the Independence police department, Truman takes a walk after a bout of flu and a brief stay at Research Medical Center, March 7, 1969.

On the afternoon of Thursday, December 28, 1972, Bess Truman – hatless, wearing a black coat and using a cane – walked out of her home at 219 North Delaware through its back door and entered a waiting limousine.

There were five limousines in all. The first carried Mrs. Truman and her daughter, Margaret. Other cars held Margaret's husband, Clifton Daniel, their four sons, and members of the Truman household staff. Their destination was the Truman Museum in Independence, the site of the main memorial service for Harry Truman, who had died two days before.

The ceremony was the principal maneuver of Operation Missouri – what the U.S. Army called the former president's funeral. The plans had been in existence since the early 1960s, and the six-hundred-page document called for thousands of soldiers to play various roles, with events stretching over several days. The funeral procession was supposed to include nine black horses, a caisson to bear the casket, a horse holder for the traditional military riderless horse, other horse caretakers, and a veterinarian.

But much of that never appeared in Independence.

Though former president Truman had signed off on the original plan, he also had asked that his family's wishes be considered, and ultimately a far less elaborate service occurred. This

was largely out of respect for Mrs. Truman. Then in her late eighties, she was fatigued after the twenty-two-day ordeal that her late husband had endured before finally passing away. But several observers also noted that the simplified funeral was much in keeping with the former president, who often had disdained pomp, especially when it concerned himself.

In the early 1960s Truman had been contacted by officers with the U.S. Fifth Army, stationed at Fort Sam Houston in Texas, to discuss plans for the funeral. Early in the discussions Truman had announced that he didn't want his body to be taken to Washington to lay in state in the Capitol rotunda. Neither did he want to be buried in Arlington National Cemetery.

"I would like to be buried out there," he said one day at his Truman Museum office, pointing out the window to the museum courtyard. "I want to be out there so I can get up and walk into my office if I want to."

At the end of the planning process, Truman reviewed a slide show detailing the planned funeral service. According to one account, the presentation had ended with an uncomfortable

silence, which Truman broke.

The plans looked fine, he said, adding, "I sure wish I could see it myself."

After Truman's death, a motorcade was substituted for the elaborate procession, and various heads of governments did not attend. Instead, the federal government scheduled a separate memorial service in Washington on January 5.

But even in its abbreviated form, the Truman funeral in Independence involved three thousand soldiers. Of those, about three hundred members of Battery D of the Missouri National Guard reported right away. Their first responsibility was to stand guard during the repose period on Tuesday and Wednesday outside the Carson Chapel funeral home of Independence.

After Truman died on Tuesday morning, December 26, at Kansas City's Research Hospital and Medical Center, his body was taken to the Carson funeral home. Mrs. Truman had viewed her husband's body for the last time there, a few hours after his death. Then the light brown mahogany casket had been sealed.

Early on Wednesday after-

A hearse carrying the flag-draped coffin of Harry S. Truman passes the Truman home on December 27, 1972, on its way to the gravesite at the Truman Library.

noon, eight military pallbearers carried the former president's casket from the funeral home to a hearse, their path flanked by forty-four soldiers. The hearse then traveled the fifteen blocks from the funeral home to the Truman Museum. Along the route, 856 members of the U.S. armed forces stood, each separated by ten steps and each saluting as the hearse passed. The motorcade eased by the Truman home, where all but one of the window shades had been drawn. From that window, Mrs. Truman watched the procession pass.

When the hearse arrived at the Truman Museum's south portico

at 1:15 P.M., twenty-one Air Force jets roared overhead. That afternoon, President Richard Nixon and former president Lyndon Johnson flew into separate airports and paid visits to the Truman Museum within minutes of one another.

But Operation Missouri was not long on limousines. Far more numerous were the buses of the Kansas City Area Transportation Authority, which operated free shuttles from the parking lot of the Harry S. Truman Sports Complex to the Truman Museum, often running a bus every three minutes.

Mr. Truman's body lay in state in the front lobby of the Truman Museum from 3 P.M. Wednesday, then until 11:26 A.M. on Thursday.

Thousands of Kansas City area residents waited for an average of two hours to file past a closed casket draped with an American flag bearing forty-eight stars, the number of states in the Union when President Truman occupied the White House. But the visitors did not so much want to view the former president's casket as to show their respect. The line stretched from the museum doorway, down the driveway, and out to U.S. 24. "Everyone walked quickly through the east door, around the casket and out the west door," a Kansas City Star reporter noted. By 4:15 A.M., more than 26,000 people had filed through.

Later, early on Thursday afternoon, Mrs. Truman rode the limousine to a back entrance to the Truman Museum. The crowds that had waited in line were gone by the time the funeral guests began

to arrive, showing their invitations to members of the military honor guard.

Among those present in approximately 250 seats in the small auditorium of the Truman Museum were W. Averell Harriman, former ambassador to the Soviet Union; John Snyder, former treasury secretary; and Clark Clifford, former special counsel to Truman.

But there was also Robert E. Sanders, the Independence resident who had painted the Truman home; George Miller, Harry Truman's barber; Thomas Hart Benton, the artist who had rendered the mural in the Truman Museum's front lobby; William Story, a library guard; Vietta Garr, the Truman family's longtime cook and assistant; Rose Conway, Truman's personal secretary; Mike Westwood, the Independence police officer who served as Truman's bodyguard and com-

panion for nearly twenty years; and about thirty members of Battery D, Truman's World War I artillery unit. The guest list, as printed in The Kansas City Times, included friends like Independence lawyer Rufus Burrus and onetime Independence postmaster Edgar Hinde, who dated their friendships with the former president back to the 1920s.

One reporter noted the juxtaposition of Truman's generation with a later one. "As the cars drove up to the entrance of the library, a few young persons in miniskirts or maxi-length hair were escorted in by the military," she wrote. "But the greater number were older men and women, some with canes. There goes Averell Harriman and Clark Clifford . . . Mrs. Eddie Jacobson, widow of Truman's partner in his early haberdasher days."

The service started at two P.M. and lasted just over thirty

Arrayed across the south lawn of the Truman Library, then current members of Battery D fire a twenty-one-gun salute at the end of the funeral of Truman, who commanded Battery D during World War I.

minutes. Mr. Truman's casket rested on the stage of the auditorium. The Reverend John Lembcke, rector of Trinity Episcopal Church, where Harry and Bess Truman had been married in 1919, read from the Twenty-seventh Psalm. W. Hugh McLaughlin, grand master of the Missouri Masonic community, read a short statement. There were no long eulogies, reflecting the belief of the former president that a person's life should speak for itself.

The ceremony then moved from the auditorium to the museum's outdoor courtyard. After all visitors and officials were in place, the family, led by Mrs. Truman – now being seen in public for the first time since her husband's death – walked to the chairs provided them.

"Man, that is born of a woman, hath but a short time to live, and is full of misery," said the Reverend Lembcke, beginning the committal service. "He cometh up, and is cut down, like a flower . . ."

Mrs. Truman accepted the folded flag from her husband's casket. The service ended with a twenty-one-gun salute from the six 105mm howitzers of Battery D of the Missouri National Guard, positioned on the library's front yard.

Surviving members of Battery D lay a wreath at Truman's grave on March 18, 1973, before holding their annual St. Patrick's Day party.

Residents of Independence, Missouri, know an election is near when presidential candidates start being sighted near the Harry S. Truman statue in Independence Square.

Bill Clinton began his 1992 campaign with a speech at the Truman statue on Labor Day. Then he walked across West Maple Avenue to Clinton's Soda Fountain, the site of Truman's first real job, to soak up any available Truman energy.

Bob Dole made the last appearance of his 1996 presidential campaign below the bronze Truman at three A.M. on election day, a few hours before the polls opened. Iowa has its presidential caucuses. Independence has the Truman statue.

But that is only where the Truman infrastructure of Jackson County begins.

Landmarks bearing Truman's name include his own museum, a Kansas City medical center, an Independence high school, a sports complex with separate baseball and football stadiums, a Grandview shopping center, his home, and the four-lane road running adjacent to it.

Drivers approaching the Truman district in Independence know they have arrived when they see signs bearing the silhouette of a walking hat-wearing man carrying a cane.

Once they have parked, visitors can follow in the walking man's steps. A new tour includes plaques set in the Independence sidewalks, alerting visitors to the spots where Truman lived as a boy, worked in a drugstore, married, voted, played poker, had his hair cut and – in his later years – admired a particular gingko tree on his regular walks through his hometown.

Truman's legacy across Jackson County is arguably more palpable today than it was when he died in 1972.

Occasional Jackson County residents may claim a casual attitude toward the local Truman landmarks. Don't let them kid you. The gasp seemed audible in 1996, when the National Trust for Historic Preservation included the "Truman historic district" of Independence on its annual list of endangered historic landmarks.

The neighborhood deserved the designation. The area that Truman had made familiar to Americans in the 1950s, when photographers often followed him on his regular walks, had grown threadbare by the mid-1990s. Many of the district's larger homes had been subdivided into apartments, with tenants' cars clogging the narrow streets.

Property values were stagnant or, when adjusted for inflation, even in decline.

In one celebrated instance, the façade of the house diagonally across from the Truman home collapsed.

A local neighborhood renovation project, which also carried the Truman name, offered residents property tax abatement for home renovations. Hundreds of residential homeowners have since brought their properties up to code. The celebrated collapsed façade was repaired and that same home is now included on the Truman walking tour.

And on the website of the National Trust for Historic Preservation, the Truman historic district's status in 2003 was described as "saved."

It's appropriate that so much area steel and glass bears Truman's name, given that his mark on Jackson County remains recognizable. His contribution to the Kansas City skyline was the downtown Jackson County courthouse. His mark on the county's rural districts are the quality roads whose installation he supervised as the county's presiding judge.

And yet the visitors who routinely line up at the Truman

Presidential Museum & Library in Independence likely are not there seeking details of Jackson County road building.

They come instead wanting to learn more about the man who

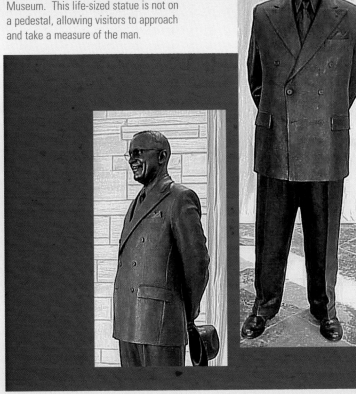

A bronze statue of Harry Truman has recently been placed in an alcove in the Truman Museum. This life-sized statue is not on a pedestal, allowing visitors to approach and take a measure of the man.

when many representatives of the graying nation of World War II veterans came to the Truman Museum.

The national memory of Harry Truman underwent a revival in the

like Clinton and George Bush to detail at length their admiration for Truman. (One reporter asked McCullough who would win the 1992 election. McCullough predicted that Harry Truman would win.)

Other biographies, by Truman scholars Robert Ferrell and Alonzo Hamby, followed. So did an HBO movie based on the McCullough book, starring actor Gary Sinise in the title role.

The Truman Museum launched a fundraising campaign. The money raised bankrolled the renovation of the Truman Museum, with permanent exhibits on Truman's presidency and personal life opening in 2001 and 2004 respectively.

Among the many new features at the renovated museum was a second bronze statue of Harry Truman in Independence. This sculpture, standing in a new glass alcove of the Truman Museum, was life-sized and not placed on a pedestal.

This allows Truman Museum visitors to approach the sculpture and take a personal measure of the man.

This is the moment when visitors to Truman's Independence invariably pull out their cameras. It is here that many realize what several presidential candidates have realized before them: Harry Truman is good company.

made a discernible difference in either their own lives or those of their parents or grandparents. This was clear during the fiftieth anniversaries of various World War II battles in the mid-1990s,

1990s, after David McCullough's 1992 biography of the thirty-third president brought the Truman story to a vast audience. The book's appearance, during a presidential election year, prompted candidates

ACKNOWLEDGMENTS

This project could not have gone forward without the assistance of the Harry S. Truman Presidential Museum & Library in Independence, Missouri. Michael Devine, director, and Scott Roley, deputy director, made *The Kansas City Star* and its book division partners in telling the life of Harry S. Truman in a new way. Thanks to them, as well as to Kathryn Knotts and her colleagues at the Harry S. Truman Library Institute.

Liz Safly, of the museum's research room, is a legend among Truman researchers and now, again, I know why. Many thanks to Liz and her colleagues in and around the research room, including Dennis Bilger, Carol Briley, David Clark, Randy Sowell, and Amy Williams.

Clay Bauske, museum curator, provided constant perspective and guidance.

Mark Beveridge, museum registrar, went beyond the call of duty, not only bringing forth poignant artifacts from Harry Truman's life but also providing captions detailing their significance.

Pauline Testerman, the museum's audiovisual archivist, found scores of photographs both familiar and otherwise. Ray Geselbracht, special assistant to the museum's director, shared his knowledge of the Truman terrain in Jackson County, as well as his photographs of many spots.

At Eisterhold Associates Inc., Gerard Eisterhold and his staff allowed us access to their database of facts and photographs.

At *The Kansas City Star* John Richey in the newspaper's imaging department scanned hundreds of photographs but always found time to scan one more. Thanks to him and his colleagues. Tammy Ljungblad, *Star* staff photographer, brought this project to a different level, not only photographing many Truman artifacts but also following the former president's trail across Jackson County.

Brian Grubb, who designed the book, brought to the project the enthusiasm of a longtime Independence resident who often saw Bess Truman on her front porch.

Thanks to Clifton Truman Daniel, the former president's eldest grandson, for contributing his foreword, and to Margaret Truman Daniel for permitting excerpts of her mother's letters to appear.

All of this depended upon Donna Martin, who as editor routinely kept several balls in the air.

Thanks, finally, to Debra, who encouraged me in this, as well as to Charlie, Jessica, and Sam, who now get the computer back.

Brian Burnes

BOOKS

Daniel, Clifton Truman. *Growing Up With My Grandfather: Memories of Harry Truman.* Birch Lane Press, 1995.

Ferrell, Robert H., ed. *The Autobiography of Harry S. Truman.* University Press of Colorado, 1980.

Ferrell, Robert H., ed. *Dear Bess: The Letters from Harry to Bess Truman, 1910-1959.* W.W. Norton & Company, 1983.

Ferrell, Robert H. *Harry S. Truman: A Life.* University of Missouri Press, 1994.

Ferrell, Robert H., ed. *Off the Record: The Private Papers of Harry S. Truman.* Harper & Row, 1980.

Ferrell, Robert H. *Truman & Pendergast.* University of Missouri Press, 1999.

Hamby, Alonzo. *Man of the People: A Life of Harry S. Truman.* Oxford University Press, 1995.

Kirkendall, Richard S. *The Harry S. Truman Encyclopedia.* G.K. Hall, 1989.

Larsen, Lawrence H., and Nancy J. Hulston. *Pendergast!* University of Missouri Press, 1997.

McCullough, David. *Truman.* Simon & Schuster, 1992.

Miller, Richard Lawrence. *Truman: The Rise to Power.* McGraw-Hill Book Company, 1986.

Montgomery, Rick, and Shirl Kasper. *Kansas City: An American Story.* Kansas City Star Books, 1999.

Paxton, Mary Gentry. *Mary Gentry and John Gallatin Paxton: A Memoir.* Privately published, 1967.

Robbins, Charles. *Last of His Kind: An Informal Portrait of Harry S. Truman.* William Morrow and Company, Inc. 1979.

Truman, Harry S. *Mr. Citizen.* Geis Associates, 1960.

Truman, Harry S. *Memoirs. Vol. I: Year of Decisions.* Doubleday, 1955.

Truman, Harry S. *Memoirs. Vol. II: Years of Trial and Hope.* Doubleday, 1956.

Truman, Margaret. *Bess W. Truman.* Macmillan, 1986.

NEWSPAPERS

The Kansas City Star.
The Kansas City Times.
The Examiner.

RESEARCH MATERIALS

Much of the material used in writing this book came from the vertical files kept on various topics at the Harry S. Truman Presidential Museum & Library in Independence.

PHOTOS AND ARTIFACTS

All photos, unless otherwise identified, are the property of either *The Kansas City Star* or the Harry S. Truman Museum & Library.

The listing of artifacts below gives either the accession number or location of the artifact in the Truman Museum & Library.

INDEX